WISH YOU WERE HERE

Wish You Were Here tells the stories of seven girls who worked as redcoats in Butlin's Golden Age from the 1950s to the 1970s. From pranks and feuds to falling in love and forging lifelong friendships, Knobbly Knees winners and beauty queens alike can now discover the touching and gloriously funny highs, lows, secrets and scandals of those at the very heart of the world's most famous holiday camp. Forget *Hi-de-Hi!*, this is what it was really like. Times have changed, but the friendships and bonds formed between those redcoats, and those who also worked or holidayed at Butlin's in those sunlit days, will endure forever.

WISH YOU WERE HERE

WISH YOU WERE HERE

by

Lynn Russell & Neil Hanson

Magna Large Print Books
Long Preston, North Yorkshire,
BD23 4ND, England.

British Library Cataloguing in Publication Data.

Russell, Lynn & Hanson, Neil
   Wish you were here.

   A catalogue record of this book is
   available from the British Library

   ISBN   978-0-7505-4054-4

First published in Great Britain by HarperElement 2014

Copyright © Lynn Russell & Neil Hanson 2014

Cover illustration by arrangement with mirrorpix

Published in Large Print 2015 by arrangement with
HarperCollins Publishers

Magna Large Print is an imprint of Library Magna Books Ltd.

Printed and bound in Great Britain by
T.J. (International) Ltd., Cornwall, PL28 8RW

Butlin's logo and archive material on
pages 244, 387 and 391–393 are
reproduced courtesy of Butlin's.

For Hilary, Mavis, Valerie,
Valda, Sue, Terri and Anji

Introduction

This is the true-life *Hi-de-Hi!* story of the Butlin's girls – the women who worked at Butlin's holiday camps during the company's Golden Age, from the opening of the first one at Skegness in 1936 to the 1970s when they were in their prime, before the growth of cheap air travel and overseas package holidays sounded their death knell.

In *Wish You Were Here* we have drawn on interviews with many of the legendary Butlin's redcoats, but we have also spoken to waitresses, bar staff, chalet-maids, chefs, kitchen porters, office staff, security men and the many other staff who kept the camps running, as well as to holiday-makers who loved Butlin's and returned there year after year.

Many redcoats also returned season after season, and some married other redcoats and built their lives around Butlin's. Others were merely passing through, but even then, they often took away with them experiences and memories that they would draw on and treasure for the remainder of their lives.

The camps began and thrived in an era when – true to their caricature image –

seaside landladies really did kick their guests out straight after breakfast and often did not allow them to return until 5 or 6 p.m. Billy Butlin always claimed that the idea for his holiday camps came from the sight of dejected holiday-makers traipsing along the streets of Barry Island under leaden skies while they waited to be allowed back into their 'digs'. 'I felt sorry for myself, but I felt sorrier for the families with young children as they trudged around, wet and bedraggled, or forlornly filled in time in amusement arcades until they could return to their boarding houses,' he claimed in his autobiography, passing over the fact that he probably owned the arcades where these families were spending their holiday money.

Inspiration had struck and Billy began hatching the idea of resorts where holiday-makers could escape the British weather – and be entertained – all day, every day. Even better, his camp staff would also look after the children, no matter how young or old, leaving parents free to please themselves for possibly the only time all year.

Billy Butlin was already rich and successful when he launched his holiday camps. The son of an ill-matched couple, he'd had a restless upbringing. His mother came from a family of travelling showmen, but his father was the wastrel son of a wealthy family, a 'remittance man' who went into voluntary exile in South Africa in return for the allowance paid by his long-suffering relations. The marriage soon ended and Billy's childhood was spent moving between South Africa, England and Canada. His education was sketchy at best, but he was quick-witted and hard-working.

He enlisted in the Canadian Army in the First World War and then worked in a department store before returning to England in 1920, working his passage on a cattle ship. He made his way to his showman uncle's winter quarters near Bristol and used his last thirty shillings (£1.50 then and about £75 today) to rent a hoopla stall from him at the first fair of the season in a boggy Somerset field. Unlike most showmen at the time, whose prizes were so infrequently won that the metal ones often had to be cleaned to remove the rust, Billy's were relatively easy to win. That, together with the free advertising of prizes branded with the Butlin's name being carried around the fairground by the winners, acted as such a successful promotion for his stall that he made ten times the profits of his rivals.

He expanded rapidly, and by the end of the 1920s, he was operating a string of arcades, amusement parks, fairground pitches and zoos all over the country. He was an inveterate gambler, always willing to back his instincts and hunches with serious money, though not all of his gambles succeeded. He lost his pride and joy, a beautiful American limousine, in a card game. He won it back the next night, but then lost it again on a toss of a coin. However, his gamble on holiday camps – he borrowed to the hilt to launch his first at Skegness and nearly went bust before it opened – paid off in style.

The boarding house keepers with whom Billy was competing were often their own worst enemies. Quite apart from driving their guests out from morning till evening, many charged the holiday-makers extra for anything they used. Having a bath was invariably subject to an extra charge and some boarding house keepers even charged for the use of salt and pepper.

Billy Butlin had set his prices at a level he believed working people could afford, coining the eye-catching slogan: 'A week's holiday for a week's pay'. That included accommodation, three full meals a day and free entertainment, for an all-in price of from £1. 15s to £3 a week, depending on the time of year, the equivalent of £90–£150 today. The slogan was slightly misleading, since the price was per head, so for a family of four, the breadwinner would have needed almost a month's wages to pay for a week at Butlin's.

The very first Butlin's holiday camp, at

Skegness, opened in 1936. Billy already had a large amusement park in the town and knew the area well. He chose it partly because of its good transport links and closeness to several major urban centres, though the cheapness of the land and the small local population – meaning fewer people to object to his plans – must also have been influential factors.

After scouting the coastline around the town for weeks, Billy Butlin found what he was seeking: a 200-acre turnip field at Ingoldmells, a couple of miles outside of Skegness. Having bought the field, he set to work. He designed the camp himself, sketching plans and jotting ideas on the back of cigarette packets. His background as a showman was evident in his chosen designs – like a fairground, the camp was to be awash with bright lights, vivid colours, music and noise, but there was to be a kind of glamour, too. The main buildings were arranged deliberately to evoke the great ocean liners of the era, regarded as the height of sophistication. Painted brilliant white with coloured detailing, the buildings formed a line with a tower in the middle, echoing the bridge and funnel of a liner.

Billy's original aim had been to create a camp for 1,000 people with 600 chalets, but it proved so successful that before the first season was out, the capacity had to be more than doubled and it eventually accommodated close to 10,000 holiday-makers. Some of the chalets even had bathrooms, but the majority of holiday-makers had to use communal bath houses and toilet blocks (though even those were a step up from the slum housing in which many still lived).

Campers were made to feel welcome from the moment they arrived. As the buses bringing visitors from the station pulled up inside the camp, a tannoy announced, 'You have now arrived at Butlin's holiday camp. We hope you had a pleasant journey and that you will all be very happy here.'

To help them achieve that happiness, Butlin's Skegness was lavishly equipped with a theatre, a Viennese dance hall, a beer garden, a fortune teller's parlour and Ye Olde Pigge and Whistle – a half-timbered mock-up of an Elizabethan inn. The landscaped grounds contained rose gardens, a swimming pool with cascades and a fountain, a boating lake and all sorts of sports facilities.

Billy was also one of the first to recognise the commercial possibilities of the emerging celebrity culture. He hired the aviator Amy Johnson – a national heroine after making the first ever solo flight from England to Australia – to attend the opening ceremony of the Skegness camp, and when the cricketer Len Hutton scored a record 364 against Australia in 1938, Billy paid him £100 to appear on stage with a bat made from sticks of Skegness rock while Gracie Fields bowled to him. The champion boxer Len Harvey was also paid to spar with a boxing kangaroo.

However, when the camp first opened, it seemed as if Billy's grand plan was going to be a failure. People in that era were often quite shy and reserved, and 'showing off' or 'making a spectacle of yourself' were frowned upon. Almost everybody wore their best clothes when they went to the seaside, and most people didn't go swimming in the sea at all, though paddling in the shallows with their trousers rolled up or their skirts lifted a decorous few inches was quite acceptable. As one female holiday-maker recalled, 'Everybody used to point and stare when people came onto the beach in a swimsuit. It was terribly daring to have a swimsuit on at all!'

As Billy walked around the camp, he noticed that very few of those first campers were using the facilities or taking part in the activities. Most of them were keeping themselves to themselves and many looked bored. Desperate for a way to liven them up, Billy asked Norman Bradford to take on the task of cheering up the campers. A gregarious, outgoing character with a good sense of humour, Norman took to his task with gusto, chivvying the holiday-makers into joining in with the activities, putting on a free drink or two to loosen everyone up and keeping them entertained with a string of corny jokes. Norman also claimed to be the originator of the 'Hi-de-hi!' catchphrase, to which his audience would respond 'Ho-de-ho!'

Within a very short time of these innovations, the camp was beginning to buzz. With his characteristic willingness to back his hunches, Billy decided that if British holiday-makers couldn't enjoy themselves without outside help, then he would employ an army of helpers to make sure they did. They needed a uniform to make them instantly identifiable, so Billy bought a job lot of red blazers; the Butlin's redcoat had been born.

Despite the hoary old joke that was soon circulating among Butlin's campers – 'I'm going to join the escape committee' – most people seemed to like being told how to enjoy themselves. Many of them had more than enough things to worry about during the rest of the year and actually relished letting someone else take the strain of organising their holiday activities for them. And if they didn't want to do something, they could always say no, although they needed to be strong-willed, because the redcoats could be very persistent.

Billy was quick to spot problems or opportunities and even quicker to take advantage of them. 'Can't' was not a word to be found in his vocabulary, as the Butlin's archivist and former redcoat Roger Billington discovered when Billy decreed that water-skiing should be made available to campers at Minehead, and put Roger in charge of organising it.

'But we've never water-skied before,' Roger said. 'We've never even taken the speedboat out.'

Billy gave him a withering look. 'There's a library in Minehead, isn't there? Well, get a book on it.'

None of the activities we now identify with Butlin's was invented by its founder. All of them – mass catering, resident entertainers, chalet patrols, semi-compulsory jollity and participation enforced by perpetually smiling staff with a ready stream of catchphrases – were features of the smaller holiday camps that had existed since the later years of the previous century, and of those camps owned by Billy's business rival, Harry Warner. Still, Billy made them seem new by practising them on a scale never seen before and promoting them with all his showman's chutzpah and razzle-dazzle.

His formula fitted a ready-made gap in the market, but he also benefited from a piece of very fortunate timing. Until 1938, only two million Britons were able to afford to take an annual holiday and most of them were middle- or upper-class people for whom Butlin's all-in, all-mates-together style of entertainment was likely to be anathema. However, in that year, the Government passed a bill compelling employers to provide all full-time employees with one week's paid holiday a year. At a stroke, the number of Britons able to afford a holiday trebled to six million, and many of them, mostly skilled and unskilled working people, began finding their way to Butlin's.

Not even the outbreak of war in 1939 – just three years after he had opened that first camp, when his second at Clacton was only a year old and the third, Filey, not even completed – could ruin Billy or derail his ambitions. When war was declared, the camps were acquired by the Government as military bases. The Army took over Clacton, the Royal Air Force got Filey and Skegness was taken over by the Navy and rechristened HMS *Royal Arthur*.

Billy also had to make a wartime alteration of his own. In the late 1930s, the targets on the shooting range at his Bognor amusement park were effigies of Nazi leaders: Hitler, Goebbels, Goering and von Ribbentrop. After the retreat from Dunkirk in 1940, however, with a German invasion now expected at any moment, Billy Butlin hastily arranged for the targets to be removed, lest invading Nazis should catch sight of them and decide to use Butlin himself a target.

At the instigation of his friend General Bernard 'Monty' Montgomery, Billy was also hired to provide entertainment centres for soldiers on leave and to construct new military camps at Ayr in Scotland and Pwllheli in North Wales. Like his existing camps, he negotiated a deal for each one, which allowed him to buy them back at the end of the war at a knockdown price. With a hasty refit and a lick of paint, Butlin's was ready to accept holiday-makers again almost as soon as the last shot was fired.

Billy Butlin's camps proved hugely popular and hundreds of thousands of people flocked to them every year. Although changing times eventually saw them go out of fashion, causing many of the camps to close in the 1980s, the remaining ones have been re-invented and remodelled for twenty-first-century tastes. Three camps – at Bognor, Minehead and Skegness – survive and thrive to this day, and the name Butlin's still evokes a smile of recognition in almost everyone, whether or not they ever went on holiday there themselves.

Wish you were here? Many still do.

Hilary

One

Hilary Cahill was in her late teens when she first heard of Butlin's in 1957. Born in 1940, she grew up in Bradford in a solid working-class home. Her mum worked in Whitehead's mill in the city and her dad was a foreman at Croft's engineering works, so although they were never wealthy and lived in a back-to-back terraced house, with two good wages coming in there was always food on the table.

Her mum was a dark-haired, attractive and lively character. She absolutely loved to dance. It's where Hilary got her own love of dancing from, because her mum taught her when she was small. However, her dad couldn't dance to save his life. 'He used to claim that it was because he'd never had any shoes when he was young,' she says, 'and only had boots, but that sounded like a bit of a lame excuse to me. He was still using the same excuse when I was a teenager! My mother and I tried to teach him over and over again, but whatever we tried, it just didn't work. He had two left feet and that was the end of it! All the mills used to have these big dances once a year and we used to go to all of them, dressed in our best clothes. The real top bands used to play at them, so they were great. My dad used to hate it, though, when we all went to the works' dances and my mum would be dancing away with people while he was just sitting there, looking on.'

Her dad was so strict that Hilary was still forced to wear little white ankle socks even when she'd left school, but she had a strong independent streak, so she used to go out on Tuesday nights wearing the ankle socks, telling her dad that she was going to the Guild of St Agnes at church, like a good Catholic girl, but then sneak off to the dance hall instead. She'd take off her ankle socks and put them in her bag, put on a bit of lipstick and then dance away with her friends until it was time to go home. However, her dad obviously suspected that she wasn't quite as good a Catholic girl as she was pretending, because one night he followed her. As she was walking along she felt a hand on her shoulder, and there was her dad looking absolutely furious. 'I want you back in the house, now,' he said. 'Get those socks back on your feet and wipe that dirt off your mouth.' She was more embarrassed than frightened, but she knew that there was no use in arguing and that it was the end of her Tuesday-night excursions to the dance hall.

Her brother was five years older than her and almost as strict as her dad. He used to go to the same dance hall as Hilary and her friends and, she says, 'He always kept his beady eye on me!' She didn't mind that – she quite liked the idea of her big brother being around. They were good pals, despite the age difference between them – and five years was a lot at that age. He didn't snitch on her to her dad, but he would certainly let her know if he thought she wasn't behaving like his little sister was supposed to. After her brother left school, he worked as a wool sorter and then did his National Service. She didn't see him for almost two years because he was serving out in Cyprus during the troubles there, and she missed him a great deal.

Hilary went to a Catholic school in Bradford, but, looking back, she couldn't say it was a very good education, and like the majority of her school year, she left at fifteen with no qualifications. Her first job was at J. L. Tankard's carpet and rug factory in Bradford. She was employed in the finishing department, doing hand-sewing. It was all piecework and hard graft, but as young girls do, she and her workmates had a few laughs along the way.

One of her friends, Brenda, was a dab hand at doing hair and used to style theirs for them in the toilets at work. The girls would give her some of their 'tickets' – the slips of paper detailing the piecework jobs they'd done – so that she didn't lose out financially from the time she was taking off work to cut their hair. 'The Grecian styles were in then,' Hilary says, 'so we were all there at work with steel wavers and pin curls in our hair, singing along to the songs on the radio.' After work they all used to go dancing together. Once she was paying her own way in the household, Hilary's dad had to ease the restrictions on her, and from then on she and her mates were out every night of the week, either in the Sutton Dance Hall, the Somerset, the Queen's or the Gaiety. 'We used to go all over to dance,' Hilary says.

Hilary and her workmates used to pay into a kitty to save for all sorts of things, including what they called the 'Christmas Fuddle'. It took only a penny or twopence a week each, but when Christmas came around, that was enough to buy plenty of drinks, crisps and sausage rolls, and on the last day before the Christmas holidays they would stop work at lunchtime and wolf down the lot! Very few of them drank as a rule, but they certainly made up for that at the Christmas Fuddle. Deaf to parental warnings to 'never mix your drinks', they drank bottle after bottle of Babycham, Cherry B, Pony and Snowball – so much so that Hilary was pretty ill one year, and when she got home her parents weren't impressed by the state she was in. The next morning, suffering her first hangover, Hilary wasn't very impressed either.

As well as the kitty for the Fuddle, Hilary and the other girls were also saving for a holiday together, having made up their minds to go to Butlin's at Skegness the following summer. They saved up all year, putting away whatever they could afford. Hilary used to put five shillings a week (25p) into a little tin towards her holiday, and saved half a crown (12½p) for clothes and shoes. She had to give her mum money for her board as well, and whatever was left after that she'd usually spend on going dancing.

There were fixed holiday times in all the industrial towns and cities then, when factories and mills would shut down for their annual clean-up and overhaul; an avalanche of, say, West Midlands car workers would descend on the holiday resorts one week, followed by Lancashire mill workers the next and Yorkshire miners the week after. In Lancashire mill towns the annual holidays were called 'Wakes Weeks', in other areas they were called 'Feasts' and in Bradford the holiday was known as 'Bowling Tide' – which was nothing to do with bowls, since Bowling was one of the Bradford districts and 'tide' was the local word for a holiday, as in Whitsuntide.

One woman from Bradford remembers her holidays as always being a bit of a home from home, because everyone from her street went on holiday to the same place at the same time. 'You knew everyone when you got there, because it was all people from your street. I mean, you weren't with any strangers, because even if you didn't know them as such, you knew their faces.' Since all the mills and factories in an area would shut down for the same week, tens of thousands of people were going on holiday at once, and they had to book far in advance – months or even a year ahead – because popular destinations like Butlin's became full up very quickly.

In the 1940s and 1950s, when Butlin's was at its peak, there were virtually no package holidays, and only the well-off could afford to travel abroad, so the holiday camps had a vast semi-captive market. The chalets may have been basic, but at a time when many young couples spent their first years of married life under the roof of one of their parents, a chalet at Butlin's was often their first real taste of domestic privacy.

Very few families owned a car and the fact that everything you could want was in one place at Butlin's was another powerful attraction. Once they got there, wives were freed from the toil and drudgery of factory work or housework – or both – for a whole week; few families could afford to stay for a fortnight. An article in *Holiday Camp Review* in 1939, 'Holiday Camps and Why We Go There', even claimed the camps were pioneering women's rights. 'At a camp alone a woman gains that pleasing sense of equality. The girl of eight, the maiden of eighteen, the grandma of eighty, rank with the boy, youth and grandpa without any sort of distinction. They are campers, first, last and all the time. Age and sex do not matter.' It's hard to think of any other British institution at the time where similar claims could be made with a straight face.

Unless they were in a self-catering chalet to save money (and they weren't introduced until the 1960s anyway), there was no cooking, washing or cleaning for the women to do, and even childcare could be handed over to the nursery nurses or the redcoats in their signature red jackets, white shirts and bow ties, white trousers and white shoes. The children were marched off to sports tournaments, swimming galas and the Beaver Club (for small children) or the 913 Club (for nine- to thirteen-year-olds), or, if the weather was wet, to the endless array of rides, games, sports and competitions held in the ballroom and children's theatre. So while their kids ran wild in safety, parents could swim or play sports if they felt energetic, or put their feet up and relax if they didn't. They could sunbathe if the weather was fine, doze in an armchair if it wasn't. They could play bingo or even booze the day away in the bar if they felt like it.

Even those with smaller children were liberated from their responsibilities to a certain extent. While parents ate at the oilcloth-covered tables in the dining hall, the under-twos were fed their puréed beef and carrots and stewed apple in a separate 'feeding room' in the nursery, where rows of babies in highchairs ate their baby food away from the other campers – or at least that was the theory. The babies were supposed to stay there until their parents and older siblings had finished their own meals in the dining hall, but the babies often had other ideas and would howl the place down until their parents collected them. Some put their little children in their prams outside the dining-hall windows, lining them up so that the babies could see their parents through the window. One camper recalled that, even from the other side of the glass, the babies' screams could be heard above the clatter of cutlery and the noise of conversation.

Parents were also free to dance in the ball-room, watch a show in the theatre or drink in the bar in the evenings, while 'chalet patrols' – nursery staff in their blue uniforms and capes – marched or cycled up and down the lines of chalets, listening for crying babies. Freed from the burdens of childcare and factory or domestic drudgery for a week or two, many couples also rediscovered the pleasure they had taken in each other's company in the early years of their relationships – although for others, the unusual amount of time spent with their partner could also have the opposite effect!

In 1957 Hilary and her friends went to Butlin's at Skegness for the first time. Four of them went, sharing one chalet. Hilary's brother had a car, a Morris 1000, and he offered to take them there, so they all squashed in with their suitcases piled on the roof rack and set off. They had driven only a few miles down the road when the car broke down. When they should have been driving in through the gates of the camp at Skegness, they were still sitting in the broken-down car, waiting for a tow truck.

It was pouring with rain all day and by the time they got to the camp they were tired, bedraggled and fed up. Like all the girls, Hilary's friend Brenda was on her first trip away from home, and her mother had bought her a brand-new suitcase to take on holiday. It was so wet that the handle disintegrated and fell off as she was carrying it through the camp. Despite the trials and tribulations of getting there, however, as

35

soon as they saw Butlin's, they absolutely fell in love with the place.

All along the road leading to the camp there were tall flagpoles with different-coloured flags flying, and there was always a row at the front of every Butlin's camp, too, 'You could see them flying from about a quarter of a mile away,' one camper recalled, 'and as you drove up to the main entrance, the first excitement was seeing all those flags blowing in the wind. When I saw that, I knew that I wouldn't be seeing much of my parents for a whole, wonderful week.'

As they turned in through the gates, the girls could see the tropical blue colour of the big outdoor swimming pool, and the theatres, dining halls and other main buildings, all freshly painted in brilliant white with the details picked out in bright primary colours. Rocky Mason, a former redcoat and entertainments manager who spent most of his working life at Butlin's, can still recall similarly vivid memories of his very first sight of Butlin's as a boy. He'd grown up in 'a very dreary city, covered in mill smoke. It was very dull and the sky was always grey. When I got to the camp I felt as if I'd suddenly walked into utopia – it was so colourful, so warm, so friendly. There were lights across the roads, there were banners fluttering in the breeze, there seemed to be music coming from every direction. The swimming pool was the most beautiful, beautiful thing I had ever seen, there were flags all around the pool and it was a stunning colour of blue. I saw rows and rows of chalets, all with different-coloured doors and windows – red, yellows, blues, greens, orange – it was just a gorgeous place to be and there seemed to be laughter coming from every building.'

Hilary couldn't have imagined a greater contrast with Bradford, which was a very wealthy city then but also a very drab and grey one. There was a near-permanent pall of smoke hanging over the city, fed by hundreds of mill chimneys, and the golden-coloured sandstone of the buildings was stained ink-black by decades of coal smoke and the sulphurous winter smogs.

The rest of Britain was just as dreary during the 1940s and 1950s. The last phase of wartime rationing only ended in the mid 1950s, and even though 'utility' clothing was no longer the only option, clothes were still invariably made of wool or cotton, in black or muted shades of green, brown or grey. Television – for those families that owned a TV set; it was still a luxury item – was broadcast in black and white. The first colour television broadcast in Britain did not occur until 1967. Radio was still dominated by 'received pronunciation' and the Reithian requirement to inform and educate, rather than entertain. And even in the late 1950s or early 1960s, most of the music played on the BBC Light Programme would have been equally familiar to listeners in the 1930s. Given this backdrop, the Butlin's camps, with their rows of colourful flags, bright-blue swimming pools and dazzling white buildings with vividly painted doors and windows, must have looked positively psychedelic to 1950s eyes.

Butlin's was impressive enough by day, but by night it was staggering. You could see the glow from all the lights from miles away – and there were thousands of them. It had the same level of impact then that Las Vegas has today, and Hilary and her friends had simply never seen anything like it. She couldn't get over how huge the camp was, either (when full, it held something like 12,000 people then), and the lines of chalets seemed to go on forever.

The individual chalets themselves weren't quite so impressive. They were tiny, and had a little sink in the corner with a small mirror over it, a curtain across a tiny alcove to serve as a wardrobe, a small table, one chair and four iron, army-surplus bunk beds. That was it. Hilary remembers noticing that the bedspreads matched the curtains – blue with white yachts on them – and that the same motif edged the tiny mirror above the sink. Butlin's kept these the same for years. Although there wasn't much spare room, it suited the girls fine. They were only sixteen or seventeen, and until then they'd always been on holiday with their parents, staying in boarding houses or campsites. Hilary doesn't think any of them had ever even stayed in a hotel, so to be off on their own, with their own separate chalet, tiny though it was, seemed quite sophisticated.

The redcoats made quite an impression on Hilary, too. The girls all looked very smart and glamorous to her, but they were friendly, too, and seemed to be absolutely everywhere, organising everything, making sure everyone was having a good time. Hilary and her friends had a ball while they were there, dancing every night, chatting and flirting with boys, and generally doing all the things their parents wouldn't have approved of. Some of the girls even destroyed their holiday snaps before they went home – not because they were doing anything particularly wrong, but the photographic evidence of them just talking to boys or having a drink or cigarette in their hand would have been enough to get some of them, including Hilary, into serious trouble.

It continued to pour with rain for almost the entire week. The only fine day was the Friday just before they went home, so they spent the entire day, Hilary says, 'running in and out of the chalet, changing our clothes and then taking another set of photos so that when we went home, we could show our friends the photos and make it look like we'd been having wonderful weather and a really great time every day of the week!'

Despite the weather, they had all loved their first holiday at Butlin's – so much so that before they left to go home they all said: 'We're definitely coming back, and what's more, we're going to have two weeks next year.' So as soon as they got home, they booked the next year's holiday and began saving for it straight away. By the time the second year came round they all had steady boyfriends, and Hilary was actually about to get engaged to hers – a boy called Dave – but nothing, not even that, was going to get in the way of her holiday, so she took a deep breath and said to him: 'All of the girls are going on holiday together. We booked it a year ago and even though I'm going to be getting engaged to you, I'm still going on holiday with them, without you.'

She's still not sure what she would have done next if he'd said that he didn't want her to go, but he just shrugged and said, 'Okay,' so that was that.

That second year, 1958, there were twice as many of them: eight girls, four to a chalet. The camp was packed with crowds of people all having a good time, and as they strolled around, the group of girls met up with gangs of boys and chatted and flirted with them, and then went dancing in the ballroom every night. Even though none of the girls really drank, they would still call in at Ye Olde Pigge and Whistle early in the evening. The bar was huge and had a fake tree in the middle of the room and a half-timbered, mock-Tudor 'street' down one side, with the 'windows' opening onto the bar. It was just as bizarre as it sounds! They'd stop in there for a little while, chat to the boys and have a soft drink, and then they'd go to the ballroom. They would still be there, dancing away, when the boys all came through after the bars had shut, and then they'd be dancing with them and generally having a good time until the ballroom closed down for the night.

One night they were chatting to a group of boys, and one of them was a real joker. He wasn't tall or short, broad or skinny, or particularly handsome, but he stood out from the crowd and Hilary can still clearly remember him. This lad was asking Hilary what she thought she was going to do with her life when one of her friends butted in and said: 'Don't bother asking her. It's too late for her, she's already spoken for. She's getting engaged when we go home.'

He just looked Hilary straight in the eye and said, 'It's never too late, until you're standing at the altar in front of that man

41

with his collar on back to front, saying "I will".'

She just laughed at the time and thought no more about it, but when she got home, what he'd said kept coming back into her mind. She did get engaged to Dave and, as girls did in those days, she began saving and putting things away for her 'bottom drawer'. She might buy a pillow case one week, a towel the next and a saucepan the following week, and put them all away in the bottom drawer of her dressing table, ready for when they set up home together. 'It was how people did it in those days,' Hilary says. 'You had to save for everything and buy it a bit at a time, whereas now people just go and buy what they need on credit, all in one go.'

At that point in her life, Hilary could easily have gone ahead and got married, and would probably have had a child before she was twenty, but she went to the cinema with Dave one night and there was a travel documentary showing, the short film they always put on before the main feature. 'Usually I was bored to death with them,' she says, 'but this time, as I was watching this film showing all these exotic places in different parts of the world, I thought to myself: you're only eighteen, and there's a whole world out there you haven't seen and know nothing about. There and then I decided that I was too young to get married and wanted to see a bit more of life before I was ready to settle down, so I broke off the engagement with Dave straight away. He was a lovely lad and he took it very well. I mean, he was upset at first – we both were – but I was sure I'd made the right decision and I didn't go back on it.'

Hilary went back to going dancing every night with her friends and was really enjoying herself. None of them were engaged or married, or even going particularly steady with anyone, so, still inspired by that short film she'd seen, Hilary said to them: 'Why don't we all go off somewhere together, like Australia, or Canada, or anywhere, really? There's got to be more to life than we've seen so far. Let's go and find out what we've been missing!'

It wasn't that she was unhappy at home; she had a very happy home life. Her parents had just moved from the back-to-back terraced house she'd grown up in to a new house on an estate called Holmewood. 'It's not got a good reputation these days,' she says, 'but when they moved in there, just after it was built, it was wonderful. It had a bathroom and all the mod cons that we'd not had before.' So her life was comfortable, she was happy enough and not short of anything, but she just felt that she wanted to do something else and see more of the world than Bradford.

So in early 1960 Hilary and her three closest friends made up their minds that, yes, they'd go off somewhere together and have an adventure! Based on little more than the fact that it had looked beautiful and very different from Bradford on the travel documentary Hilary had seen, they decided they would all go to Canada, so they applied for visas, got all the forms and filled them in. However, a couple of the girls then started to get cold feet, and the other one started going out with a boy and didn't want to leave him, so in the end Hilary was the only one ready to go. She didn't feel let down or fall out with the girls about it – 'They were very good friends to me then, and I'm still friends with them over fifty years later. I go on a night out with them all every now and again, and two of them still live in the same village as me now' – and it didn't shake her own determination to do something different before she settled down.

Two

Hilary freely admits that she wasn't brave enough to go off to Canada on her own. She was so disappointed to miss out on the trip that she said to her friends, 'Well, I'm going

44

to do something. I'm not just going to stay around Bradford for the rest of my life.' A couple of days later, she saw a Butlin's advert in the local paper and decided that she wanted to work for them. She thought to herself: there are things going on all the time there, and I'll not just be working, I'll be enjoying life as well. She certainly did that, but having only seen Butlin's from the other side of the fence as a holiday-maker, she didn't realise quite how hard she'd have to work.

She applied to be a redcoat, and although she wasn't an entertainer – she couldn't sing, play an instrument or do stand-up – she could certainly dance; she had learned tap and ballet when she was younger, after all. She went for an interview at a hotel in Leeds and was a bundle of nerves going in there, but the man who was interviewing her was very friendly and put her at ease. She told him she could dance and liked meeting new people, and after they'd chatted for a while he offered her a job as a redcoat at Skegness.

Hilary didn't start right at the beginning of the season – not everybody did. The camps opened to the public at the beginning of May but weren't as busy then as they were in high summer. So instead, Hilary started working in mid May and then went right through until the end of the season in September. When she arrived, she found that some of the redcoats had been there for a few weeks already (they would prepare for the new season and hold themed activity weeks at the camps from mid April), and quite a lot of them had worked for Butlin's before, at Skegness or one of the other camps, so they helped her and the other newcomers to settle in. She was excited and also very nervous, but she found that she felt at home right away and loved every minute of it. 'I don't know if I was a typical redcoat,' she says. 'In fact, I don't know whether there is a typical redcoat at all, but I certainly wasn't a real extrovert, and I never had a great deal of confidence, though it developed over the years.'

The redcoats' jackets were laundered for them, but they had to wash the rest of their clothes themselves. Luckily, the white pleated skirts and blouses that Hilary and the other girls wore were drip-dry, so they just had to wash them and hang them up. They were allowed two each, but they'd always try to get an extra one, as it did make life a little easier: one on, one spare and one in the wash. Redcoats always had to be smart – Hilary wore white stilettos all day, apart from when she was on the sports field – and they all had to have a little white handkerchief showing in their top pocket and to wear their Butlin's badges. They issued a different badge for every camp, every year, and people used to collect them. 'You'd sometimes see campers coming in', Hilary says, 'with what looked like about a hundred badges pinned to their hats or coats.'

During the week, Radio Butlin's at Skegness used to wake the campers with 'Zip-a-Dee-Doo-Dah', and there would be similarly jolly music all day, every day, except for Saturday – leaving day – when they were woken to the wistful strains of Mantovani's 'Forgotten Dreams'. The solemn music would continue all morning as the campers wandered around looking sad at the thought of going home. Some tried to cheer themselves up by booking for the following year before they left.

The redcoats would see the same families coming to the camp year after year. Some of the wealthier families 'hardly ever seemed to be away from the camp at all', Hilary says. It's a testament to the strength of the connection many of the campers felt that one woman, who had been to Butlin's over fifty times, even asked for her ashes to be sprinkled onto a flowerbed at her favourite Butlin's camp after she died, because, according to her daughter, 'This is where she called home.'

Hilary had to learn the rules that the redcoats had to follow, and there were pages and pages of them. 'You couldn't go dancing with just the pretty girls or the handsome men, or dance with anyone more than twice, and you had to seek out the reluctant dancers, the shy people and the wallflowers, and get them on the floor as well. You weren't allowed to have anything in your pockets, because it spoiled the lines of your uniform, and I used to smoke then, so it was a struggle to know where to put your cigarettes. One of the boys, a black guy who had an Afro, used to keep his cigarettes and his lighter hidden in his hair!'

Hilary fell foul of one of the numerous Butlin's rules when the local paper sent a photographer along to take a picture of the tug-of-war contest they were holding on the sports field. When the paper came out, right on the front page there was a picture of Hilary standing up and cheering on one of the teams. She was delighted to see herself in the paper, but then her heart sank. She knew she'd be in trouble when she saw that the photograph clearly showed her holding a cigarette, with a rolled-up Butlin's duty roster sticking out of her jacket pocket. Staff members weren't allowed to smoke when they were standing up – Hilary could never understand why, but you had to sit down if you wanted a cigarette. Sure enough, when the entertainments manager saw the picture, he called her into his office and gave her a dressing down.

At Skegness the redcoats put on various sporting events and had to go around the camp often literally dragging people out of the dining room or wherever they were to take part. The campers were divided into 'houses', like in public schools – in Skegness's case, named after the royal households of Kent, Gloucester, Windsor and York – and the redcoats had to persuade them into volunteering for all these competitions. They may have been on holiday, but the redcoats would make them practise every day and then take part in the events themselves. There was one gang of guys at Skegness who were there for two weeks. Hilary got hold of them in the first week and, after a bit of coaxing, got them doing the five-a-side football and a few other events. They actually won the football competition and were presented with their prizes: Wilkinson Sword razors, since the company was sponsoring the event. At the start of the second week she tried to get them to play football again, but they all said, 'No, we're on holiday. We were practising and playing all last week, and all we got at the end of it was a lousy razor each.'

'You won't get them again this week, I promise,' she said. 'I'll make sure they give you a really good prize this time.'

In the end they agreed to do it, but they

warned her: 'If we get those razors again, you're going in the pool, fully clothed.'

So they played and won the five-a-side competition yet again. Everyone was lined up on the sports field at the end of the week when all the prizes were being given out. When their names were called, sure enough the prizes turned out to be more 'lousy razors'. They didn't even take them, they just turned round, stared at Hilary and then came running towards her. They picked her up, carted her off and threw her in the pool fully clothed, and of course the other campers absolutely loved that!

As well as running the competitions, the girl redcoats had to make sashes and rosettes for them as well, which involved going down to the camp stores to get the material and then cutting them out and stitching them together. 'You had to do all sorts for your team,' Hilary says, 'but if they won the overall competition at the end of the week, you got a small bonus. The redcoats were always very popular with the campers, and you would often get them saying, "Come and have a drink with us," but we hardly had any time to spare. You might have got an odd ten minutes to go and have a quick drink with someone, but that was about it.

'It was hard work, of course,' Hilary says, 'but there was always a real buzz and a feeling of excitement in the air. If something good wasn't happening right now, then you knew that it would be before long. I loved meeting all the different people who passed through the camp, I loved the shows and entertainment and above all, of course, I loved the dancing!'

The working day normally finished at quarter past eleven with the redcoats singing 'Good Night Campers', but after that they still had to fit in rehearsals for the Redcoat Show – a weekly cabaret in which almost all of the redcoats performed sketches or songs. Other entertainment put on for the campers included such timeless favourites as knobbly knee competitions and beauty and talent contests galore. In later years, the Holiday Princess of Great Britain, the Glamorous Grandmother of Great Britain and the Miss *She* fashion competition were even televised. People came to Butlin's to be entertained and to have a good time, and the redcoats had to make sure that happened. As another former redcoat recalled: 'We would organise competitions, whist drives, snooker, football, darts, Glamorous Granny, Holiday Princess, as well as all the children's competitions. We would act as bouncers in the Rock 'n' Roll Ballroom, we would dance with campers in the Old Tyme and Modern ballrooms, some would act as lifeguards for both pools (indoor and outdoor), we would sit up till gone midnight doing the late-night bingo and then still be up for first-sitting breakfast at 7.30 a.m., smiling away as if our lives depended on it ... and our jobs certainly did!'

Every night the redcoats were allocated their duties for the next day. If Hilary was down to do darts or some other competition that she found boring, a lot of the other girls would swap with her. They hated having to do the ballroom duties, like the Old Tyme, afternoon tea and morning coffee dances, whereas Hilary absolutely loved those, so the system worked perfectly. 'I'd be there with my long white gloves on,' she says, 'and as long as my partners could dance, I didn't care what they were like, I just loved it!'

In the ballroom in the evenings the redcoats would get everyone doing the Chopsticks. They called it that because the music they used was 'Chopsticks', but it also described what they did. Four redcoats would kneel down, each holding two long bamboo canes, and they'd begin banging them up and down and moving them in and out in time to the music. The campers – either volunteers or those conscripted by the redcoats – lined up in a long column and took it in turns to hop or dance in between the canes without getting their legs trapped. 'When Jimmy Tarbuck was working as a redcoat,' Hilary remembers, 'he used to lift the canes so high you practically needed a step ladder to get over them! And of course when the campers tried to do it, they'd be falling all over the place. So it was a bit of a giggle for everyone.'

They'd do a limbo competition, too, not that it was any more serious. The redcoats would raise the bar to make it easier for the old and the overweight, but, Hilary says, 'We'd have it practically touching the floorboards for anyone we thought was taking it too seriously!'

Hilary and the others also had to go 'swanning around' the dining room while the campers were eating their lunch or tea, trying to sell them raffle tickets to win a car. The redcoats were all given targets and had to sell a certain number of tickets each month, and if anyone did really well, they might get a little bonus as a reward; 'It was really high-pressure stuff.' The draw was to be made at the end of the season and the first prize really was supposed to be a car, though Hilary doesn't remember anyone ever winning one. 'Things are different now,' she says, 'but back then there was a bit of an "anything goes" mentality.'

Butlin's had been a success from the start, but the camps really boomed in the post-war period, driven on by Billy Butlin's risk-taking, entrepreneurial spirit and his flair for generating publicity, even if it involved telling a few white lies along the way. Long-serving redcoat and entertainments manager Rocky Mason recalls the time when Billy phoned a journalist on *The People* and told him that he was buying the *Queen Mary* to turn it into the largest luxury floating holiday camp in the world.

The story made headlines throughout the world. A few weeks later, the journalist phoned Billy to ask if there had been any developments. 'None at all,' Billy replied. 'But how else could I get £100,000-worth of publicity for the price of a phone call?'

However, Billy wasn't the only one with an eye for a publicity opportunity. In 1949, while he was surreptitiously trying to check out the competition at the Brean Sands camp of his rival Fred Pontin, Billy was unwittingly photographed having a drink at the bar. To his incandescent rage, the picture was then used in a Pontin's brochure with the slogan: 'All the best people come to Pontin's!'

Billy Butlin had always thought big and was ever willing to gamble money on the newest and most eye-catching attractions. He opened his own airports next to some of the camps, allowing some holiday-makers to arrive by air, but also offering them pleasure and sightseeing trips. There were chairlifts and miniature railways at all his camps, and he also installed the UK's first commercial monorail at Skegness. Some of the camps had vintage cars and famous old steam railway engines, which kids loved to clamber all over. But one of the greatest attractions at Skegness, both for the campers and for Hilary, was an elephant. Billy had been using animals as attractions since the early 1930s, when his Recreation Shelter in Bognor featured a zoo with bears, hyenas, leopards, pelicans, kangaroos and monkeys, and a snake pit where Togo the Snake King would stage regular shows. And both Filey and Skegness also had ex-circus elephants.

Hilary had always loved elephants. She had ridden one at Belle Vue Zoo in Manchester when she was a child and had never forgotten it. 'It was a really big thing for me to see an elephant there at Skegness. And you can just imagine the faces of the children – and the adults – who were staying at the camp when they realised they could actually see a live elephant strolling through the camp with his keeper.'

Sadly, though, the elephant, called Gertie, came to an unfortunate end during Hilary's first season. The trainer would lead Gertie up and down the camp every day and Gertie would do tricks, like picking up the trainer's eight-year-old son with his trunk and putting him on her back. The kids used to love it, and there would always be a little procession of them following Gertie around.

She also used to go in the shallow end of

the swimming pool and blow jets of water out of her trunk, washing herself and drenching anyone within range. She'd been doing this for years without coming to any harm, but one particular day, for no obvious reason, Gertie started walking down the pool, away from the shallow end and towards the deep end. Her trainer kept on shouting at her to stop, but Genie just kept on going, and when she got out of her depth, she drowned. Even though Gertie hadn't been at Skegness for long, for the staff, it was like losing a family member. It had happened in full view of the holiday-makers as well, so they were just as upset about it as the redcoats. Some of the kids were inconsolable. They had to drain the water and bring in a crane before they could get the elephant's lifeless body out of the pool, so it was very traumatic for everyone.

Soon after she had started working at the camp, Hilary had got chatting to one of the other redcoats, a Londoner called Bill, who did general duties and also ran the sports events and competitions, including the boxing and wrestling matches, as he was a boxer himself. He wasn't a typical redcoat at all, because he was public-school educated, and with her working-class background in Bradford, Hilary had never met anyone like him before. Redcoats weren't allowed to socialise with each other during working hours – it was one of Butlin's strictest rules

– but Hilary and Bill would meet up after work and on their days off and they soon started going out together.

Like some of the other staff, Hilary stayed on for an extra two or three weeks at the end of the season to help out with the Christian Crusades Week (when hordes of religious people descended on the camp to hold their revival meetings) or other special events that some of the camps put on. There was also a Ballroom Week at many of the camps, when competitive ballroom dancers arrived from all over the country. After the last waltz of the evening, as the dancers left the floor and went back to their chalets, one woman still vividly remembers the excitement she felt as a young girl crawling round the ballroom floor on her hands and knees, collecting all the sequins that had fallen from the women's ball gowns.

Once the camp had closed down at the end of September, Bill, who had found a job at Selfridge's, was heading back to London for the winter, so Hilary decided to go with him. She started working as a waitress at the Imperial Hotel in Russell Square, but hated every minute of it. The head housekeeper, who was in charge of the staff, was 'a real hard case', she says with a shudder, 'and so were most of the other women who worked there, so it wasn't a pleasant place to work at all'.

After a few weeks of that, Hilary said to Bill: 'I can't stand it there and I'm feeling homesick, too, so I'm going back home to Yorkshire.'

'All right,' he said. 'I'll come back with you, then.'

Bill managed to get a job in Leeds doing credit-enquiry reports, and since Hilary's parents had already met him and knew they were serious about each other, they let him live with them at their house. 'Although, of course,' she says, 'we were in separate bedrooms and strictly chaperoned, so that nothing untoward went on!'

A lot of couples at this time had to live with one or other set of parents both before and after they got married, because very few could afford to set up home on their own straight away. After they'd been living with her parents for a few weeks, Bill said to her: 'If we're going to be living under the same roof anyway, there's no point in us not being married, is there? So why don't we just get married?'

It wasn't the most romantically phrased proposal, but it seemed heartfelt, and even though they'd only been going out a few months and really didn't know each other very well at all, Hilary said yes. She was still only twenty and had not seen much of the world except for Bradford and Skegness, but nonetheless, thrilled and excited, she threw herself into plans to get married a month later, on Christmas Eve.

Bill then set off back to London for a couple of days to break the news to his father; his parents were separated and he didn't get on that well with his mother, so he was in no hurry to tell her. He was supposed to be coming back to Yorkshire on a train the following Sunday evening, but he never showed up. They didn't have a telephone – a lot of people didn't then – so there was no way that Hilary could get in touch with him or find out what had happened to him, but in any case, she wasn't too worried at first. As the days went by and there was still no sign of him, however, she began to get increasingly anxious. She didn't have a clue what had happened to him and before long she was going frantic with worry.

At last, on the Thursday of the following week, she got a letter from him, though it wasn't good news. It read: 'I'm so sorry, I'm so despicable and you must hate me, but I'm not sure if I want to get married.' It went on in a similar vein for another two pages. It turned out that instead of going to see his father, Bill had gone to Butlin's for the weekend instead: even though the season had ended, they still put on a few special weekend events at the Bognor Regis camp.

Hilary thought about it for a few minutes and then, ever resourceful and remarkably brave, she showed her mum the letter and said, 'I'm going to go and see his father.' She'd only ever met him once, and she didn't even know his address. All she knew was that it was somewhere in Tottenham. I'll find it somehow, she thought. So she cancelled everything: the cake, the ceremony and the reception, told all her friends and family that the wedding was off, and then set off to London.

She got off the train at King's Cross, found her way to Tottenham and then wandered around the streets until, by a miracle, she managed to find the right house. She walked up to the door and when she knocked on it, who should answer the door but Bill?

When she saw him, Hilary did a double take and was lost for words for a few moments, but then she said, 'I haven't come to see you, I've come to see your father,' and angrily pushed past him into the hall. When she had calmed down a little, they began to talk things over. Bill had changed his mind again and had now decided that he did want to get married after all, but his father sat them both down and offered them some advice.

'You've rather rushed into everything, haven't you?' he said. 'Why don't you give yourselves a bit more time to really get to know each other and just get engaged instead?'

His words made sense, so that's what they decided to do, but as Bill sat opposite her on the train back to Bradford, he said, 'I'm so sorry about the way I've acted and what I've put you through, but I do know what I want now. So, if you're willing, I'll have a word with your dad when we get to Bradford and see if we can put it all back on again and still get married on Christmas Eve, just like we planned.'

If Hilary had any misgivings, she swallowed them and said yes to Bill for the second time. Her father obviously wasn't pleased about the way his daughter had been treated, and when Bill asked him, at first he just shook his head and said, 'Oh no, if you really want to get married, you're just going to have to wait now, at least until Hilary is twenty-one.'

However, he gave in after a couple of days, so they rang the register office and spoke to the cake maker just in the nick of time – with Hilary having cancelled her order, he was just about to cut up the cake he'd made and sell it off! So, as they had originally planned, they got married on Christmas Eve, then caught the next train to London and had a two-day honeymoon at a hotel in Russell Square. They worked in London until the spring and then together went back to Butlin's in Skegness for the start of the new season.

As married redcoats, instead of a chalet with bunk beds, Hilary and Bill were given one with a double bed in it, and Hilary did her best to make the chalet – their first home together – as cosy as she could. She put up their own curtains instead of the Butlin's ones, and bought a little paraffin stove (even though it was strictly against regulations due to the fire risk) and used it to boil a kettle for cups of tea.

Halfway through the season, Bill was offered a promotion to deputy entertainments manager, but based at Clacton rather than Skegness. So they moved to Clacton and this time, when they got to the end of the season, Butlin's offered to keep them on for the winter and sent them to work at one of the hotels they owned, the Ocean Hotel in Saltdean, near Brighton.

It was while she was working there that Hilary met Jimmy Tarbuck, who was also a redcoat at the hotel, and another Butlin's girl, Valerie, who was to become one of her very best friends. Valerie was a redcoat, too, but was working as an entertainer because she had a great singing voice. She arrived at the hotel two days after Bill and Hilary, and the two girls hit it off straight away. Even though Hilary was newly married to Bill, she and Valerie were always together. Whenever they had time off or a break, they would get together for a drink, a few laughs and a dance. They learned all the new dances that were coming in, like the twist, the Watusi, the mashed potato and the locomotion – at the time it seemed like someone was coming up with a new dance every couple of weeks.

Coronation Street had just started on ITV and they both loved it, so they were always trying to sneak off duty and go to the television room to watch it. The ballroom at the hotel doubled as the venue for the cabaret shows, and Valerie and Hilary were often on duty together operating the spotlights and changing the colours of the acetate filters to suit whatever dresses the singers were wearing. However, the start of the shows coincided with *Coronation Street*, so, desperate to watch it, the girls decided that they would get two of the guests' kids to do the lights while they sneaked off for half an hour. Children under the age of twelve weren't allowed at the hotel, so Valerie said to Hilary: 'All we've got to do is find the two tallest boys' – they had to be tall to be able to change the filters and operate the lights – 'and give them the sequence of acetates for the first half-hour, because *Coronation Street* only lasts half an hour, so we'll be back before they get any further into the show. Simple!'

They found two tall boys who both jumped at the chance – they'd do anything for the redcoats, and playing with the spotlights sounded like good fun. So after giving them their final instructions, Hilary and Valerie left them saucer-eyed with excitement and went off to the television lounge.

Coronation Street was already hugely popular, its gritty realism, ordinary-looking characters and northern dialect a stark contrast to the 'drawing-room and French-windows' settings and received pronunciation of most other television programmes at the time, so a lot of the hotel guests were already in there with the lights off watching the show when Hilary and Valerie sneaked in. They sat down out of sight on the floor at the front and whispered to the guests: 'Don't let anyone know that we're in here, will you? Or we'll get into trouble!'

'It was funny,' Hilary remembers, 'because a lot of the guests came from the South of England and they just didn't believe what they were seeing on the screen when *Coronation Street* was on. They kept saying to us, "It's ridiculous, people just don't change the wheels of their bikes in their front rooms," but we said, "Oh yes, they do in the North. Believe me, we've seen it!"'

Their plan worked; the girls' young deputies did the job perfectly and no one noticed. When the boys went home with their parents at the end of their holiday, Hilary and Valerie found another pair to take over. To start with, all went well again, but one night, they'd only been in the TV lounge for about five minutes when they heard the entertainments manager shouting, 'Where are they? Where the hell are they?' And they didn't need to be told who 'they' were. They tried to sneak out but walked straight into him and had to stand there, rather shame-faced, while he tore them off a strip. When he paused for breath, Hilary said, 'How did you know we weren't doing the lights?'

He burst out laughing. 'Because it was like World War Two was starting all over again inside the ballroom. There were searchlights flashing all over the sky!' The two boys had got bored with just focusing on the performers and had started swinging the lights all over the ceiling, pretending to shoot down enemy aircraft. The audience were in hysterics, but the artists who were performing on stage were rather slower to see the funny side.

As well as working in the Brighton hotel, the girls also went to the various campers' reunions and promotional visits that Butlin's held in cinemas, theatres and ballrooms all over the country during the winter. It was just one of the ways they tried to build loyalty in their campers and encourage them to book again the following year. People who'd made friends at one of the Butlin's camps would arrange to meet up at the reunion, and redcoats would put on entertainment for them. On the Friday night it was like a show night at one of the camps, complete with all the entertainment, just to remind those who had been to Butlin's what it was like, and show those who hadn't what they were missing. Then on Saturday morning they would put on a big free film show at the local cinema. 'There would always be kids queuing up to come in for the show,' Hilary says. 'And some of them broke our hearts because they were so poor. You'd see them standing out there in the freezing cold with no coats, no socks, and their little shoes with the soles worn through.'

Hilary and Valerie were always well aware that there were many people who were much worse off than they were, which helped to put any of their own troubles into perspective. A lot of disabled people, especially children, used to come to the camps with their parents or carers. 'Even though they were only there for a week,' Hilary says, 'you often did get very attached to them, and it was the sort of job where you had to go and find them and make sure that they were having the very best time they could.'

While working at the hotel, Hilary also became friends with a few other redcoats, and has remained so to this day. Her friends Des and Mair met each other there and, like Hilary and Bill, later got married, and there was Rocky Mason, who also came from

Bradford. 'Perhaps because there were only a few redcoats working in the hotel,' she says, 'we formed a really close-knit group, almost a family. We got to know each other so well and I really became close to them all.'

In the spring of 1962, Bill was promoted again and sent to work at Minehead as assistant manager. Hilary went with him and became assistant chief hostess, but she still kept in close touch with Valerie and her other friends from the hotel in Saltdean. The camp at Minehead was brand new. When they were building it, there had been a lot of objections from the locals, because some of them didn't want a holiday camp built there at all, but Billy Butlin always seemed to get his way in the end. He even managed to turn the one occasion when councillors defied him to his advantage. Having built the Heads of Ayr hotel in Scotland, Billy applied to the council for a late licence for the bars. His application was refused and when Billy told the councillors that he would rather demolish the hotel than run it without the late licence, they treated it as a bluff – whereupon Billy called in the bulldozers and flattened his newly built hotel. If that seemed to be cutting off his nose to spite his face, it proved to be good business in the long term, because no other councils were brave enough to call his bluff after that. The camps at Bognor and Minehead both went ahead despite vigorous local opposition, though at Minehead Billy used charm instead of bulldozers to win them over. He said to all the objectors: 'When it's ready, we'll invite you all along and you can come and look around.'

So when the camp was ready to open, they laid on an inspection and an afternoon tea for the local people. Hilary was given the job of meeting some of them at the gate, showing them round the camp and then taking them for afternoon tea. There were a lot of ladies from the Minehead Women's Institute there and they must have had a nice afternoon, because at the end of it they had a whip-round and tried to give her a tip. She had to tell them, 'I'm sorry, ladies, but we're not allowed to accept tips' – it was yet another of Butlin's rules. However, a couple of days later, a letter arrived for her, thanking her again and sending her a cheque for the amount they'd raised in their whip-round: £2. 10s (£2.50). Her wages were only about £4 per week then, so it was a very nice bonus, and Hilary was so touched by that gesture that she kept the letter and still has it today.

As a hostess, Hilary was in charge of the competitions and dealing with all the prizes – 'and there were so many competitions', she says with a sigh. A lot of them were sponsored by companies such as Lux Soap and

Smiths Clocks, and the prizes for those were the sponsors' responsibility. Butlin's provided the rest of the prizes, and Hilary was given an allowance of nine old pence (about four pence today) per camper for the prize fund. In high season, when there might be 10,000 holidaymakers there, it added up to quite a lot of money, but earlier and later in the season it was a lot less. No actual money ever changed hands, because the camps had plenty of shops where she could obtain prizes, so she'd just go around them, choose what she wanted and the shops would then debit the value of what she'd taken against the prize fund.

There were prizes for all ages: toys for the small children, sports stuff for the older ones, scarves and handbags for the women and free holidays at the end of the season for the winners of the bigger competitions. The day after they'd given out the prizes was always bedlam in the camp offices, because people who'd won a prize would often bring it back and try to swap it for something else, either because they had already won the same thing earlier in the week, or simply because they didn't like what they'd got.

The redcoats would always get a bit of stick from the parents of children who hadn't won prizes, too, especially the parents of the kids in the Bonny Babies competition. 'Everyone always thought their baby was the most beautiful baby in the world and wanted to win the prize to prove it,' says Hilary, but dealing with complaints was all just part of the job. There was never any trouble with the competitions that were just a bit of fun, though, like the Knobbly Knees contest, or when they had campers doing stupid things on the sports field, like chariot races and pram races, with grandmothers in the prams instead of babies. There were one or two anxious moments, particularly when one granny was pitched out of a pram during a race and knocked out cold. Nowadays her relatives would probably have been phoning the lawyers before her head touched the ground, but when she opened her eyes a couple of minutes later, all she wanted to know was: 'Did we win?'

The redcoats also had campers throwing eggs to each other and trying to catch them. At first, the eggs they were handing out weren't real, and the campers would be throwing them to each other and stepping back a few paces every time, but of course eventually the redcoats would swap the pretend eggs for real ones, and when they tried to catch them, a succession of campers would be splattered with egg yolk.

They'd also get campers to take their shoes off for a barefoot race across the field. As soon as they said 'Go' and the campers had gone haring off over the grass, the redcoats gathered all their shoes together and then threw them up in the air so they came down again in a heap. When they got back, puffing and blowing from the race, the campers had to spend ages sorting out whose shoes were whose. 'You couldn't get away with that stuff now,' Hilary says, 'because people would either punch you or sue you for emotional trauma or something, but we got away with it back then!'

When the redcoats meet up at reunions now, they all talk about those days and say what happy times they were. 'They certainly were,' Hilary says, 'but it was hard, hard work as well. You were so tired sometimes, but then you were working from eight in the morning until midnight, or even later, and the camps were so big.' The redcoats often found they were at one end of the camp for one event and then had to go right to the far end of the sports field for the next, and they'd only have half an hour's break in between them. Hilary had a bike for a couple of seasons, so getting around wasn't so bad, but those who didn't have a bike couldn't even take five minutes off, as it would take half an hour to walk across the camp. So there wasn't much free time, but there was, Hilary says, 'still a lot of fun and a lot of camaraderie'.

Three

Hilary and Bill worked at Minehead from when it opened until the end of that season, 1962, and it was to be their last Butlin's camp. By then they were both thinking it was time to move on. They were ready to start a family. 'We didn't really associate that with working at Butlin's,' says Hilary. 'I know people after us did manage to bring up their children while living on the camp, but I didn't want that for my family.'

So they both resigned at the end of the season and Bill began working for Top Rank, managing the Hammersmith Palais and then the Empire in Leicester Square, but it all started going downhill for him – and for them – from that point on. In the end, Bill's problems cost him first his career, and then his marriage. They were still living in London and it was, Hilary says, 'just an awful, sad time'.

Luckily, Valerie was in London at the time, too, with her husband Mike, and Hilary used to see her most weekends, so at least she had a friend she could turn to for support. Hilary left Bill for several months in 1963. It was the year that President Kennedy was assassinated and she can remember her dad sitting on the sofa and crying while he was watching the news on the television. She then went back and stayed with Bill for a while, hoping that things would improve. Before long, however, it became obvious that he wasn't going to change his ways, so in the end she had to leave him for good in 1965. She went home to Bradford and moved back in with her mum and dad.

Hilary met the man who was to become her second husband, Bernard, on a night out in Bradford the following year. She had actually been at school with him, although she hadn't really noticed him at the time. He'd also been to Butlin's in Skegness on holiday when she was a redcoat there, but they only met properly for the first time at a nightclub in Bradford, the Lyceum Rainbow.

Bernard had been in the Merchant Navy but was home for good when he met Hilary. They got on well, started going out together and Hilary began divorce proceedings against Bill soon afterwards. However, divorce was not so easy to obtain in those days, and whether through accident or design, on several occasions when a court date had been set Bill failed to turn up at the designated time and the hearing had to be postponed. Hilary finally divorced him and married Bernard in 1969. They had two children together, both boys.

Bernard and Hilary kept pubs together and had The Shoulder of Mutton in Baildon, near Bradford, for seventeen years. 'So I suppose in a way I was still doing a redcoat-type job,' she says, 'and still entertaining the public, even then.'

When their children were small, Hilary and Bernard took them to Butlin's for holidays two or three times, and one year Hilary even judged a competition, just like she'd done in her redcoat days. Most of her old friends had moved on by the time she went there on holiday, but Rocky Mason was still there; he had been promoted from redcoat to entertainments manager by then. It was a strange feeling for Hilary, watching the redcoats at work, rather than being part of it with them. 'I couldn't stop myself from watching them, of course, checking what they were doing and rating them on how well they were doing it! They were great family holidays for us, because they still had all the entertainment and everything, and once you had paid the price to go there, everything was free. I still think it was the best possible holiday and the best value for families with children, especially compared to the cost now when you take your children or grandchildren somewhere, and every ride, ticket or show costs you an absolute fortune.'

Bernard was a very good husband to Hilary

and a wonderful father to their children, but tragically he was killed when he was only forty-five years old, 'He was just crossing the road,' she says, her voice still showing her bewilderment, 'and two taxis were racing each other, driving like lunatics, and one of them hit him.'

He was not killed instantly, but Hilary thinks that he was clinically dead by the time he reached hospital, though he was kept on a life-support machine for some time. 'It was heartbreaking,' she says. 'The boys and I also had to make the decision about whether to donate his organs. We decided to do so, and his heart, liver and kidneys were used in transplants, so we were at least giving other people the life that had been denied to Bernard.'

Hilary grieved for her husband for a long time, but gradually she rebuilt her life, and though she never remarried, she says, 'I've had my moments since then! I've a lovely family, two sons and two lovely grandchildren, and of course I've got my friends.' Among them is Valerie, of course, and another Butlin's girl, Mavis, whom Hilary first met at Minehead but then lost touch with for many years. Like the other redcoats of their generation, they had all started to get computers and explore the internet, and about five years ago, Valerie said to Hilary one day, 'There's this site I've found called Forever Butlin's and you should go on it.'

A few days later she rang Hilary again, really early in the morning, and said, 'I'm heartbroken and I haven't slept all night.'

'Why, whatever is the matter?'

'I've been on that Forever Butlin's site again,' Valerie said, 'and I've seen all these obituaries of people we used to know,' and she began reeling off the list of names. However, a few days later she called her again and this time was much more cheerful, telling her that she had also found people they had worked with, like Rocky Mason, who were still very much alive. She had sent them an email mentioning that she was in touch with Hilary and had then had a long phone conversation with Rocky. 'I've given him your number, too,' she said. 'So he'll be calling you as well.'

Sure enough, Rocky phoned Hilary and they had a good long chat about the old days and what they'd been doing since, and he also told her about a reunion they were planning in Scarborough at the old Butlin's hotel there. Not long after that Mavis phoned Hilary, having also got her number from Rocky.

Although Mavis and Hilary had worked together at Minehead, they hadn't really been close friends at the time, and hadn't seen each other for almost forty years. However, it turned out that Mavis was living only a few miles away from Hilary, so they met up in Leeds, got on like a house on fire and became firm friends. They met up again at the Butlin's reunion in Scarborough, and still meet regularly now. 'It's all sitting down somewhere, eating and drinking lots, and talking our heads off!' says Hilary.

A few years ago Hilary returned to Butlin's, this time with her grandchildren, Oliver and Maddie. They went to Butlin's in Skegness, but this time she didn't stay in a chalet; they rented a caravan on the adjoining site and walked onto the camp every day. 'It was nothing like it was in the years when I was working there,' she says. 'It's a very different place, but then, these are very different times.'

Today's Butlin's is a reflection of both the changing times and rising wage costs, of course, which Hilary acknowledges. 'It's a business like any other, I know,' she says, 'so it has to pay its way, and you just could not afford the staffing levels today that we had in our era, but although it's probably the nostalgia we all feel for the "good old days" as we get older, I do regret the passing of those times.'

People go away on holiday a lot these days, but when Hilary was working at Butlin's, most people who went there had to save for it the whole year round, just like she did, and that was pretty much all they had to look forward to. 'So you had to make it special for them,' she says, 'and it really was. They'd forget all their cares and worries when they went to Butlin's, and they would just have a ball. For the majority of people, I'd say that their annual holiday was one of the biggest, if not *the* biggest, things in their lives. They just lived for it, so we felt a responsibility to make sure that the holiday lived up to their dreams.

'We had a permanent smile fixed to our faces and no matter how you felt on the inside, you just had to keep smiling. It didn't matter what was happening in your personal life – you might be miserable and heartbroken off duty, but when you put on that red jacket you'd think to yourself, they don't want to know about your problems, they've come on holiday to get away from all that.'

Since Bernard's death, Hilary has travelled all over the world with her friend Dorothy. 'I've drawn on the confidence that Butlin's instilled in me in those days to do it,' she says. 'I've been to the Caribbean, I've seen the Great Wall of China, the geysers and glaciers of Iceland and the midnight sun in Norway, and during my travels to Japan, I visited Hiroshima. It was one of the most moving experiences of my life, seeing the devastation that wars create. I've also been to Korea and found the grave of Bernard's brother, who was killed in the Korean War. None of his family had ever been there, but I laid flowers on his grave and my son Danny did the same a few years later, so he's not been forgotten.

'I never regret my time at Butlin's,' Hilary says. 'It was not only great fun; it was a great life experience, too. A lot of things happen throughout your life and the things you learned at Butlin's, especially how you are with people and how to deal with them, come back to you, and they do help you through.'

Mavis

One

Mavis Idle began working at Butlin's as a musician and redcoat in 1959. She was born Mavis Wilcock in Dewsbury, Yorkshire, in the summer of 1938 in her grandmother's terraced house. Unable to afford to rent let alone buy a house when they got married, Mavis's mum and dad were still living with her grandmother at the time. Even when they eventually got a house of their own, it wasn't that far away – just two doors along the street. It was an old type of terraced house, with no bathroom and a toilet outside in the yard. Like most people they knew, they would get the tin bath out on a Friday night and the whole family would take it in turns. Although it lacked modern amenities, it was a decent house, stone-built, very solid and in a good street, and Mavis had a very happy childhood there.

Her father had a job winding coils for an electrical transformer company, while her mother looked after Mavis and her little brother, Roy. They were a musical family. Her father used to play the harmonica pretty well, Roy played the guitar for many years, though he eventually gave it up, and

Mavis played the accordion.

One of her relatives on her grandma's side used to make concertinas and accordions for a living, and Mavis often wonders if her interest in them stemmed from that, but as far back as she can remember, she always wanted to play the accordion. Her dad often used to take her to shows at the Dewsbury Empire Theatre when she was little, and she was so small that she would have to sit on the steps down the aisle, because she couldn't see the stage otherwise. She can still remember the tingle of excitement she felt as the house lights began to dim and the orchestra struck up. The shows staged there were always variety bills in those days, and they almost always started with a musician. Whenever it was an accordion player, Mavis used to say to her dad: 'When I get big, I want to have one of those.'

She kept on and on at her parents about it and in the end, when she was still only about six or seven years old, they bought her an accordion. It was only a tiny one, but still it felt so heavy to little Mavis that she could hardly pick it up. She enjoyed playing it from the start, though. 'My granddad always wanted to listen to me playing it,' she says, 'or at least he said he did! And he helped me a lot with it. When you start on the accordion, you just learn the keyboard to begin with, using your right hand, and then you learn to do the bass – the buttons – with your left hand afterwards. Granddad used to say to me: "It's all right you learning the keyboard, and then learning the left hand, but when you come to put it all together and you've got to pull the bellows as well, what are you going to do then?" And we'd burst out laughing together. I can still remember how thrilled he was when I did it for the first time.'

Mavis was a pretty good dancer as well when she was small. She danced from when she was a tot until she was about nine, and with the rest of her dancing school she appeared in her first pantomime at the Empire Theatre when she was five. 'So that was the beginning of my show-business career!' Mavis says with a laugh. It was a big theatre, seating 2,000 people, and although the pantos they put on there were all home-grown, they were some of the best in the whole of the North, with future stars like Hylda Baker and Morecambe and Wise among the guest artistes and most performances sold out weeks in advance. People came from all over Yorkshire to watch them.

Mavis appeared in the pantomimes until she was nine, but then had to choose between dancing and the accordion, because to do both was just too much of a commitment. She loved dancing, but she loved her music even more, so she gave up her dance classes and concentrated on playing the accordion.

This was probably just as well, because soon afterwards, in January 1947, she was involved in a serious road accident and damaged her foot badly. She had been to a dressmaker who had made a coat for her. On her way home, Mavis got off the bus and crossed the road. She already had one foot on the far pavement when a coal wagon passed so close behind her that its rusty mudguard caught in her coat. She let out a shriek, less in fright than in horror at the damage to her new coat, but the impact then span her around and threw her into the side of the lorry, while one of its wheels ran over her foot, crushing it.

Mavis doesn't remember anything for two weeks after that. She was in hospital for quite a while, and if she had still been having thoughts of being a dancer at that stage, it would have been a very difficult time for her, because the specialist who was treating her said, 'I'm afraid you won't ever be able to wear high heels, and you won't ever be able to dance, and you won't ever be able to play sports.' However, this just made her all the more determined to prove him wrong. And although there has been a weakness in that foot ever since, while she was still at school, she played all the sports, like hockey, tennis and rounders, and when she grew up, she not only wore high heels, but danced in them as well.

When her baby brother Roy was due to be born – he was nine years younger than Mavis – her parents sent her to stay with an aunt in Kent for a couple of weeks to keep her out of the way. When Mavis got home, she discovered that she not only had a new baby brother, but a new accordion as well, because her father had bought her a proper, grown-up one. It had belonged to her music teacher's son, a brilliant accordionist who had tragically died very young. Her teacher often used to say to her, 'You play like my Jack used to play,' and he really wanted her to have the accordion, but money was so tight that for quite a while her parents couldn't afford even the modest price he was asking. However, in the end her dad found the money and bought it for her. She was so thrilled when she saw it, she could hardly speak.

Mavis passed the eleven-plus and went to grammar school, and had a vague idea in her mind that she'd like to do something connected with art when she grew up. It turned out that her career would not be in art, but in music, and she started working as a professional musician when she was still very young. She had carried on with her accordion lessons and practised really hard, and by the time she was twelve years old, she was good enough to be playing on stage.

A friend of hers who 'did a bit of singing'

told her that a comedian called Ken Idle was holding auditions for a concert party he was putting together, and she asked Mavis if she'd go with her. Ken had been in the forces doing his National Service, but was now looking to make a career in entertainment, and as a first step was planning to put on shows for charity. So Mavis and her friend went along to the auditions together, which were being held at the house where the concert party did its rehearsals.

Mavis was petite and nimble, with a dancer's natural grace, but she was also painfully shy at the audition, so much so that she could hardly speak, and she was very much in awe of Ken, who was twelve years older than her – twice her age at the time. The other musicians weren't as old as him, but even the youngest of them was four years older than her. Although she was so young, Mavis was fine once it was time to play her accordion for them – it never bothered her to play her accordion in front of strangers or on stage, because she knew she could do it – but 'I couldn't have spoken on stage to save my life!' she says. 'Even when I was a lot older, I could never even introduce a song; I just didn't talk on stage at all.'

She passed the audition and started playing with the concert party, and continued doing that for the next couple of years. The troupe had separate boy and girl singing groups, but Mavis rarely sang; she mainly just played her accordion. Eventually, the four boys decided to break away, as they'd had enough of just playing for charity and wanted to start playing the working men's clubs and making some money from their music. They asked her if she'd play accordion with them. She was only fourteen and still at school, but she jumped at the chance.

So instead of playing the odd concert party, usually in the daytime at weekends, Mavis was now out several nights a week playing the clubs. It certainly wasn't the way to great riches; 'I remember the first club we ever played,' she says. 'They gave us three pounds ten shillings for our night's work, and that had to be shared between five people! However, we were convinced we were on the path to fame and fortune and we gradually got more and more bookings. Sometimes we even got slightly more money as well!'

Every time they had a booking, Mavis would hurry home from school and grab a sandwich, the boys would then pick her up in the van and they would be off to whatever club they were playing at that night. She'd be sitting in the club's dressing room doing her homework before they went on stage. Her exams were looming and she was beginning to panic about them, so she'd do some of her homework, then do the spot on stage, then come rushing off stage, do some more homework in the interval and then go back on stage. By the time they'd packed up their kit and driven home again, it could easily be midnight, or even later. It was a crazy schedule, but they kept working the clubs for quite a few years.

Looking back now, Mavis is amazed that her parents didn't try to put a stop to it. 'To be honest,' she says, 'I think they were quite intrigued by it all. They couldn't believe what was happening; it was a whirlwind for all of us! When we were playing somewhere local, they used to come and watch us, and we eventually got to the point where we had coach-loads of people – friends, and even a few fans, I suppose – coming to see us wherever we were playing.'

Mavis left school when she was sixteen. She had it in mind that she was going to be a fabric designer, but when she told the school careers officer this, he put her right off the idea, telling her there was a new machine that had just been brought out that could print hundreds of different designs.

'He was talking nonsense, of course,' Mavis says. 'It wasn't like today when they have computers that can do all sorts of fabulous things, but I didn't know that at the time.' So she ended up in a rather less stimulating work environment: the accounts office of the British Rail goods department.

It was a job, at least, but she was still playing in the clubs at night and often not getting to bed until the early hours, so she admits that she probably wasn't the most wide-awake or efficient accounts clerk British Rail ever had.

Over the next couple of years, the group went through three different line-ups and eventually dwindled to just three people: Dave, Ken and Mavis. So they formed a trio and carried on doing the clubs for a while, calling themselves The Verdi Three. Mavis chose the name, just because the accordion she used was a Verdi III and she liked the name.

When Mavis had joined the group at just twelve years old, the gap between her and Ken had seemed like a chasm. He was everything she wasn't at that time: mature, poised and confident. He was a grown man who'd been away in the Army, and had been working as a professional musician and comedian, and she was just a kid, a schoolgirl, who happened to be able to play the accordion. She was more than a little in awe of him. 'Though I might have had a bit of a teenage crush on him as well,' she says, 'he was really more like a much older brother to me.' By the time she was seventeen, however, that began to change, and despite the age gap there was definitely some chemistry between them. They started spending time together off stage as well as on, and although they never really went courting (as they called it in those days), because they were always on stage in the evenings, and very rarely went out on a proper date, just the same, they were going out together from 1955 onwards.

When Mavis told her parents, they were nervous about it at first, especially her mother. Mavis remembers her asking, 'What happens if he meets someone his own age and doesn't want you any more?' Both her parents came round to the idea fairly quickly, though. They knew Ken pretty well by then, because five years before, when Mavis had started playing with the band, her dad had made Ken promise that he would always make sure she got home safely. So he'd always see her to the door and say hello to her parents and sometimes, if it wasn't too late, he'd pop in for a cup of tea before he went home.

Rumours had started going round her school that Mavis was going out with a band-leader from the moment she had started playing with the group. 'It made me laugh at the time,' she says, 'because it sounded like I was going out with Joe Loss or Mantovani!' So when she actually did start going out with Ken several years later, her friends were already quite used to the idea, and most of them didn't really react to the news. There were inevitably some people who showed their surprise. A couple of her friends said, 'Why are you going out with an older man?' One even asked her if she was going out with Ken just because he was so popular. (Working as a comedian, Ken often had the audience in hysterics when he was on stage, and he was fairly well known locally as a result.) Most people, however, just accepted their relationship.

In the summer of 1956, Mavis and Ken went on holiday to Butlin's Skegness with another couple. Mavis had been away without her parents before; when she was fourteen she went to Morecambe with a friend, which they both thought was very grown-up, even though they stayed in a boarding house run by her friend's aunt, so they weren't completely unchaperoned. Before she went to Skegness with Ken, however, she'd never been to Butlin's and didn't really know a lot about it, other than the things she'd read in magazines.

The camp seemed enormous. Mavis can remember walking along the road that ran between the rows of chalets on one side, and the shops, bars and theatres on the other, and she could just see the big old-fashioned merry-go-round at the entrance to the fun fair right at the far end – 'It looked miles away!' she says. The camp was like a mini-town and she felt sure she'd always be getting lost, but once she got used to it, it no longer seemed as vast as it had on that first morning.

The camp also seemed to have a glamorous air, even if it was sometimes only skin-deep, with its 'marble' columns that were actually painted plywood. Another girl who made her first visit to Butlin's at the same time remembers being overwhelmed by the facilities, which were quite unlike anything she had ever seen before. She still recalls how 'gorgeous and opulent' the ballrooms were, with their chandeliers and the smell of polish from the gleaming dance floor.

The redcoats also made quite an impression on Mavis. Speaking of when she later became a redcoat herself, she says, 'If we were not quite idolised, we were certainly very popular and admired by the campers, and I think I felt the same about them when I first went there as a holiday-maker. They always looked amazing and were always smiling and chatty, and very friendly.' She doesn't know if she really got the most out of Butlin's at the time, because she was too shy to enter most of the competitions, though she did a few of the sports and games. Ken certainly wasn't shy about getting up on stage, but then he'd been doing it for years. Mavis wasn't the same kind of performer.

They could only afford to stay for a week,

but Mavis and Ken had a great time while they were at Butlin's and loved all the entertainment, including the Champagne Spinner in the ballroom on a Friday night. This was a big dial at the side of the stage, which had numbers painted round the edge and an arrow in the middle. The redcoats would spin the arrow and if it was pointing to the number of your table when it stopped, you got a bottle of champagne – at least, they called it champagne; it was fizzy and went 'pop' when it was opened, and best of all it was free!

Mavis even quite liked the stream of Radio Butlin's announcements over the tannoy, apart from the early-morning ones, which would ease you out of a deep sleep with what was supposed to be soothing music.

Two

Mavis and Ken got married eighteen months later, in the spring of 1958, when she was nineteen and he was thirty-one. They carried on performing with Dave at the working men's clubs until the spring of 1959 when they saw an advertisement for an audition for Butlin's. They were all a bit fed up with constantly having to load and unload their equipment and drive for hours to get to yet another club that didn't pay much, and the thought of regular money – even if it was quite modest – plus free bed and board, with sun, sand and seaside thrown in, sounded pretty good.

All three of them went and auditioned at a hotel in Leeds. There were other groups everywhere, and microphones and loudspeakers all over the place. A lot of them were rock groups, with guitars, drums and 'plenty of rock 'n' roll attitude', and Ken, Mavis and Dave weren't sure how well their somewhat gentler music would go down, but they passed the audition and were offered a contract at the Butlin's camp at Ayr. They were to be employed as musicians, playing in the bars and doing background music for the competitions.

Mavis's mother was heartbroken when they set off, and Mavis felt pretty emotional about it as well. She was still only twenty and had never been away from home for more than a few days, yet now she was going to be away for a whole season: five months. They packed two great big trunks with clothing. At that time they had 'a big, old car, a bit like a taxi with a drop-down boot lid at the back', so they piled the trunks on top of that and then the three of them drove up to Ayr. It was the first time Mavis had ever been there, but then it was also the first time she'd ever been to Scotland.

They travelled through the night, with no real idea of how far away it was, nor of how long it would take them to get there. In the event, they got to the camp at about 5.30 a.m. It was only just getting light and the camp gates were still locked at that time of day. They drove up to the entrance and when they got out of the car, a huge Alsatian came bounding up to the gates, barking and growling and baring its teeth. On first impressions, with the locked gates, snarling dog and arc lights illuminating the barbed-wire fences, it seemed more like a prison camp than a holiday camp, but then the night security guard came to their rescue, called off the dog and let them in. He saw that they were absolutely shattered from driving all night, so he said, 'Come and have a cup of tea and sit in the gatehouse with me until everyone else is up and doing.'

They waited until the other staff had arrived for work and then walked over to the main office, introduced themselves and showed their contracts. After their forms had been checked, the first thing they had to do was get their photos taken for their staff cards. 'It was a bit like being arrested,' Mavis says, smiling at the memory. 'You had to hold up a number while they photographed you. We had no time to spruce ourselves up after having been up all night and we looked a state! I've still got my photo and it's hilarious! I just look bewildered and bedraggled.'

They were then allocated a chalet and issued with their uniforms. Musicians usually wore green jackets rather than red ones, and had to live off camp in rented houses and 'digs', because there wasn't enough staff accommodation available for everyone on the camp. However, the entertainments manager told them that if they were willing to do a few general redcoat duties when they were not playing their instruments, they would be given red jackets and allowed to live in chalets on site. That sounded like a good deal to them, so they became Butlin's redcoats, too.

They found their chalets, and as Dave was not part of a couple, he had to share his with another single redcoat whom he had never met before. When Ken and Mavis walked into theirs, the first thing they saw was that they'd been given a chalet with bunk beds, which was not exactly ideal for a newly married couple. So they went back up to the office and said, 'Bunk beds? What? Do me a favour. We've not been married twelve months yet!'

They promised to find Mavis and Ken a chalet with a double bed and they moved into it the following day. It was late April, right at the beginning of the season, so the chalet hadn't been occupied all winter and it was cold, damp and very basic. Mavis did her best to make it a bit more homely, though since there wasn't any heating, the only way to keep warm was to put on extra clothes or fill a hot-water bottle from the hot tap in the shower block – if there was any hot water – and rush back into bed with it.

There wasn't much time off anyway, because the work was harder than they had expected. All the redcoats had to help with the big clean-up to get the camp ready for the season, and they also had to learn to find their way round the camp, because, like London policemen, redcoats were expected to know everything, from the location of the nearest toilet to how to reunite a lost holiday-maker with his chalet.

They had to play backing music for all the competitions throughout the day and then play their own set in the bars in the evenings. They also played in the Redcoat Show every Friday night – the cabaret in which all the redcoats did a 'turn' – and had to do a bit of dancing in that as well. Playing the music wasn't hard, of course, because after their years of playing in clubs that had become second nature to them and they loved it; it was continually shifting their instruments and equipment from one location to another that they found exhausting.

All the redcoats, entertainers and musicians used to get a weekly rota to show them where they were working and what they were supposed to be doing. Most Butlin's camps were on flat coastal plains, but the Ayr camp was on a hilly site, and although most of the camp was at the bottom of the hill, there was a section at the top where they used to hold competitions, singing contests and other events. For some reason, Mavis, Ken and Dave ended up with a rota that had them doing a half-hour show at the top of the hill and then another half-hour show immediately afterwards at the bottom of the hill. So with the other contests elsewhere in the camp, plus their evening session in the bar, they were having to move their kit four or five times a day. Mavis had her accordion, which was heavy enough, but then Dave had his drums and Ken his bass, and they had microphones, amps and speakers, too. Ken worked out that they were spending more time moving their gear than they were actually playing it. At the end of each gruelling day, Mavis reflected ruefully that one of the main reasons they'd come to the camp in the first place was because they were fed up with constantly having to do this when they were playing the clubs. And to make matters worse, it rained and rained and rained, pretty much non-stop, for what must have been five or six weeks.

Butlin's had just finished installing a chair-lift at Ayr and Billy Butlin, accompanied by the South African singer Eve Boswell, arrived to perform the official opening ceremony in the June of 1959. All the redcoats had to congregate at the bottom for the send-off as Billy and Eve got into the chairlift – but the manager had warned the redcoats beforehand: 'As soon as the chairlift sets off, you've all got to run to the top, so that you're there to greet them again when they get off.'

'I suppose he thought that if we did, it would look like there were twice as many redcoats as there actually were!' Mavis says. So as soon as it began to move, they all set off and began sprinting up the steep hill. It was 500 yards, but they just about beat the chairlift up there, though they must have looked a strange collection, puffing and panting, and with their faces as red as their blazers!

Any thoughts that Mavis and the others might have had about the chairlift making their lives a little easier were soon dispelled, because it was forbidden to carry anything on it. They continued carting their equipment up and down the hill and put up with their ridiculous rota for another three weeks, but Ken and Dave then went to see the entertainments manager and said, 'We're really not happy with this schedule. Can you not change the rota to make it a little bit easier on us?'

The entertainments manager just said, 'I'm sure we can work something out. Just leave it with me, lads, and I'll see what we can do.'

A week went by and there was still no change in their rota, so they went back to see the manager. This time he said, 'Oh, it's okay, lads, you seem to be managing all right as it is.'

They lasted another week and then they went back to see him for a third time. 'Look,' Ken said. 'We're not happy with this and you're not doing anything about it. So unless you do, we're going to quit.'

'You can't do that,' the entertainments manager said. 'We're just coming up to peak season. What's your reason for wanting to leave, anyway?'

Dave, who never said much but had a very dry sense of humour, pulled a long list of their grievances out of his pocket and started reading from it, until the manager cut him off in mid-flow. Although he wasn't happy about the idea of them leaving, he still wouldn't do anything to meet their complaints, so they handed in their notice on the spot.

The night before they were due to leave, they were playing their last set in one of the bars, performing on a stage with a little cur-tained rail right round the edge of it, when one of the bosses at Butlin's head office,

Wally Goodman, who organised the entertainment for the company, turned up. 'He was a lovely guy,' Mavis says. 'Very short, with a beard and a moustache with twirly ends. We didn't even know he was there until suddenly his head popped up over the top of the curtained rail and he said, "When do you finish?"'

'Tomorrow!' Ken said.

'No, no, I mean, what time do you finish tonight?' Wally said. 'I want to talk to you.'

He told them that he didn't want them to leave and was willing to do whatever he could to deal with their grievances, but by then it was too late; they had already arranged a series of bookings elsewhere. They finished that evening and went straight down to London as soon as they had packed their bags – another overnight drive.

They spent the next few months mainly doing shows on American army bases around the South of England. The shows were good fun and they enjoyed doing them, but then, out of the blue, they got a message from Wally Goodman at Butlin's, saying, 'Are you available at Christmas?'

They had planned to go back up to Yorkshire – they already had quite a few club and cabaret bookings there – but Ken said, 'Well, we could be... What have you got in mind for us?'

It turned out that the band at the Butlin's Metropole Hotel in Blackpool had fallen out with the management and walked out. Christmas was the worst possible time for that to happen, as there were non-stop shows and pantomimes and the hotel managers now suddenly found themselves with no musicians to play at them. So Wally made them a very good offer. It was a great venue and guaranteed work, with nice accommodation in the hotel itself. The alternative was to spend the winter travelling from club to club, often driving for three or four hours after the show through ice and snow to get to the next venue, and then staying in what were often pretty dingy, miserable digs. It was obvious which was the better deal, so Ken phoned the agent in the North who had lined up the club and cabaret bookings for them and said, 'Look, we may not be able to do those bookings you arranged after all.'

'The agent's language down the phone at hearing that news was pretty choice,' Mavis says. 'In fact, we never worked for him again after that, but we liked Wally and we really wanted to work at the Metropole, so we stuck to our guns and that's what we did.'

The management at the Metropole were certainly desperate to have them there, because as soon as they arrived, before they'd even had time to put their bags down, the manager said, 'Right, you've got a rehearsal in half an hour!'

So they did Christmas and New Year at the Metropole and ended up staying there for the whole winter. They then went down to Sussex at the start of the new season, where Wally had booked them to open the newly built Butlin's camp at Bognor. When they got there, it turned out that it was still a work-in-progress, with builders and other tradesmen still frantically trying to complete the camp. It had to open a bit later than the other camps, because when the season started, a lot of the chalets and other buildings still weren't finished.

Mavis, Ken and Dave arrived there thinking it would be fine – but that proved to be more than a little optimistic. As so many of the chalets weren't ready and Butlin's had already taken bookings for them, they and indeed most of the staff had to live off camp when they first got there, because otherwise there just wouldn't have been enough chalets available for the campers.

One of the biggest problems was that the contractors had diverted part of a river when they were building the camp. It then began to rain very heavily and the river flooded as it tried to resume its former course. A lot of the ground was waterlogged and what was going to be the sports field became just a sea of mud. All sorts of things that the builders had buried underneath the sports field then began to appear through the surface mud as the waters started to recede: rubble, Wellington boots, bits of metal and even a broken-down digger all had to be extracted from the glutinous mud. So there was a lot to put right and certainly plenty of reasons why some of the campers might have felt aggrieved when they turned up for their holidays.

'The day the camp finally opened was horrendous,' Mavis says. The Butlin's management had decided that the reception area didn't really matter as much as the rest of the camp. Their main efforts had been devoted to getting as many of the chalets, bars and other public rooms finished as possible, and the reception had been left as something of a bomb site.

Mavis and the others were all waiting in reception, wearing their brand-new redcoat uniforms, ready to do the 'meet and greet' when the first campers of the season started to arrive. They were soon streaming through the doors, but because the reception wasn't quite finished and was a mess of rubble, unplastered walls and empty doorways, the campers must have assumed the rest of the camp was like that, too. A lot of them just put their bags down and refused to move. They were up in arms, demanding to be transferred to other camps or given their money back.

'We were stuck in the middle of it,' Mavis

says, 'and because we were wearing red coats, we were copping most of the flak. Campers were pulling at our sleeves, shoving us and jostling us, shouting and swearing at us, and we couldn't really offer them anything either, so it was just awful. All we could do was say to them, "Just come and see the rest of the camp. It's lovely, honestly. It's only the reception that isn't finished."'

Gradually they persuaded most of the campers to do just that, and as they'd promised, the rest of it was in much better shape. Although there was still a hard core who kept demanding to be moved to other camps or given a refund – and in the end the camp managers had to oblige them – when the rest of the campers saw the entertainment areas and the finished chalets, most of them were happy. That opening day at Bognor could have been a catastrophe, and it was a testament to the calming and persuasive skills of the redcoats that it didn't end in a riot!

Some of the campers even managed to see the funny side of the situation and had a few laughs with the redcoats about it. One camper was given his key and he set off to find his chalet but was back in reception ten minutes later, handing it back in. 'I won't be needing that,' he said.

'Why not?' the manager said, fearing that he'd have to hand out another refund.

'Because there's no door on the chalet, so there's nothing to lock.' He was laughing about it, though, and when they found him another chalet and gave him a bottle of champagne as compensation for the trouble he'd been put to, he was happy enough.

Another camper, who'd booked one of the more expensive chalets with a bathroom, was still creased with laughter when he came back into reception. He had a bathroom in his chalet all right; the only problem was that the jerry-builders who had been working on it had somehow managed to finish the external walls without noticing that they'd left a cement mixer inside. More champagne and a change of chalets solved the camper's problem, but the builders then had to demolish one of the original chalet's walls to get the cement mixer out again.

The Verdi Three were booked to play every lunchtime and evening in the massive bar, called Ye Olde Pigge and Whistle, just like in the other Butlin's camps. Mavis can still remember the chaos that greeted them when they went to play their first set. 'We set up our gear and started playing, even though there were electricians up ladders still putting lights in, and joiners finishing some of the fittings. The rhythm must've got to them, though, because eventually they were all hammering and banging in time with the music, so it didn't sound quite as bad as it could have done!'

The first set of holiday-makers had proved in the end to be pretty philosophical and good-humoured about the camp's teething troubles, and eventually the staff, builders and other tradesmen managed to solve all the problems, so it turned out to be a really good season. Mavis, Ken and Dave stayed on for the winter as well, running a social club at the camp for the residents of Bognor. The local people could come along, play indoor bowls or snooker, go swimming or use any of the other facilities, and The Verdi Three would play a bit of dance music for them in the afternoons and evenings. There was a membership fee, but it wasn't expensive and they loved it so much that many would bring a flask and some sandwiches and stay there all day.

However, that winter there was another disaster when one of the glass walls around the swimming pool shattered. The pool was next to the ballroom and had glass walls so that people could sit and have a drink in the seating areas around the edge of the dance floor and watch the swimmers under the water through the glass. One of the panels must have had a fault in it, because a crack snaked across it and then, seconds later, it gave way altogether. Fortunately, there was no one in the pool or the ballroom at the time, but a torrent of water – thousands of gallons – came flooding out and swept right across the ballroom. The dance floor was feet-deep in water, and all the carpets, sofas and chairs in the surrounding areas were saturated. No one could believe that such bad things were still happening; it was as if the whole place was jinxed.

The Verdi Three had left all their instruments and equipment down in the ballroom, ready for their next set, so they had to grab all their gear and take it upstairs out of harm's way, and then pitch in with everyone else to try to minimise the damage and clear up. Every member of the staff, from the camp manager right down to the kitchen porters, rolled up their sleeves and got stuck in. Someone had dialled 999 and a fire engine soon arrived to pump out the worst of the water, while Mavis and the rest of the staff were all running around with mops and squeegees, clearing up the puddles, rolling up the sodden carpets and carrying the soaked furniture outside in the hope that it might dry a little in the sunshine. They worked all day and into the night, and the catering people also laboured tirelessly, making stacks of sandwiches and endless cups of coffee to keep everyone going. Ken always told Mavis that she made a big mistake when she and Dave volunteered to do the washing-up afterwards, because they found what looked like a thousand dirty cups and plates stacked up waiting for them.

They made some good friends at Bognor and at another brand-new Butlin's camp, Minehead, when they were sent there the following year. The company had learned a lot of lessons from the previous year's mistakes, and Minehead's opening in 1962 was much smoother than Bognor's, so much so that when The Verdi Three played their first set, there was not a single electrician or joiner in sight! The one thing that the opening of the two camps did have in common was that both sites were awash with mud due to flooding. At Minehead, Butlin's solved the problem by excavating a trench right round the low-lying site and piling up the earth they'd extracted into a steep bank. Making a virtue out of a necessity, the trench was then converted into the camp's boating lake.

Minehead had all the usual range of Butlin's attractions, and a few newer ones as well, including one of the Hawaiian-style Beachcomber Bars that were opened at several camps during the 1960s, allegedly after Billy Butlin had seen the Beachcomber Bar at the Mayfair Hotel in London. The one at Minehead had fibre-glass palm trees, totem poles, fake hibiscus and jacaranda flowers, plastic parrots and pelicans, 'Hawaiian' barmaids in grass skirts serving exotic cocktails and even a 'wrecked ship' projecting out of one wall. The pièce de résistance was the volcano that erupted on the hour every hour, accompanied by a mock tropical storm, complete with the sound of thunder and lightning and torrential rain.

It was while working at Minehead that Mavis met another redcoat, Hilary, who was to become one of her closest friends. She actually met Hilary's husband Bill first, because he was assistant manager there and was the first person who greeted Ken and Mavis when they arrived. She met Hilary soon afterwards, but they lost touch after Ken and Mavis left Minehead, and it would be many, many years before Mavis saw Hilary again.

Three

By the time they began working at Minehead, Ken and Mavis were already thinking that they might want to start a family. They knew that if they did, they would have to split up the trio and stop working as redcoats, because that job was so demanding of their time and energy that it simply wouldn't leave room for family life as well.

Butlin's management had already been asking Ken if he would be interested in becoming an entertainments manager with the company. He was an obvious choice, as he'd always been good at organising the business side of things for the group and his years of working in the clubs had also given him great contacts in the industry.

He had said no at first and they'd carried on as they were for a while, but eventually Ken and Dave sat down together, had a long chat and decided it might be wise for both of them to look at a change of direction. Butlin's was also willing to train Dave for a management role, so they dissolved the trio at the end of that season. Dave went off to Butlin's at Pwllheli and became an assistant entertainments manager there, while Ken was offered the job of entertainments manager at the Ocean Hotel in Brighton, and Mavis became the chief hostess there, organising all the competitions and prizes.

It was part of Mavis's job to look after the stars appearing at Butlin's. 'It was one of the nicest things about becoming chief hostess,' she says. 'We made friends with a lot of them, because they would come back to do shows time and again. Bob Monkhouse came there often – he was an absolutely brilliant comedian and a lovely man as well.' Many other comedians frequented Butlin's, including Dave Allen, Freddie 'Parrot Face' Davies,

Norman Vaughan and Colin Crompton, who'd made his name on the *Wheeltappers and Shunters Social Club* television show. There were also singers like Frankie Vaughan and the Canadian Ted Hockridge, and television personalities like Hughie Green, who was a really big name at the time. 'It was nice to meet them and get to know them,' Mavis says, 'but we still had our feet on the ground and didn't get "enraptured" with it all.'

There were also many old-fashioned variety and novelty acts who extended their careers by appearing at Butlin's, some travelling from camp to camp and appearing virtually full time during the season. Among them was 'Dare Devil Peggy' – not a woman, but a man with a wooden leg, who dived from a high board into a small tub of water – Mario, 'Europe's Champion Stock Whip Manipulator'; Wilson, Keppel and Betty doing their legendary 'Sand Dance'; a hypnotist called Peter Casson and a reformed pickpocket, who used his skills to pinch wallets, purses, watches, handkerchiefs and even ties and braces from the campers he lured onto the stage, though they always got their property back at the end of the act!

Billy Butlin had always hired big names in entertainment and many redcoats dreamed of similar showbiz stardom, with one describing the camp shows as 'a microcosm of show business. You had hierarchies among

114

the entertainers on the camp: first the principal comedians, then the review company and the review stars, then the compère and then the redcoats, who were still minor celebrities.'

Despite this veneer of glamour, the reality was often rather more prosaic. For every one who made it, there were a thousand others who never got closer to the bright lights of fame than the Redcoat Show on a Friday night, the last show before that week's batch of campers would depart and the new influx arrived. Nonetheless, most were happy with their lot, whether they stayed for a season or a working lifetime.

Some redcoats were also travelling the road to stardom in the opposite direction. One barman working at a camp in 1967 knew a former pop star, Mick, who was back on the bottom rung of the ladder. Mick had been a singer with a pop group that'd had an enormous Top Ten hit with their debut record. Sadly, the group proved to be the archetypal one-hit wonder and their fall was as meteoric as their rise. Within eighteen months the closest Mick could get to showbiz stardom was leading the campers in a rousing chorus of 'Roll Out the Barrel' in the bar on Saturday nights.

After Brighton, Mavis and Ken went to work at Filey for a couple of years, still hoping that they'd be able to start a family soon. She can remember being backstage in 1969 and watching the American moon landings between sets on a little television that the stage manager had set up in the wings. 'Even watching it on that tiny little screen was amazing,' she says. 'I couldn't quite believe what was happening.'

For the first few winters, while their Butlin's camp was closed, Mavis and Ken took a touring show out into clubland, appearing with about a dozen other performers, all of them people they'd met at Butlin's. There was an organ and drums, two singers, Ken as comedian and Mavis playing accordion, and a really good balancing act as well.

They had a van to get them and their equipment around, although it was a slow business then, because there weren't many motorways. They had done it all before, of course, in the days when they were playing clubs all the time, so they thought they knew what to expect, but still, it turned out to be quite an experience, because some of the clubs and accommodation they were booked into were, she says, 'beyond belief!'

The winter of 1969-70 was a hard one, and Mavis can remember waking up in their freezing-cold digs in Sheffield one morning, looking out of the window and not being able to see their van because it was completely covered in snow. Their landlady kept her false teeth in a glass in the hallway and never had them in when she was in the house. 'She used to talksh like thish to ush wishout shem!' Mavis says. She would always put them in before she went out to the shops, though.

When they went into her house, it was always quite dark and smelled of boiled cabbage, no matter what the time of day. The landlady never put the lights on in the lounge area. They assumed at first that it was to save money, but before long they realised there could be another reason. Two lads were staying there who had a shooting act, and one day they were sitting in the lounge cleaning their guns and one of them put the light on so he could see what he was doing. Mavis then realised why the lights were always off – because the place was absolutely filthy. The landlady used to serve their evening meal around her big 'farm' table, and she always made sure that the light was off in there as well, so they never knew what they were eating, which was perhaps just as well. Most of the time, they would get fish and chips on the way back from a gig, rather than eat the meal waiting for them back at their digs.

The landlady also had a strange domestic arrangement, because her husband lived at the bottom of the garden in a big shed. Every so often, when his wife was out, he'd come wandering up to the house in his pyjamas. They were a bit nervous of him, but he usually wandered off again quite peaceably after scrounging a cigarette from Ken.

They also played a few clubs around Leicester and stayed at a cheap hotel there, which was also not without its quirks. 'All the beds were really old-fashioned, iron-framed ones with ageing springs,' Mavis recalls. 'They all squeaked like mad whenever anyone sat on them or slept in them, and if anyone was making love, it sounded like they were doing it in a scrap-yard! So all night long, whenever anyone turned over in bed, you could hear this metallic squeaking and groaning sound. We all finished up sitting on the stairs for the rest of the night and chatting to each other because no one could get a wink of sleep.'

They did a couple of winters in Blackpool as well, and Mavis always enjoyed Christmas at the Butlin's hotel there. 'It was always lovely,' she says. 'There was a great atmosphere and it was also very comfortable. However, we also stayed at a Butlin's camp one Christmas and that was a lot less fun, because the chalets were freezing cold and so were the bars and the ballroom. We did put some heaters in those, but we were fighting a losing battle, because you didn't get rid of two or three months' winter cold overnight, and you still had that damp atmosphere that didn't do much for anyone's Christmas spirit.'

Ken and Mavis next went to Ayr, where Ken spent three years as manager, and they then did another three years at Filey. Her mum and dad came there on holiday while Mavis and Ken were working there. Although her mum enjoyed most things about it, it was also something of an ordeal for her, because she was very shy and easily embarrassed. When Mavis's mum and dad first used to go to working men's clubs together, if her mum wanted to get up and go to the ladies in the middle of the evening while one of the acts was on, she'd be absolutely terrified, because she was afraid that everybody would be watching her. When they came to Filey, Mavis reserved them one of the best tables, near the stage at the Midnight Cabaret, but when her mum saw where Mavis had seated them, all she could say was: 'Do we have to sit quite so near to the front?'

Mavis's dad laughed and said, 'What are you talking about? People would kill for these seats! Sit down and don't make a fuss!'

When Mavis and Ken were off duty, there were plenty of things to do and it was, she says, 'amazing what you could do at Butlin's. As well as all the entertainment, music and dancing, you could do just about any sport or pastime you could mention, from football and swimming to archery and art classes. You could even watch showjumping – stars like Harvey Smith used to appear there.'

Like Ken and Dave, a lot of the other men they had worked with became managers and assistant managers. When they did, they had to give up the Butlin's red jacket and wear a navy-blue blazer instead. When Mavis saw them again, she observed, 'It was funny how many of them said to me: "I really miss my red coat," because everybody loved the redcoats – or at least the campers did; the other staff sometimes weren't so sure! When they put the blue blazer on, the campers didn't really know who they were, and however good a job they did, they weren't as involved with the holiday-makers as the redcoats were. If you were a good redcoat, when you walked into a bar, you never had to buy a drink, because the campers were queuing up to buy you one. You never had to buy anything, because they were always saying, "I'll get that, come and sit with us," just because they wanted to be with you. And anyway, it was part of the rules of our job that we had to sit with the campers; we weren't ever allowed to sit down with another redcoat, because we were there to entertain the campers, not ourselves.'

Four

All the time they had been working for Butlin's, Ken and Mavis had still been trying for a family, but for many years it looked like it was never going to happen. They were married in 1958, and as the 1960s and the early 1970s went by, they still hadn't had a child. 'After a while we just sort of gave up trying,' she says. 'We both thought, it's just not going to happen, we're never going to have a family.'

Despite that, in 1976, completely out of the blue, Mavis got pregnant. She didn't even realise it at the time. She hadn't been feeling right for a few days, so she went to see the doctor at the camp, whom she'd got to know quite well by then. He gave her a quick examination and then said, 'Will you come out to my surgery?' – he had his own surgery outside the camp – 'and I'll be able to do some more tests there.'

He didn't tell her what he was testing her for and said that it would be the next day before he got the results, so she was worried, fearing that she might have some terrible illness, and didn't sleep well that night. The next morning, the secretary from the medical centre rang her and said, 'Mavis, can you come down, because your test results are back and the doctor wants to see you?'

So she went, not knowing quite what to expect. The doctor knew that they had been trying for a family for years – they had been to see him a couple of times to find out if there was anything he could advise them to do to improve their chances – and as soon as she walked in, he said, 'So, what happened this year, then? Did you get yourself a boy-friend?'

She didn't get what he was talking about at first and just said, 'Why, what do you mean?'

'I mean that you're pregnant.'

She just couldn't believe it; she was so thrilled she could hardly speak. When she got back to the camp, Ken was in a meeting with the other managers over in the Beach-comber Bar, so she couldn't tell him straight away. However, his deputy, Derek, was in the office when she went in and asked, 'How did you get on at the doctors?'

She was so excited that she just blurted out 'I'm pregnant'.

'What? Does Ken know?'

'No, I haven't told him yet. I can't go in, because he's in a meeting with the other managers.'

'Well, I can,' he said. 'Wait here and I'll tell him.'

So he went over to the Beachcomber Bar. There was a security grille separating the bar area from the rest of the room. Derek was on one side of the grille, frantically waving and signalling to Ken, who was sitting on the other side of the room with the rest of the managers. Eventually one of them noticed Derek and said, 'Ken, I think someone is trying to attract your attention.'

Mavis would no doubt have preferred Derek to say something like, 'Ken, Mavis needs to see you urgently,' so that she could break the wonderful news to him herself, but Derek was so excited on her behalf that before Ken had got halfway across the room to find out what he wanted, he had shouted out 'Mavis is pregnant!'

None of the staff were supposed to drink on camp before six in the evening, but this was one occasion when that rule was definitely going to be ignored. Ken broke up his meeting, came straight back to the office and gave Mavis a hug that nearly broke her ribs. 'Seeing as it's a special occasion,' he said, 'my bar's going to be open early today!'

Ken didn't drink when he was working as a rule, but he knew he was going to be in for a big night that evening, so he said to Derek, 'Stick with me all night and don't leave me for a moment, because everyone will be trying to buy me drinks and I'm only going to be drinking whisky, nothing else.' Despite his best intentions, however, by half past ten that evening his friends had to carry him back to his chalet.

Mavis phoned her mum and dad that night to tell them the news. Her dad just said, 'After all these years? I can't believe it. You've either made a big mistake or you've gone crazy!' Then her mum snatched the phone from him – she could hardly speak for crying because she was so happy for her.

Ken tried to wrap her in cotton wool while she was pregnant. Even though the baby wasn't due until early the following year, he took her back home to her parents before the end of the season to make sure she would be all right, and then went back to Butlin's to finish the season. He had always said to her, 'If we have any children, we won't bring them up at Butlin's,' because they'd seen what happened when other people tried to do that. 'The children would often get really spoiled,' Mavis says, 'because everybody would make such a big fuss of them, and trying to juggle your work and your family life in such a full-time job was also far from easy, so that was the decision we made.'

At the end of the season, Ken decided it was time to leave and take a less all-consuming job at Ashton under Lyne, organising the entertainment programme for the local council. The job itself was all right, but the stress of travelling from Dewsbury to Ashton under Lyne and back over the Pennines on the M62 motorway every day was horrendous for him, especially in winter, when there was often fog, snow and ice to contend with.

One morning in January 1977, when she was eight and a half months pregnant and Ken had gone off to work early as usual, Mavis was at home looking through the baby clothes they had bought for about the hundredth time when the phone rang. When she answered, she heard a woman's voice, saying she was calling from Ashton under Lyne. At first Mavis thought it was someone from Ken's office, but then she felt her heart give a lurch as the woman said, 'No, it's the hospital. We've got your husband here, and we're keeping him in under observation. Perhaps you'd like to come over.'

'Should I come now?' she said.

'No, there's no immediate cause for panic, just come when you're ready.'

Even though the woman wouldn't tell Mavis what was wrong with Ken over the phone, it all seemed very calm, so she rang her brother and said, 'Ken's in hospital in Ashton, can you take me over there?'

He asked her if she wanted to go right away, but he had his own business to run and Mavis knew that he was very busy, so since the hospital had said there was no rush, she just said, 'No, just when you've got time.'

'Right, I'll be up for you shortly.'

He turned up an hour or so later, drove her over to Ashton under Lyne and dropped her off at the hospital entrance while he went to park the car. Mavis went inside and found her way to the ward. When she told the duty nurse who she was, the nurse took her into a side room, sat her down and made her a cup of tea. That really set the alarm bells ringing, as Mavis was thinking to herself, they don't usually do this, do they?

Her brother came in and gave her a look as if to say 'What's going on?' but then the nurse came back and said, 'I'm afraid your husband's had a heart attack.'

He'd driven all the way from home to Ashton under Lyne with a box of Rennie on the seat beside him, thinking he just had indigestion, but then he'd had a heart attack in the office and was crawling around the floor in agony when one of the other managers found him. Ken had been rushed to hospital, but because of Mavis's pregnancy, he had begged them not to tell her. It was the first either of them knew about him having a heart problem. When she saw him he was weak and obviously very shaken by what had happened, but he managed a smile and told her in a slurred voice: 'Don't worry about me, I'll be fine.'

However, while he was still in hospital, he had two more heart attacks in that first week alone. Mavis was fifty miles away from him, on the wrong side of the Pennines, and so heavily pregnant that she couldn't drive. She was obviously worrying herself sick about Ken and the baby, so in the end the hospital arranged for her to go over to Ashton and give birth there, just so she could be near him. As a result, their beautiful daughter, Anna Marie, was born by Caesarean section in the maternity unit of the same hospital where Ken was in intensive care. Almost the first thing Mavis thought as she was cradling her baby was: we've waited all these years and now he's never even going to see this baby.

In the end, Ken came out of intensive care the day after Anna Marie was born. So they brought him over to the maternity unit in a wheelchair and for the first time he held his daughter in his arms. Quite a few of their Butlin's friends also came to see them while they were in hospital, and the knowledge that so many of their friends were there for them was a real boost.

As she'd had a Caesarean, it took Mavis a while to heal, and in the end she and Ken were released from hospital on the same day. Her mum and dad came over from Dewsbury and brought them home with them, and the three of them ended up living in the terraced house Mavis had been born in – her grandmother's old house, just two doors away from her parents. 'So I was right back where I started all those years before!' she says with a smile. 'It was just as well, for without them I really don't think I would have been able to manage. Ken's heart condition meant we couldn't risk him going upstairs, but luckily we had a studio couch, so he slept on that in the living room. Anna Marie had to sleep in her pram because we didn't have room for a cot, but she was still so tiny that she was fine in the pram.'

Ken seemed to be recovering slowly and was doing quite well until the first week in October. It was the Harvest Festival at church and Mavis had taken Ken his breakfast and then put a basket of fruit together for the celebrations. She had got Anna Marie dressed and in her pram and they were just about to set off for church when Ken called out to her, 'Get an ambulance, quick!'

He had another massive heart attack that morning. Her mum looked after the baby while Mavis went to the hospital with Ken. She was sitting outside the intensive-care unit as they were trying to save his life and all she could think was: I'm going to walk out of here without a husband.

Thankfully, Ken once more had the

resilience and the medical care to get through it, but by then his health had been wrecked. He never fully recovered, and even though he lived for another twenty-four years, he was only a shadow of the person he had been and never went back to work again, which, Mavis says, 'he found very hard to take, because he was a proud man and he'd always been so active'.

Her mum and dad were a constant help and support to them, and of course they doted on their grandchild. Mavis and Ken also had a very good friend who used to come and take Anna Marie out in the pram every single day. Whatever the weather was doing, rain, snow or shine, he would always come to take her out, just to give Mavis a little bit of time to herself. They had such good friends from their Butlin's days, too, and they all kept in touch and came to see them regularly.

Although it was never easy, they managed somehow, and Mavis remains convinced that it was Anna Marie who pulled Ken through and kept him going for so long. When the district nurse came round to check the baby for the first time after Mavis had brought Anna Marie home, she said to Mavis, 'This baby has been sent for a reason. She's given your husband something to live for.'

'He knew he was living on borrowed time,'

Mavis says, 'and he was so hungry to see her grow up and go through all the stages of her childhood. Each one – the first time she smiled, the first time she sat up, her first tooth, the first word she spoke, the first hesitant step she took – was another milestone reached, but there was always another goal Ken had set himself. He just couldn't wait. He used to say, "Now I just want to see her go to school," and when that happened there was always something else to look forward to and live for. He kept going all the way through her childhood and when she was growing up, becoming a teenager and then a young adult. She adored him as well. He was at home all the time, of course, and they used to sit together on the sofa and watch kids television programmes, and he'd teach her all sorts of things – she learned such a lot from him. She could read and do her numbers before she'd even been to nursery, because he taught her them.'

Anna Marie inherited her parents' talents and their love of entertainment, too. Mavis bought a little accordion for her when she was small and taught her to play it. 'Although she was doing quite well with it,' Mavis says, 'in the end she decided she preferred dancing, so she went the other way from me and gave up music to concentrate on dance.' When she grew up, she went to college to do dance and drama, and then became a professional dancer. Mavis took Ken to see their daughter in some of the shows she did, and of course he absolutely loved that.

So even though it was hard for all of them at times, their life together was far from being all doom and gloom. One year, when Anna Marie was very young, they took her to one of the Butlin's hotels, which they all enjoyed. She never followed in her parents' footsteps and worked as a redcoat, though as Mavis says, 'It wasn't really the same place by the time Anna Marie was growing up.'

When she was in her teens, Anna Marie said to them one day, 'I know I've been to one of the Butlin's hotels, but I've never been to one of the holiday camps. You talk about it so much and yet I don't really know what went on there, so will you take me?'

So Ken and Mavis took her down to Bognor for a week and 'she absolutely loved it', Mavis says. 'But it was a strange and rather unsettling experience for us, because it was all so different; everything had changed. On the Friday night they still did the big Au Revoir [when all the campers had a big party before they went home the next day] and we went into the ballroom and started watching it, but after a few minutes Ken just said, "I'll have to go outside." I followed him out and he said to me, "I just can't stand to watch it," because it wasn't what we had known in all our years at Butlin's.

'When we worked there, we were there to give people a good time. They came expecting it and they always *did* have a good time. We'd have bank managers and accountants rolling up their trouser legs and entering the Knobbly Knees competitions and things, and they just didn't care; they were away from home, nobody knew them and they were just there to have fun. They let their hair down, they really went to town, and that was what was so funny and really made me laugh, but I suppose that changed. There was an innocence then, but that's gone now. Those days are over and I don't suppose they'll ever come back.'

Ken and Mavis went on several other holidays with Anna Marie and they had some great times together, but Ken's heart condition was always in the back of their minds. Ken couldn't do any lifting or anything strenuous, and even though they took every precaution, there were always new health scares. 'In all those twenty-four years that he lived after that first heart attack,' Mavis says, 'there was only one when he didn't have to go back into hospital at some time or other during the year for fresh treatment. They used to give him all these tablets, and they were trying out all sorts of new drugs on him, but a lot of them used to affect him quite badly and give him all sorts of side-effects, and sometimes it was the reaction to the tablets, not his heart, that put him back in hospital.'

They just tried to laugh it all off. Mavis used to say to him with a smile, 'You know what, Ken? I've spent more than enough birthdays and wedding anniversaries sitting in front of the television with you, with a glass of lemonade in my hand! Where's the champagne?'

They moved to a bungalow in the 1990s, as it was easier for Ken to manage without stairs. He was lying in bed one morning in 2001, just like any other day. Mavis had been down to the corner shop and got him the morning paper and then made him a cup of tea, as usual. She was sitting in the kitchen reading a magazine when she heard a noise from the bedroom. 'It was the sound the newspaper makes when it falls on the floor,' she says, 'if you've fallen asleep in bed and let it drop from your hand. I thought to myself, he's just dropped the paper, but I went to check, and when I walked into the room, he was lying back on his pillows and had gone very white. At first I thought he'd just fainted, but then I realised it was more serious. I called the ambulance at once and then tried to give him resuscitation, but I found it very hard to do and I think he was probably dead before the ambulance had even got there.

'The ambulance crew took over then. So I stood there, with tears pouring down my face, while they worked on him – and they did work really hard to try to save him – but it wasn't to be. So I never had the chance to say goodbye to him or exchange any last words with him, but we'd been man and wife for forty-three years, and there wasn't much that hadn't been said after all that time, and I've so many memories of him to treasure.'

Anna Marie was in London when he died and Mavis had to ring her up and tell her. She was heartbroken, and Mavis thinks her daughter felt even worse about it, because she hadn't been there when he died. She kept saying, 'I'm not going to go away again,' but Mavis said, 'You certainly are. You have not done all that work and training for nothing. Your father would want you to carry on, and so do I.'

Anna Marie kept working as a dancer and, one year, while she was working as a dancer on a cruise liner, Mavis went out to the Caribbean on the ship with her and had a fortnight out there. 'I saw Anna Marie dance every day and we had a wonderful time together,' she says. Ken's heart condition had meant that he couldn't sail or fly, so they'd never been abroad. It was the first time Mavis had ever been out of the country.

She also had a lot of friends at her local

134

church, where she had always been very involved in things, and that helped pull her through, she says. And, of course, she had her friends from Butlin's as well. 'They all kept me busy and I think that's the secret for anyone who's lost a loved one. You can sit there and cry forever, but it's not going to bring them back and it's not going to help you either, so right from the start, whether I wanted to or not, I made myself go out every single day, even if it was only down to the corner shop.

'It was a long time ago, almost thirteen years, and it's different now of course, because you do learn to live with it – you have to – but at the beginning it was hard to go on sometimes. And you never know how other people, your friends and acquaintances, are going to react to something like that. Some people try to avoid you, not because they're cold or heartless, but because they just don't know how to cope with it or what to say to you, so they keep out of your way. There were some people like that, but I had plenty of good friends there to help and support me, and of course I had Anna Marie.'

Mavis is always very busy and she's still remarkably fit and supple. 'I must owe that to good genes,' she says. 'Though I do get an awful lot more aches and pains than I used to!' It's a long time now since she last played music professionally, but she's still got her accordion and plays it for her own pleasure – 'I sometimes think I'm the only person in Britain who still plays one!' she says with a laugh. 'There were quite a lot of accordionists around in the days when I was growing up, and it's still a popular instrument in Italy and Germany, but you don't often see accordionists over here any more. I don't play it now as much as I used to, but I've always thanked my stars that I learned to play it when I was young, because it's taken me all over and given me a life of experiences I would probably never have had in any other way. But of all those experiences, it's Butlin's that still stands out for me.'

When Ken and Mavis were working at Butlin's, because they were playing music all the time, they weren't as involved with the other redcoats as the ones who were on general duties. So although she worked alongside many of them and recognises them when she sees photos of them as they were then, Mavis wasn't close friends with many of them at the time. Mavis's years as a redcoat and chief hostess overlapped with those of another Butlin's girl, Valda, for example, but she has only got to know her more recently through the Butlin's reunions they've been to. The first one Mavis went to was at Scarborough, in the Grand Hotel – once one of the Butlin's hotels.

She's been to lots of reunions since then and loves to meet the people there, some of whom – like Hilary, whom Mavis met at Minehead – she hasn't seen for forty years. When Mavis got back in touch with Hilary, despite all the years that had passed, it was, she says, 'as if we'd seen each other only the day before'. They are now the best of friends. They are both Yorkshire lasses, who are now on their own, and they live just a few miles from each other, but they have many other things in common, too. 'Hilary's had a rough time in her own life – she's lost two husbands – but she does really well,' Mavis says. 'She copes with it, and just gets on with it.'

When they meet regularly for lunch in Leeds, they often find themselves still sitting there, chatting about their lives, when the other customers have all long since gone. They always travel to the reunions together and share a room. There is sorrow as well as happiness at the reunions, because apart from the husbands they've lost, the gaps in the ranks remind them, Mavis says, 'that we're losing a lot of people now. I suppose you get to an age where you start losing your friends on a regular basis, and it's not going to change for us from now on.'

Mavis absolutely loved every moment she spent at Butlin's – even the times when she was lugging her accordion across the camp in the pouring rain! 'It was such an exciting time,' she says. 'I wouldn't have missed it for anything. We always say at the reunions, "We had the best time," and I really think we did. I don't think it's the same now as it used to be. That may just be our prejudices; maybe the people who are working as red-coats there now think it's the same for them; maybe they feel that now is their time, just as we did about ours. All I can say is that it was the best of times for me and for us, and when we were there, we lived like a family, in a home from home, and we really looked after each other. There were lots of goings-on, of course – we were young, after all – but we were a real family. We were close then and we're still close now, all these years later, and I know that we'll stay close for the rest of our lives.'

Valerie

One

Valerie Knibbs came from a poor working-class background, growing up in a slum district in the old Jewellery Quarter in the centre of Birmingham. She was born in 1942, while her father was away fighting in the war. She didn't set eyes on him until she was five years old. Before then, she says, 'My dad was only a photograph that my mum showed me.' When he came home at the end of the war, Valerie can remember going with her mother to Snow Hill Station in Birmingham, standing on the steps watching soldiers pour off the train and wondering which one was her father, and then saying, 'There's my daddy!' when she recognised the man in the photograph coming towards them. He was about five foot six inches tall and very thin and hollow-cheeked at the time, though he filled out later on. He'd brought her a present of a doll back from Italy. She was absolutely thrilled with it, because it was the first doll she'd ever had.

She had a brother, Malcolm, who was three years younger than her. The family lived in one rented room in a crumbling Victorian house in an area that had been heavily bombed during the war and was still pocked with rubble-strewn, weed-infested bomb-sites. Once her younger brother had out-grown the drawer in which he slept when he was small, Valerie had to share her single bed with him. 'Though you'll hear lots of people joke about having a coat on the bed instead of a blanket, we really did – that was all we had to keep warm,' she says.

There was no bathroom or toilet in the house, just an outdoor WC and a tin bath hanging on the back wall next to the dolly tub and washboard that her mum used to do the washing. They would have a bath once a week on a Friday in front of the open fire, always providing that there was enough money for coal – and often there wasn't. As young children they used to get sent down to the coal yard to try and pick up bits of coal, and they'd get told off by their mum if they brought back what she called 'slack' – small pieces of coal and coal dust, rather than bigger lumps. There was no electric light; they had gas mantles, which gave off a strong odour and burned with a continuous hissing noise.

There was no light at all in the outside toilet, which was very dark and smelled of damp. The newspaper that they used as toilet paper – cut into squares and threaded on a piece of string – was also damp. 'It wasn't a pleasant experience at all,' Valerie says. 'I can smell damp and wet paper a mile off, even today!' Newspaper had several other uses. Sheets of it were also spread on the table as a makeshift tablecloth, and when they were soiled, they were screwed up tightly into balls and used to light the fire.

Her mother was very thin and a really hard worker, always scrimping and saving to try to make ends meet. Her father would give her a little housekeeping money out of his wages, but that was it; what was left over was his to spend as he saw fit. Unlike children today, Valerie and Malcolm were left on their own a lot while their parents worked. Even when she was really quite little, no more than three years old, her mum would leave her in the evenings while she went to work. 'We really were latch-key kids,' she says, 'who let ourselves into the house and saw to ourselves a lot of the time, and as I'm always telling my children and grandchildren, we didn't have cereal for breakfast; we just had a piece of bread with a little bit of sugar sprinkled on it and a cup of hot milk, and that was it, that was our breakfast.'

Her father worked as a lorry driver and her mum was a machinist in a metal-working factory. During the war they were making munitions, but when the war was over they went back to making parts for cars. Valerie was taken in to see the factory one day. 'It really was awful,' she says. 'Filthy and deafeningly noisy, with dust filling the air, piles of metal cuttings on the floor and no facilities at all. As I looked around, even as young as I was, I can still remember thinking to myself, I don't want this when I grow up.' That wasn't the way her parents saw it; Valerie says the only careers advice she and her brother ever had from their parents was when they said to Malcolm, 'Your father is a lorry driver, you'll be a lorry driver,' and to Valerie it was: 'Your mother works in a factory. It was good enough for her, so it'll be good enough for you.'

The house next door was not divided up into bedsits like theirs. It was owned by a factory owner, Mr Tidsdale, and his wife. They had lived there for many years and had stayed there even though the area had become more and more decrepit. Mrs Tidsdale would sometimes let Valerie go round and play on the upright piano they had. Of course, she couldn't really play it, but she'd sit on the piano stool and plink-plonk away on the keys. She remembers how the house always smelled of apples and how much she used to love going round there; it was perhaps the first hint she'd had that there were possibilities in life other than drudgery in a dead-end job and a grim, hand-to-mouth existence.

When Valerie was still only five, the family moved out of the area and went to live in Hamstead, a mining village a few miles north of Birmingham. They lived in a prefab house built by the forced labour of Italian or German prisoners of war. 'It would seem very crude and primitive to modern eyes,' Valerie says, 'but it had a bathroom, an inside loo, a stove in the living room, a cooker with an oven in the kitchen and a little garden at the front and back. Coming from where we'd been living, it seemed very posh indeed to us.' There were only two bedrooms, though, so Valerie still had to share a room with her brother – and with her new baby sister, Christine, who was born soon after they moved there.

Valerie's parents could not afford a television, but further up the road there was a family who were much better off and owned a black-and-white TV. Valerie would go and stand outside their house when *Watch With Mother* was on. She couldn't hear it, of course, but looking in through their window, she could see a little puppet horse – Muffin the Mule – bouncing about, and two flowerpot men – Bill and Ben. 'I foolishly thought that if I stood there long enough, I'd get invited in to watch the television, but of course we were the poor family in the road, and that never happened. When we did get a television, many years later, it was still so exciting that even when the programmes had ended for the day, we'd leave it switched on and keep staring into the static on the screen, hoping that it would come back on again!'

Like many families then, there were a lot of arguments between her parents. Perhaps the long separation during the war was partly to blame for that – most couples in Britain had to make a similar adjustment – and it didn't help that they were still desperately poor. The Women's Voluntary Service (WVS) used to come round in a van, giving away plants for the garden and second-hand clothes for the children, and that was where all their clothes came from. Valerie can remember having only one pair of pants and having to wear them for a couple of days, then wash them and put them on top of the oven in the hope that they would be dry enough to put back on again the next morning. They were made of such thick cloth that they never were, so she'd have to go to school wearing damp pants and in winter they would chap her legs terribly. She also often had to go to school with cardboard inside her shoes, because there were holes in the soles.

They could never afford a holiday when she was small. The first time she can remember going on holiday was when she was eight or nine years old, and that turned into a disaster. Her father had rented a battered old caravan at Weston-superMare. It was the only one they could afford, but it was practically derelict. Her father was making their breakfast one morning while the children sat either side of the little table by the stove. He tried to light the gas to boil the kettle, but the gas pipes were so corroded that the gas was leaking. It ignited beneath the stove and a tongue of flame flashed out and burned her sister's legs as she sat at the table. She was taken to hospital in Weston-super-Mare and had to have skin grafts on both legs. Although they could have sued the owner of the caravan for compensation, her parents had no money and could not afford to go to court, so they got nothing. Their first ever holiday was memorable for all the wrong reasons.

Valerie's mum and aunt used to sing together in the pubs at weekends– 'Not for money,' she says, 'just because that's what everybody did then. On Friday, Saturday and Sunday nights, people went to the pub and would have a singsong.' As part of their preparations for a night out, Valerie can remember the two women rubbing a brown liquid onto their legs and drawing a black line up the back of them with a soft pencil to mimic the seams on stockings.

The pubs were always dense with cigarette smoke, which her mum contributed to by chain-smoking untipped Woodbines, and her mum and Auntie Nen used to take snuff as well. Valerie can remember them sniffing up pinches of snuff from the backs of their hands, staining their nostrils dark brown. She would be taken to the pub with them, but when they got there she'd have to sit on the steps outside, with a bottle of Vimto and a bag of crisps if she was lucky, and she would be there till closing time – she thinks it was 10 or 10.30 p.m. at the time – in all sorts of weather. While she was sitting there, she'd hear her mum and Auntie Nen inside, singing their hearts out, and she'd sing along, sitting on the cold, damp steps outside.

After her father came home from the war, her parents would go to the pub together and Valerie was left at home on her own to look after her brother and sister. 'You'd be locked up for leaving children at home with no one to look after them today,' Valerie says, 'but back then it was just the way it was.' By the time they got home from the pub, she was usually asleep in bed, but she'd hear the noise of them coming in – they always brought other people back with them. They'd then get her up and she'd be put on show, with her parents saying, 'Valerie will sing.' So she'd stand up and sing for them while they and their friends got more and more drunk, and then fights would break out. 'There were always arguments and fights,' she says. 'It was just the norm in those days.'

Valerie went to Dorrington Road School. Starting school can be daunting for any child, but it was made worse at Dorrington Road because the school's windows were still covered with thick paint from the wartime blackout, casting a forbidding gloom over the classrooms. The children wrote on slates with sticks of chalk. 'The chalk dust got down your throat,' Valerie says, 'and the squeaking of the chalk as it scraped along the slate made you shudder. The highlight of the day was the mid-morning break at around 10.30, when a lady would arrive with a large enamel jug and tin cups full of piping-hot cocoa. I soon learned to get myself first in the queue, because if there was any left over, I would have finished mine by then and was ready to get seconds.

'Breaktime was also the first time that I ever took something that didn't belong to me. Each day we took in a snack to have with our drink and we all had to put them in a box until break-time, when the teacher would give them out again. One day, when she presented the box to me, there were only two packages left. I knew which one was mine: a piece of bread spread with white lard and sprinkled with salt, wrapped up in the ever-useful newspaper. The other one was in shiny wax paper and, without hesitation, I chose to take that one. When I opened it up, there was a piece of cake with jam in the middle. Not believing my luck, I lifted the lid of my desk and scoffed the lot in seconds. As I wiped the sticky evidence off my face, I had a pang of guilt as I heard a little boy wailing, "This isn't mine!" as he opened the newspaper and saw my lard sandwich. While I learned to be at the front for the hot cocoa, being last in the queue was the best place when we started to get school dinners, as you would always get any extra food that was left over – when you were hungry, you developed a strong sense of survival.'

Free school milk had been introduced by the Labour Government just after the war, and when she started school, Valerie soon worked out what happened to the spare milk if a child was away from school. 'I found out where they put the empty crates and the leftovers,' she says, 'and every day on my way home I would pinch two bottles of milk. My mum obviously knew where it was coming from, but she never questioned me about it, nor did she query it when I walked in with a few potatoes, onions and carrots I had pinched from the allotments. With a couple of bones from the butcher, they made a good meal. Thieving from the allotments then escalated to taking some of the empty beer bottles left behind the "outdoor" – the off-licence. I took them back through the front entrance and got the penny deposit back. I'm not proud of it now, and I would have been mortified if my own children had ever done anything like this, but we were desperately poor and I was always hungry.' There was no money for books or anything like that either, and Valerie's education was sketchy at best. When she left school aged fifteen, she had no qualifications and the best that her head teacher could find to write on her school certificate was: 'Valerie's sense of humour will be invaluable to her.'

After leaving school, she worked in an office job for a while, but then started working for the General Post Office (GPO) as a telephonist, and singing with a local band in the evenings. She saw an advert in the local paper for entertainers to appear at the Good Companions club in Sutton Coldfield. 'So I went along with my little two-shillings-and-sixpence music copy,' she says, 'and sang "Apple Blossom Time", which I hadn't rehearsed properly, so I don't know how many times I went round and round apple blossom time, because I'd forgotten the words!' Nonetheless, she sang well enough to be taken on. So with 'a really nice little group of musicians', she began doing a lot of singing for charity, going into prisons, mental hospitals and old people's homes, performing for the inmates or residents.

Eventually she joined a semi-professional band and began singing with them in clubs around Birmingham, but it was at this time that things started to go very wrong at home. There had been problems since she was very young, and in that era, what went on behind the closed doors of the family home tended to stay hidden. So there had been trouble for a long time, but things really came to a head after Valerie left school and started work. 'What happened is still very, very personal,' she says, 'but suffice it to say that it was far better for me to be out of the home at that time.'

Things got so bad that the leader of the band she was singing with came and picked her up from home and took her to his house, where he lived with his wife and two young children. However, she knew she couldn't stay there forever. So the next morning she rang Bill, the pianist with the band, and asked if she could stay with him and his wife for a little while. 'They were only in their early twenties themselves, had just got married and only had a one-bedroomed flat, but, God bless them, straight away they very kindly said, "You'll come home with us tonight." By the time she got there that evening they'd put together a bed frame out of some pieces of wood, found a mattress and made up a bed for her in their lounge.

She was very much aware that Bill and his

wife were newlyweds, so, trying to keep out of their way as much as she could in the evenings, she'd do her own shift at the GPO and then volunteer for all the extra hours that were going. There was a noticeboard where a lot of the women workers advertised for people to cover some of their hours for them, especially from four to six in the afternoon, which was often a difficult time for women with kids. The GPO was also always asking for volunteers to work overtime from six until ten in the evening – women weren't allowed to work any later than ten o'clock then; only men worked nights – so she'd volunteer for that shift as well. Not only was she earning extra money, she was keeping out of her hosts' way as well.

Valerie knew that she couldn't go on living like that indefinitely, but when she began looking for somewhere to live, she very soon became aware that on her wages, she couldn't afford to rent a flat on her own either. As she was wrestling with that dilemma, she heard a couple of her friends in the band talking about being a redcoat at Butlin's. Although she'd never been to a holiday camp, and had never before considered working at one, she'd obviously heard about Butlin's. 'It was the holiday for working-class people and families then,' she says. 'It was like going to Disneyworld is today. And of course everyone who'd been to Butlin's on holiday always came back with tales of the redcoats. And for a woman in that era, the glamour of being a redcoat was on a par with being an air hostess!'

There and then, she decided to apply. She was seventeen years old by now, but she discovered that the minimum age for working at Butlin's was eighteen. However, she wasn't going to let that stand in her way, so she lied about her age and told them she was eighteen. There were no computers then and no quick way for employers to check the age of their prospective employees, so she got away with it.

Valerie was still singing with the band, and her day job was with the GPO as a telephonist, so that's what she had on her CV when she went to the Butlin's interview at a hotel in Birmingham. It was a very stiff interview – in fact, there were two sets of interviews to get through – but she was determined to succeed. 'Not only did I want it as a job,' she says, 'I desperately wanted it as a home, and I would have said or done anything to make it happen. The wages were only a couple of pounds a week, but it didn't matter about the money – I wanted Butlin's to be my home.'

Two

Valerie was far from unusual in viewing Butlin's as something of a safe haven. For staff even more than campers, Butlin's often provided a refuge; it was a place where young people could take their first tentative steps into the world of work, where students could earn money in the long vacation and where the unemployed or the down on their luck could seek a fresh start. Young adults from broken homes, parents from broken marriages or even those who had been on the wrong side of the law could find an alternative home and a family of sorts, together with a sense of self-worth and belonging.

The camps also offered many young people their first taste of life away from their homes and local communities, and often their first encounters with people from different regions, for staff and campers came from all over Britain. Another redcoat, Gail, who had led 'a very cosseted life up till then', said of her time at Butlin's that it 'certainly opened my eyes to a few things. It was the first time I'd ever met someone who'd been to prison – he was the boyfriend of one of the other girls, and, despite having been in prison, he was such a nice chap. Another girl's boyfriend was on the run after deserting from the Army. He'd climbed the fence to get into the camp and was living in her chalet with her, hiding from the camp security.'

If Butlin's offered them a hint of freedom and very often their first paid work, many young people – particularly those from quiet, rural areas – also found the camps a safer and less threatening environment than an unfamiliar town or city far away from home. In some senses at least, Butlin's was a home from home, where meals and accommodation (though sometimes in houses off site to free up chalets for paying guests) came with the job. There was even a camp doctor and dentist, although just as you wouldn't have expected to find a Claridge's trained chef in a Butlin's kitchen, you were unlikely to be treated by a doctor from the upper reaches of the medical profession in the Butlin's Medical Centre.

Someone had told Valerie that Butlin's really wanted people who loved children, so when she went in for her interview, she says, 'I went on and on about how much I loved children.' It seemed like a good idea at the time, but the result was that, although she was duly taken on at Butlin's at Filey, it was not as a redcoat entertainer but as a camp 'Auntie', who looked after the kids all day. 'I lasted precisely one week!' she says with a laugh.

Luckily for her, someone who was supposed to be working at Radio Butlin's didn't turn up, so Valerie switched to doing that instead and became a redcoat. 'It was like winning *Britain's Got Talent* for me!' she says. Every day she would wake up the campers with the words: 'Good morning, campers, this is Valerie. This is just a reminder that it's 7.15 and the first sitting of breakfast will be at 8 a.m.' And then she'd play something soothing like 'Sleepy Shores' or 'Cavatina' to wake them up gently.

Not everyone was grateful for the early-morning call. One former redcoat recalls that some campers took to bringing a pair of wire cutters on holiday with them in their luggage. 'One of the first things they did was to cut the wires to the speakers in their chalets, and at the end of the week, one of our regular jobs was to go around and reconnect all the wires that had been severed. The speakers were always the most damaged pieces of equipment on site, and some had to be repaired every single week.'

Every Saturday morning, all the redcoats had to line up to greet the campers as that week's influx began arriving. Any dancers or musicians who wanted to live on camp had to do fifteen hours of redcoat duties in return for the use of their chalet, and the

157

dancers were usually put on reception duties on the Saturday. 'All the men arriving for their week's holiday were licking their lips at the sight of all these gorgeous redcoats,' Valerie says with a laugh. 'They must have spent the rest of the week wandering around trying to discover where all those fabulous redcoats had gone, because they were back in their "civvies" by then and only visible on stage in the shows.'

In those very early days, just like the rest of British society, Butlin's was very maledominated. The managers were all male and so were the house captains, though in her second year Valerie helped to change that a little by becoming the first female house captain they'd ever had. It sounds trivial now, perhaps, but in those days, even such small advances meant a great deal. Looking back, she feels very fortunate to have landed the job at Butlin's at a crucial point in her life. 'I was still only young and after the troubled life I'd had at home, I could easily have gone off the rails altogether, but Butlin's gave me not only a job, but a home and a ready-made family, too. It set my life on an entirely different and much better course.'

Just the same, showing iron self-discipline, she never spent a penny of the £2. 10s a week she was being paid, putting her entire wage into a Post Office savings account every week, because she was constantly worried about what was going to happen when the camp closed at the end of the season. There was no guarantee that she would have any work after September; she might have found herself back in the cold, cruel world, with no job and nowhere to live. She was absolutely determined, however, that she was not going to allow herself to be drawn back into the home situation she'd left behind. Saving her wages every week would at least give her enough money to avoid that fate.

Valerie rapidly made friends among the other redcoats. Her good looks and out-going personality with more than a hint of devil brought admirers, too, but the first person to ask her out was not a redcoat but a camper. In late August there used to be special weeks at the Butlin's at Filey called the Miners' Fortnight, when injured miners used to come to the camp in their droves. Valerie remembers a family coming down with their son, who was very talented – he sang in the Star Trail competition and won it – but who'd had a mining accident and damaged his spine. As a result his legs were paralysed and he was confined to a wheel-chair.

He was a handsome young man with a powerful upper body, and he asked Valerie out on a date on her day off. He had his own car, a Mini, that had been adapted for him to use, and the only thing she had to do was learn how to get his wheelchair out of the car and put it up and then fold it down again. So they went off for the day, had an evening meal and then some drinks. They got back to the camp at about half past eleven that night and parked in the car park, right at the far end of the camp. Unbeknown to Valerie, the car park was locked at midnight every night.

They 'had a bit of a kiss and cuddle' and then Valerie got out of the car and unloaded his wheelchair, but when they tried to leave the car park to go back to their chalets, they found that they were locked in. There was absolutely no one around at all, and because it was so far away from the chalets and the public areas, there was no chance of getting anyone to come and help them, so in the end their only option was to stay in the Mini all night. The security men didn't open the gates of the car park until seven o'clock the next morning, and after a virtually sleepless night, Valerie was back on duty at eight.

That relationship ended when the young man went home at the end of his holiday, but Valerie's next boyfriend was much longer lasting. The Fred Percival Orchestra used to play every night in the Regency Ballroom at the Filey camp and Valerie had to walk past the stage on her way to and from her work. She passed close to the pianist as she did so, and almost every time, the pianist called her over and asked her if the drummer with the orchestra, called Mike, could take her out for a coffee. Valerie took a look at him behind his drum kit and decided that he wasn't her type. So that time, and every time after that – because the pianist kept pestering her on Mike's behalf – she kept saying no.

Although she was putting all her wages away, the redcoats were also given coffee vouchers worth another four shillings every week, which they could use to buy cups of coffee in the café. One day Valerie had run out of vouchers for the week and as she was passing the stage, the pianist yet again asked her if the drummer could take her out for a coffee. 'For God's sake, just have a coffee with him,' he said, 'He's driving me mad going on and on about you all the time.'

'Oh, all right then,' she said, remembering she was out of vouchers. 'He can buy me a cup of coffee, just so long as he doesn't get any ideas.'

She got a shock when they did get together for that coffee, because looking at him on the stage, sitting behind his drum kit, she'd imagined Mike to be about six foot tall, but it turned out that it was the drum stool he was sitting on that was tall, not him. Valerie actually towered over him by several inches, especially in the high-

161

heeled court shoes that women redcoats had to wear every evening. However, the coffee can't have been that bad an idea, because they began going out together that very day and celebrated their golden wedding anniversary last year.

Valerie had been fretting all summer about what would happen at the end of the season, but to her great relief she was offered work for the winter at one of the Butlin's hotels, the Ocean Hotel in Saltdean, just outside Brighton. She was very lucky to get it, because all the camps closed in September then, and only a handful of the summer staff were kept on through the winter as well. However, it meant that she had to separate from Mike for the time being, because he had taken a job playing in the orchestra on a cruise liner, so they could only keep in touch by postcards and letters.

Valerie had gone to Saltdean expecting that her accommodation would at least be better than the chalets at Filey, but she found that she and the other girl redcoats were being housed in the staff quarters: six small, damp rooms in the basement, none of which even contained a sink. They all had to share one small bathroom and loo, which meant 'an army-style queue' every morning as they waited to use it.

The following summer, in 1960, Valerie

went back to Butlin's in Filey, which should have brought back happy memories for her, but instead it made her very sad, because when she went into the ballroom, there was a different drummer playing with the Fred Percival Orchestra; Mike wasn't there, having gone straight from the orchestra on the cruise liner to a booking playing at a ballroom in Dundee.

However, one day, as she was collecting her post from the office, the bandleader, Fred Percival, stopped her and said, 'Is Mike working at the moment?'

He was, but 'for my own selfish reasons, I wasn't going to tell Fred that', Valerie says with a laugh. 'So I told a little white lie and said, "No, not at the moment."'

So Fred sent a message to him and it turned out that Mike wasn't any happier being away from her up in Dundee than Valerie was at being parted from him. He jumped at the chance to come back to Filey and re-join Fred Percival's orchestra, and so he and Valerie were able to rekindle their relationship. They had to be very discreet about it, because when you wore a red jacket, you were not allowed to socialise with another staff member – you were supposed to be there for the guests, not your fellow workers. If Valerie was on first breakfast duty at eight o'clock, she would be working pretty much non-stop from then until midnight, and although they were given meal and coffee breaks, the chalets were so far away from the main camp that there was never time to go back to them in their breaks, so they just had to go to the dining hall or one of the cafés or bars. When Valerie was wearing her red jacket, she couldn't sit with Mike, she had to sit with the campers, so she would hardly see him at all during the working day.

The only time they could spend together was on their days off, when they would leave the camp and go to Bridlington or Scarborough to get a bit of privacy, or after Mike had finished playing in the evenings and she'd finished her work for the day. There was a place off camp called Reighton Hall, a big stately home that had been turned into a hotel with a late bar, where they and a lot of the other Butlin's staff used to go after they'd finished work. It was a two-and-a-half-mile walk, but that didn't put them off. They'd be there two or three times a week, staying till four or five in the morning sometimes, and then stagger back to the camp with only enough time for an hour or two's sleep before it was time to get up and smile for the campers again. 'I wouldn't have the stamina to do it all now,' Valerie says, 'but back then I was young and took it in my stride!'

That winter Valerie went back to work at the

Ocean Hotel in Saltdean, where she met another Butlin's girl, Hilary, who became one of her very best friends. While married redcoats like Hilary were given guest rooms in the hotel, Valerie and the other single girls found that they were again being housed in the staff quarters in the basement. Valerie's room was so cold and damp that she actually contracted pneumonia during the winter and spent three weeks in Brighton General Hospital.

Back at work, Valerie and Hilary were in charge of organising the competitions for the guests and soon 'had a nice little scam going', Valerie says with a laugh. The prizes were provided by some of Butlin's sponsors, but very few guests entered the competitions in the afternoons, because most of them were out strolling on the seafront, and sometimes no guests turned up at all. So there were always prizes left over and the two redcoats began filling in the forms with fictitious names and addresses, and awarding themselves the prizes. 'One year almost everyone we knew got a Smiths alarm clock for their Christmas present!'

That winter also saw a couple of hundred rally drivers and members of their rally teams take over the whole hotel for a weekend, including Pat Moss, who was Stirling Moss's sister. Valerie still shudders at what happened next. 'They absolutely trashed the place,' she says. 'It started in the dining room and as the drink flowed they were throwing all the bread rolls around. That turned into a full-on food fight and then it carried on and escalated from there.

'They came into the ballroom after that and by then they were all very drunk. We were on duty and, as we would with any other guests, if we were asked to dance it was part of our job to do so. They were getting us up to dance with them, but they were treating us as if we weren't redcoats but escort girls – or worse – and it wasn't any part of our job to have to put up with being groped and pro-positioned. I don't know what Pat Moss made of it – she was one of the few women guests there – but her companions were showing the worst kind of male attitudes from that era. There might have been occa-sional male campers who were like that, but they were few and far between, and it was shocking to see how these apparently well-educated and well-paid young men chose to behave. In the end, the senior redcoat at the time, a lovely man called Ron Stanway, who I'm still in touch with today, said, "I'm not having this," and took us all off duty and out of harm's way.'

They left the rally drivers to it and went into the dining room to try to get something to eat, because they'd had to wait until the drivers had finished eating before they could have their own meals. However, the dining room was in such a mess that all the staff had walked out in disgust and gone home, so there was no food prepared for the redcoats. Normally they weren't allowed in the kitchens, but in the circumstances Ron told them to go in there and help themselves to whatever food they could find. So they raided the fridges and made bacon sandwiches for everyone.

In the meantime the rally drivers had got the trampolines out of the sports storage cupboard and started jumping around on them, and then they began smashing up some of the chairs and throwing the rest into the swimming pool. They took the bronze bust of Billy Butlin from the dining room and threw that into the pool as well and caused an awful lot of other damage. 'They were as bad as football hooligans,' Valerie says. 'We were all upset and disgusted with them.'

Much later that night, as Valerie and Hilary were about to go to their rooms, they saw that most of the drivers had put their shoes outside their doors to be polished, as was usual in high-class hotels at the time. Nice as it was, the Butlin's Ocean Hotel wasn't that sort of hotel, so the shoes would have stayed there till doomsday and never been polished. Instead, still seething at the drivers' behaviour, Valerie and Hilary decided to indulge in a bit of childishness of their own. They collected all the shoes together from all three floors of the hotel, put a brown leather size ten with a grey suede size seven, and so on, tied the laces together, gave the knots an extra pull to make them particularly hard to undo and then put them outside doors on different floors, chosen at random as they walked along the corridors. Their only regret was that they wouldn't be able to watch the hungover drivers trying to sort out the mess in the morning.

Valerie saw one of the rally drivers later the next morning, still looking very hungover, and she said to him, 'You and your friends were absolutely disgraceful last night.'

He made a pathetic attempt to justify it, saying, 'How would you feel if you'd been cooped up in a car for so long?'

She replied, 'I wouldn't have behaved like that even if I had been cooped up in a car for twelve months non-stop.'

There were no repercussions for the girls after 'Shoegate', but Butlin's managers weren't always so lenient. Rules about relations with the guests were very strict and, in particular, under no circumstances were redcoats ever allowed to go into a camper's chalet or into a guest's room at one of the Butlin's hotels. If a girl redcoat was found in a male camper's chalet, or a male redcoat in a woman's, it resulted in instant dismissal. There was the occasional exception to the rule, however. When Bobby Butlin was learning the family business, working as a redcoat at Ayr, he was caught with a girl in his chalet. The girl's mother complained to the general manager, who gave him 'a real ticking off'. Still, a few weeks later Bobby received a letter from the girl's mother saying that she hadn't realised who he was and inviting him to call in the next time he was in Warrington!

'Billy Butlin was very straight-laced,' Valerie says. 'He might have come from a fairground background, but he was very strict. I don't know if he had a strong personal morality or if it was just good business sense, but certainly if such goings-on were allowed to go unpunished, and rumours or reports about them started to appear in the newspapers, then those looking for a stick with which to beat him would have hastened to claim that his camps were at best "hotbeds of vice" and at worst "glorified brothels".'

Billy Butlin knew all too well how quick the newspapers were to fasten onto negative news from his camps. It has long been a Butlin's tradition for the redcoats to open events and shows by calling out 'Hi-de-hi!' to the campers. When they responded with 'Ho-de-ho!' the redcoats would come back with 'Is everybody happy?' To which the answer was invariably 'Yes!' However, after one camper (whether for his own amusement or because he really was fed up) called out 'No!' a piece appeared in one of the tabloid newspapers, citing the comment without mentioning that it was only one person, and claiming that it showed 'holiday-makers are disgruntled with Butlin's'. So if Billy was paranoid about his camps' reputation, he did have some grounds for it. The feeling was that any tiny thing that happened in a camp would be greatly magnified outside it.

As a result of Butlin's strict rules, Valerie and Hilary did come very close to being sacked over another incident just a month after 'Shoegate'. While their job required them to treat every guest the same, the redcoats were inevitably more drawn to some people than others. While they were working at the Brighton hotel, Valerie and Hilary became very friendly with two young honeymooners. On their last night, a Friday, the honeymooners invited the two of them and another young redcoat back to their room for a drink. It was a married couple issuing the invitation, so it wasn't like the girls were accepting an invitation from a group of unattached men, and they never thought anything about it. They just said, 'Yes, that would be nice,' and went along to their room when they'd finished their duties for the night.

They were quite innocently sitting in the honeymooners' room, having a drink and talking to them, but it was well after dark, so the lights were on and they hadn't drawn their curtains. The hotel was arranged around a quadrangle and, unbeknown to the redcoats, a security man on his rounds was walking across the quadrangle when he glanced up at the lit window and saw their red jackets.

The first they knew of their discovery was when there was a pounding at the door and a voice shouting, 'Security! Open up!'

The girls' faces blanched as they realised they were now in serious trouble. Just like a Brian Rix farce, they began scrambling to find places to hide. Hilary ran into the bathroom, Valerie jumped into the wardrobe and after dithering and running this way and that for a few moments, the third young redcoat joined Valerie in her hiding place. They were all absolutely petrified, because they knew it was potentially a sacking offence.

When the honeymooners opened the door, the security man said, 'You've got staff in here.'

They tried to deny it, but he just said, 'I know you have, because I've seen their red jackets through the window.' He raised his voice and said, 'I suggest you come out now, whoever you are.'

Hilary, 'being a bit of a goody-goody' according to Valerie, came straight out of the bathroom and gave herself up, but because he'd said 'their red jackets', Valerie knew the security man wasn't going to be content with just finding Hilary, so she whispered to the young redcoat with her, 'I'm sorry, I was here first and, like the trade unions, it's last in, first out!' and the girl had to get out of the wardrobe. Looking back, Valerie's not proud of herself for that, but she was panicking at the time.

The security man took his two captives into the corridor, gave them a dressing down and told them he'd be reporting them to the manager in the morning. They were duly summoned to the manager's office, fearing the worst, but probably because they'd only been in a married couple's room and not an unmarried man's, he didn't sack them; he let them off with a stern warning instead.

Valerie thought she'd got away with it altogether, but the following evening she was on 'train duty', which involved going down to Brighton station on the Butlin's bus to greet all the guests arriving from London and bringing them back to the hotel. She found herself sitting next to the same security man on the bus going down there and it was fortunate that it was dark, because she was blushing furiously. Like her, he was from Birmingham, and he struck up a conversation with her about places they knew. Then, out of the blue, he suddenly said, 'Did you hear about what went on last night?'

She played dumb and just said, 'No, what?'

He told her the story about finding two redcoats in one of the guest rooms.

'Never!' she said, trying to look like butter wouldn't melt in her mouth.

He turned to look at her. 'But I know that there was another person in there as well,' he said. 'And I would suggest that if you know that other person, you tell her never to do it again.'

By then she was blushing crimson. He obviously knew it was her, but Valerie thinks that because he was also from Birmingham, he knew something of her background and that Butlin's wasn't just a job for her, it was a home. Perhaps for that reason he had made do with catching the other two the previous night and had left her hidden in the wardrobe.

Lots of redcoats were determined to break into showbiz one way or another. Lorna, one of the girls Valerie and Hilary worked with at the hotel in Saltdean, taught herself how to balance on a circus ball, and also did a fire-eating act and limbo dancing beneath a blazing pole, with Valerie as her willing assistant. On Valerie's first day helping her, Lorna sent her down to the local garage to get some more methylated spirits, but when she got there the mechanic said, 'We haven't got any left, but we've got some pink paraffin, if that'll do instead.'

'Well, can you set fire to it?' Valerie asked.

'Oh yes.'

So she came back up with the paraffin and soaked all the strings around the limbo pole with it. As soon as Lorna began her act and set fire to it, the pole went up in flames like in a scene from *The Towering Inferno*. 'Everyone was screaming and stampeding for the exit,' Valerie says. 'The ceiling was scorched and the room was full of oily black smoke. It wasn't one of my finest moments and did nothing to improve the hotel manager's temper, but we avoided burning the hotel down and managed to clean up the mess.'

Lorna did magic tricks as well, and perhaps surprisingly after the paraffin incident she continued to use Valerie as her assistant. She had two doves and a live rabbit as part of her act, and when she and Valerie went away to work at a Butlin's reunion for a couple of days, she left two of the boys, Jimmy Tarbuck and Brian, in charge of feeding and looking after the doves and the rabbit. It didn't prove a very good arrangement, because one of the doves promptly died. Hilary can remember

Jimmy saying, 'Can't we just find a pigeon before she gets back and paint it white?'

When she found out, Lorna went 'absolutely ballistic about it', so when she and Valerie had to go and work at another reunion, the boys refused to look after her rabbit. Hilary took charge instead and hid the rabbit's cage in the cupboard under the washbasin in Lorna's room. It really shouldn't have been there at all, and Hilary then forgot to feed it and, even worse, left both the cage door and the cupboard wide open. As a result, the hungry rabbit hopped out and began chewing on the closest available alternative to grass: the plush, cherry-red carpet.

The hotel manager at the time was 'a big, robust character, rather like Billy Butlin himself, except that, unlike his boss, he hated redcoats with a passion', Valerie says – 'I suppose because he had no control over us, as we reported to the entertainments manager, not him.' The housekeeper reported to him that the carpet in Lorna and Valerie's room was full of holes, and when they got back from the reunion, they were summoned to see him.

'It's about the rabbit,' he said, as soon as they walked in there.

They tried to play dumb and said, 'What rabbit?'

'It's too late for that,' he said. 'You've been

found out and now you're going to have to pay for the damage.' He told them they would have to pay £60 for a new carpet – it was a fortune, about twenty weeks' wages.

Valerie was then summoned to see the entertainments manager and when she walked into his office, he said, 'I've got Wally Goodman on the phone' – one of the directors of the company. Valerie felt sick, certain that she was going to be sacked. When she picked up the phone, Wally said, 'I understand that you're in trouble, young lady. Don't do it again. You won't have to pay for the carpet, but as punishment, next week – a week earlier than scheduled – you will be up at Filey to help get the camp ready for the new season. And whatever tasks they give you, you will do.'

She heaved a sigh of relief; whatever her punishment entailed, it couldn't be worse than the sack. When Valerie got to Filey, it was the last week in April and as bleak as only the North Sea coast can be – and she had no warm clothes with her at all. She was sent straight down to the sports fields where the chief redcoat at Filey was waiting for her. 'I understand that you've been in trouble in Brighton, Valerie,' he said. 'So now you're on jankers. See that machine there?' It was one of the old line-marking machines that grounds-men used to mark the white lines on football pitches. She had to push the machine around for the whole day and carry on doing menial tasks for the rest of the week, by which time the management decided she'd 'done her porridge' and put her back on general duties.

Three

Valerie carried on working at Filey in the summer and the Brighton hotel in the winter and she loved every minute of it – apart from that pre-season week at Filey! When she finally stopped full-time work at Butlin's in 1964, it was not because she'd had enough of working there, but because she wanted to be with Mike. He had taken a job playing with a band in the North and she had again been offered the chance to go back to the Ocean Hotel for the winter. She accepted the job at first, but at the last moment she just couldn't bear the thought of being parted from Mike again for the whole winter, so she turned down the Butlin's job and went up to South Shields where he lived.

She started doing the club circuit, singing cabaret in social clubs and working men's clubs all over the North. 'That,' she says, 'was a real education! When you sang at Butlin's, or if you stood on your head, or if you told a joke, people would laugh and applaud. When I got out of that environment and into one where people really were paying for their entertainment, that was a different world altogether. I'd had a pit orchestra or a twelve-piece band backing me when I sang at Butlin's, but in the clubs, where it might have been one man playing an organ, who was semi-professional and couldn't read your music, that was another story entirely. Every laugh, every round of applause, had to be worked for and really earned.'

It was a tough school in which to learn your trade, as Valerie soon discovered. 'Innocent as I was,' she says, 'I didn't realise that some of the clubs had strippers appearing there. It was illegal back then – girls could appear half-naked, but they had to remain absolutely motionless, because that was supposed to be artistic and was allowed. However, if they moved a muscle, they were breaking the law. Nonetheless, in some clubs strippers were performing behind closed doors.' In her first gig, Valerie was sitting on a stool centre stage, wearing 'a very lovely – or at least I thought it was lovely – pale dress', singing 'My Funny Valentine', when a red-faced, gruff-voiced man at the back of the room shouted 'Get 'em off!' Within seconds the rest of the audience had joined in, and with a chorus of lewd shouts echoing in her ears, Valerie ran from the stage in tears.

Both Mike and Valerie carried on playing the club circuit for a while, but it was now the mid 1960s, Beatlemania was in full flow and the music scene in the North was changing fast. Many of the clubs were starting to close down, and most of the remaining work was in the South, so in the end they moved to London. They found themselves 'a grotty little one-bedroom flat in Battersea' and headed off to Archer Street, off Piccadilly, which was where all the musicians who were looking for work used to go. They bumped into the comedian Dave Allen there, whom they knew from having worked with his brother Johnny at Butlin's in Filey. He put them in touch with a bandleader called Vic Abbott who offered Mike the chance of a season with his orchestra in Jersey, backing actress and singer Shani Wallis and comedian Frankie Howerd at the Plaza Ballroom.

Valerie wanted to go with Mike, but she said to him, 'I don't want to go to Jersey and just live with you, I want to get married.' So they arranged a lightning-quick wedding at Wandsworth Town Hall in June 1963 and went to Jersey for their honeymoon, with precisely £1.10s in their pocket. Vic Abbott met them off the boat and frightened them to death, because although Mike was going to be paid £21 a week – a lot of money then

– Vic told them that accommodation on Jersey was horrifically expensive and would swallow most of that.

They managed to find lodgings in the little back bedroom of a woman who had five children and was struggling to make ends meet. The room was spartan but clean. As well as a bed and a wardrobe, it contained a large bowl and an enamel bucket with a lid. 'I thought it was a waste-paper bin,' Valerie says, 'but I soon discovered my mistake. There was no bathroom and the loo was outside in the yard, so the bucket was for nighttime use instead!' They found a slightly better room a few weeks later and carried on living there for the next ten months.

At the end of their time in Jersey, Mike and Valerie went back to London 'very happy', because she had just discovered she was pregnant. They found another 'grotty bedsit', once more with an outside loo. 'I was beginning to wonder if outside loos were going to follow me around for the rest of my life!' Valerie says with a laugh.

Mike was still playing clubs and hotels in London, including The Dorchester, and Valerie was singing, but for the next couple of years they did Christmas and Easter together at Butlin's in Clacton and then Minehead. Although Mike was never officially a redcoat, he donned a red jacket for those two holiday periods.

Sadly, Valerie miscarried her baby and then had another two miscarriages over those two years. 'It was obviously very upsetting and a really bad time for us,' she says. However, in 1966, Valerie became pregnant again and this time she gave birth to their first daughter, Michelle. 'It was the year of England's World Cup win, so we had a double celebration!'

After the birth she decided that, to build a proper home for their daughter, she had to get them out of their poky little flat, and to do that, she needed to work and earn good money. She wrote down a list of goals that she wanted to achieve – 'A place to live with a bathroom and an inside loo was very high on the list,' she says, laughing. She knew she couldn't earn enough money to do all she wanted by singing, so she applied for a job as a sales representative with the perfume and cosmetic house Coty, a division of Pfizer, which was launching The House of Romney to try to emulate Avon's success in direct selling.

The advertisement specified that the person they were looking for had to have several years' sales experience, three years' driving experience and no children. Valerie failed on all three counts – she had a six-month-old daughter, she couldn't drive and she'd never sold anything – but she wasn't going to let that stop her. She applied for the job and got an interview, but when she walked into the waiting room she saw about twenty other ladies already sitting there, who had come from all over the country. 'Every single one of them had handbag, shoes and gloves in matching colours,' she says, shuddering at the memory, 'and all of them were wearing a hat. In complete contrast to that, I was wearing white plastic winkle-picker shoes, with a black handbag, a peach Crimplene dress, which I'd bought from Brixton market, and a Dannimac, which I'd folded over my arm!'

An American woman was doing the general interview before their individual meetings and went round the room getting them all to introduce themselves. A series of frightfully well-spoken ladies went first – Daphne from Ascot, Hermione from Berkshire and so on – and when it got to her turn, Valerie said, 'Oim Valerie, and oim from Battersea,' in her broad Birmingham accent. 'I nearly died from embarrassment!' she said, bursting out laughing.

However, Valerie was not the type to give up without a fight, and she went in for the personal interview full of cheeky attitude and with a big smile on my face. I said that although I did have a six-month-old daughter, I had a nanny for her (not true, I couldn't afford to go out for the evening, let alone pay for a nanny); I did drive (crossing my fingers again behind my back) and though I didn't have sales experience, I knew that I could sell and I'd prove it to them.'

There was a pause while the interviewers digested this, and then the American woman tossed a little blue cosmetics bag across the desk to Valerie and said, 'Go on, then, prove it!'

So for the next six months, dragging her cases of samples on and off buses, tubes and trains, Valerie footslogged her way around 'all the poshest and most fabulous parts of London – Battersea, Brixton, Peckham, Wandsworth and the rest–' knocking on doors, and in between times learning to drive. She drew heavily on her Butlin's experience in that job, because above all else, Butlin's had taught her how to get along with people of all sorts and all ages. She worked hard and did well, and at the end of her six-month trial, her employers were convinced and offered her the job. Luckily, she had actually passed her driving test in the meantime, so she really could drive by then, just like she'd said she could at the interview!

It was a great opportunity for Valerie at a time when employment opportunities for women with children were beginning to open up. 'Housewives and mums at home were wanting more independence and the chance to earn their own money,' she says. 'That was why Avon, Tupperware and all the other direct-sales companies were successful. They gave women the opportunity to fit their work around their family commitments and earn their own cash.'

She worked for The House of Romney for several years, during which she also gave birth to her second daughter, Amanda. She was promoted to a senior managerial role, but eventually Dart Industries, which owns Tupperware, bought out the company and changed the way the business was run. Valerie was still recruiting the junior managers, who in turn were recruiting the reps who went round selling the products, and she was still buying the products from the parent company, but Valerie was now also controlling the money and effectively running her own business.

One of the directors of Dart Industries, Peter Bunn, then left and was hired by the American company Tri-Chem to start up a new party plan company, selling ballpoint tubes of liquid paint in a range of colours that could be used to mark glass, china, linen or anything else that was hard to mark with a normal pen. It became a very successful product and Peter brought Valerie on board to work with him. 'He taught me everything I know about management,' she says, and over the course of the 1970s, she became area manager, national sales manager and then sales director.

Valerie's rise also reflected changing attitudes towards the role of women in business. Before the 1970s, there had been very few women in company boardrooms, but American companies were leading the way by appointing more and more women and UK companies began to follow. Many showed their worth and, like Valerie, became directors in their own right, paving the way for others.

'It also catapulted me into a very different lifestyle,' Valerie says. 'I was holding meetings and staying at hotels like the Royal Garden, the Royal Lancaster and The Dorchester in London.' While it was exciting, it was also more than a little daunting for her at first. 'I had only ever used a knife and fork, and a spoon for my pudding, and had been living in houses with outside loos, and now I might be sitting down at dinner with an eighteen-piece table setting in front of me, and having to deal with haughty maître d's and sommeliers!' Peter Bunn was a real mentor for her, and his generosity, patience and gentleness, along with Valerie's own eagerness to watch and learn, helped her through all that.

Valerie was now earning a very good salary and was beginning to tick off some of the items on her list of goals. She even began taking flying lessons and for the first and only time in their married life, she kept it secret from Mike. 'He's not a suspicious person at all,' she says, 'but he did begin to wonder where on earth I was disappearing to every Saturday and Sunday, so he followed me one day and discovered my secret. He was cross with me at first, because he was petrified that I was going to kill myself, but he came round to the idea and I persevered and got my pilot's licence at the age of thirty-eight.'

Eventually she was headhunted by the lingerie and cosmetics company Miss Mary of Sweden, and seventeen years after she'd begun selling door-to-door for The House of Romney, she was signing her name on letters as 'Managing Director, Cosmetics Division, Miss Mary of Sweden'. Even then, Valerie says, 'I was still drawing on the full range of experiences I'd had at Butlin's. The work I was doing was obviously very different, but I was still working in a people business; and performing on stage to a couple of thousand campers at Butlin's proved to be pretty good preparation for addressing 3,000 girls at a sales conference!'

From there Valerie joined a ceramic and glassware company, and was then head-hunted again to join Great Universal Stores. And finally, having started in entertainment, she finished in entertainment, albeit of a very different kind, by developing markets in Europe and the United States for the Ann Summers company.

Valerie had come a very long way from the slum in the Jewellery Quarter in Birmingham where her life began. She would like to think that her mother was secretly very proud of her – whenever her mum spoke to her friends about her, it was 'Our Valerie did this' and 'Our Valerie did that' – but she was never able to show or express any emotion to Valerie directly. 'She wasn't like that with my brother and sister,' Valerie says, 'so I don't know if her relationship with me was changed by those five hard years when my father was away in the war, or by what happened after he came home, but then it's something I've only really been able to address, even to myself, since my father's death ten years ago.'

Although the domestic troubles when Valerie was young meant that her relationship with her mother was less close than it might have been, she has been lucky enough to be able to help her mother financially in later life. She bought her council house for her, gave her a holiday abroad for the first time in her life and made sure she had a tumble dryer, a phone and the other modern conveniences that her mother had never enjoyed before.

'I've been very lucky,' Valerie says, 'because Mike has given me everything that my mother didn't. He gave me all the emotional support and encouragement I needed and I wouldn't have been able to have the career that I've had without that support. He always made sure that he was there to look after the family when I was away or tied up with the business. Sadly, last year Mike was diagnosed with Parkinson's disease, but being the positive, generous person he is, he's still helping others and still has a great appetite for life. I owe him more than I can say and I love him.'

The good habits that Valerie developed when she left home all those years ago are still with her. 'All those things you experience when you're young make you the person you are when you grow up,' she says. 'I still save part of my pension every month and I support my daughters and their children emotionally and financially, so that they will never have to live the kind of harsh life that I endured when I was young.' And all through her career, right from when she was in her teens and singing at charitable events, Valerie has also been involved to a greater or lesser extent in raising money for charity. Now that she's retired from full-time work, she can devote even more of her considerable energy to it and for the last few years has been instrumental in organising a breast cancer charity called Pink Day in Tenerife, where she and Mike now spend much of their time.

'I got involved because a good friend of

ours got breast cancer and is now no longer with us,' she says, 'so the charitable work I do is in memory of her, and of my brother, Malcolm, who I also lost to cancer six years ago. So I do what little I can to support efforts to eradicate the disease. I've still got the cheek to approach big companies for donations and they've been incredibly generous in supporting Pink Day.'

If that wasn't enough, her five grand-children and two great-grandchildren, with two more on the way, also keep her busy, and she's also in regular touch with her Butlin's friends. She and Hilary have remained friends to this day, ever since they worked together at the Ocean Hotel in Saltdean in the early 1960s.

One Saturday afternoon in 1985, Mike was watching the television and called to Valerie, 'Come and see this!' Fire had broken out in an old wooden stand at Bradford City Foot-ball Club, and the television cameras broad-casting the match showed the stand engulfed in flames and fans fleeing for their lives. Knowing that Hilary's boys were avid Brad-ford City fans, Valerie's first thought was to call her.

When Hilary answered with 'Hello, my darling', Valerie knew immediately that she was unaware of what was happening.

'Where are the boys?' she said.

'At the match. Why?'

'I went cold,' Valerie says, 'but I quietly asked if anyone was with her and then told her to put on the television. We had to wait what seemed a lifetime for news of the lads. Thankfully they were both safe, but as the scale of the tragedy unfolded, it became clear that several of their friends were among the fifty-six dead and the hundreds of injured.

'Hilary and I are not on the phone every five minutes,' Valerie says, 'it's not one of those relationships, but we love each other dearly and we have had such laughs together over the years.'

Valerie is not, she says, 'one of those former redcoats who goes on Facebook and moans about how Butlin's isn't the same today. Yes, they're right, it is different, but it has to be different, because it has to move with the times. And I would say that the product, from a pure entertainment point of view, is probably much superior these days. What there isn't any more is the level of interaction between the redcoats and the guests that there was in our era. A lot of that used to happen in the dining rooms; all the redcoats were allocated to a dining hall at mealtimes and were required to do the "meet and greet" with the campers. That doesn't happen now. The reds' main job is still to host guests, but they do tend to be aspiring entertainers, whereas back then they were hosts and companions first and foremost, and, if at all, entertainers only as an afterthought.'

Valerie reached the peak of her career long after she left Butlin's, but she says that she owes a lot of her subsequent success to the Butlin's training. 'It was incredibly strict. You were never late, because if you were, you would be sacked. You had to have a smile on your face all the time, and even today I still walk around smiling at everyone I pass! It's just the natural thing to do after all those years. And you get to know people, you learn about people, and I saw and mixed with all types of people in my years at Butlin's.

'Every part of my life has been touched by Butlin's, and even my smile today is a Butlin's smile. It'll be something that I'll take with me right until my last breath. So give me a red jacket and I'll put it on, and I'd just like to say, "Thank you, Sir Billy."'

Valda

One

A singer, disco dancer and northern firecracker, Valda Warwick was born in 1953 and grew up in Blyth in the Northeast. Her dad worked as a profile burner in a colliery workshop for the National Coal Board (NCB) in Ashington. Every Coal Board employee used to get free concessionary coal, and Valda can remember when it was delivered – a big mound of coal that she would have to help shovel into the coal hole. They weren't by any means living in abject poverty, but money was always tight.

Their council house was fairly well equipped for one of that era, but Valda's overriding memory is of how cold it was. There was no central heating, just an open fire in a house that was so poorly insulated and so exposed to the bitter winter easterlies – which her mother said had blown all the way from Siberia – that there would be ice on the inside of her bedroom window in the mornings. On those days Valda would get dressed under the covers, postponing the moment when she had to expose herself to the numbing cold.

Valda had one sister, five years younger

than her, who was afflicted with brittle bone disease. Her mother suffered from it, too. Strangely, it had afflicted every second child of every generation. When she was little, her sister couldn't walk, so to help her, Valda made her a sort of prototype skateboard. She'd never actually seen or heard of a skateboard before, but nonetheless that's what she came up with. She used the pastry board from a child's cookery set that she'd had when she was young and strapped two roller skates to it with a couple of leather belts. She could then sit her sister on it and she could wheel herself along by pushing her hands against the ground. 'She used to go outside on it, and play in the street with the rest of the local kids,' says Valda. Her mum was always shouting, 'Look out, be careful!' to her, because with her disease Valda's sister could have broken a bone in even the slightest fall, but she came through it all unscathed and the primitive skateboard transformed her early years.

Valda loved to play in the street, too, but her dad was very strict and also, she says, 'a bit of a snob'. He had condescended to leave the South where he grew up and come north to marry Valda's mother, but he found it all a bit 'rough and ready', and even though they lived in a council house themselves, he didn't want his own children out on the street, mixing and playing with what he called 'these council house kids'. Valda and her sister were never allowed to have any of those kids round to play at their house. However, he kept his opinions about their neighbours so well concealed that Valda can remember lots of them telling her what a 'great fellow' her father was. Her usual retort to that was: 'You wouldn't say that if you had to live with him.'

Mrs Warwick did not share her husband's prejudices. She was 'small, round and jolly, though it's a funny way to describe her', Valda says, 'because she was actually the world's biggest pessimist. She was always expecting the worst, and when it didn't happen, she'd be all cheered up again! They were different in almost every way, and the one thing I could always guarantee was that if one of my parents said one thing, the other would immediately say the opposite.'

Valda's favourite days of the week were Tuesday and Thursday, when her father always worked late at the colliery and didn't get home until eight o'clock in the evening. On those nights Valda and her sister played in the street with their friends until just before eight, when her mother would come out, stand on the step and shout, 'Valda, it's ten to eight. Five more minutes and then get yourself home before your dad gets in!' Valda knew she had to be back inside the garden, with the gate firmly shut before her dad came home, or there would be trouble.

He was by no means an ogre, though, and Valda's eyes still glow at the memory of the day she came home from school to find that her father had a surprise for her. 'Go and see what's in the front room,' he said to her. When she went in there, she saw a large cardboard box by the fireplace, and when she opened it, she found 'the most beautiful black and tan puppy, a collie crossed with at least fifty-seven other varieties'. She christened her Lassie and she and her dad trained the dog together. It was a real bonding experience for them.

Their council house had large front and back gardens that had been allowed to run wild – in summer, the grass would be almost waist-high on the girls. That didn't put them off, though, and on sunny days Valda would drag out a piece of old carpet, which they'd use to flatten the grass, and then they'd make a triangular tent out of the clothes airer from the kitchen and some old blankets and play there for hours.

As well as working at the colliery, her dad had a part-time job in a pub, which he absolutely loved, so eventually he left the colliery and became a pub landlord, running The Traveller's Rest at Blyth. It was a huge barn of a pub, three storeys high and very old. It had originally been a coaching inn and still had the stables round the yard from that era, but it was not in the best condition. The roof leaked, there was rot and woodworm in some of the timbers and the top floor of the building was so unsafe that Valda was forbidden to go up there, though she would sometimes sneak up there with her friends, pretending that it was haunted and telling them ghost stories to frighten them!

Valda's teenage years were spent at the pub and she can clearly remember one important milestone, when she was given her first taste of alcohol. Her father had a regular 'stoppyback' as it was known in the Northeast – a 'lock-in' or after-hours drinking session for his favoured regulars – when they would all go into the Snug, a small room right in the middle of the pub that had no external windows. Valda can remember sitting in there with her parents and a few regulars one night when she was about fifteen, and though she usually drank lemonade, she pointed to her father's drink and said, 'Can I just have a little taste of that?'

Her mother kept saying, 'No, no, no, don't be giving her alcohol,' but her dad said, 'Never mind a taste, I think it's high time you had a proper drink of your own.' He poured out a bottle of McEwan's Export Pale Ale and gave it to her. She remembers taking the first sip and thinking to herself, oh God, this is hideous, but she persevered and drank it down, mainly to impress her dad, and she soon got the hang of it! She suspects that her dad had always secretly wanted a son rather than a daughter, and takes his choice of drink for her – a pale ale rather than a Babycham – as further proof of that.

Valda left school a month short of her fifteenth birthday and afterwards took a string of short-lived jobs. She first worked on a bakery counter and then went to a chemist, then a factory, and after that she tried to join first the Air Force, then the Wrens and then the Army – 'I just loved uniforms!' she says with a laugh. 'But I had a dodgy chest because of asthma and failed the medical for all of them. I was absolutely gutted at the time. It was such a huge disappointment, because back then, joining one of the services was the only thing that I'd ever wanted or really tried hard to achieve.'

She also helped out at the pub in the evenings. She was too young to serve behind the bar, but she waited on tables and cleared away the empty glasses. One night, well after closing time, the usual stoppy-back was in progress when there was a knock at the door and her dad sent Valda to answer it. When she opened the door, there were two policemen standing there. Her face fell, as she was convinced they were going to be raided. 'I'll just get my dad,' she said, and went to fetch him, her heart in her mouth.

When she told him, he just smiled, walked

towards the front door and called out, 'Right you are then, lads, come on in!' and the two policemen headed for the Snug, accepted the pints that Valda's dad pulled for them and settled down with the other regulars.

In common with most pubs at the time, there was an off-licence attached to The Traveller's Rest, a small room with its own outside door and a little serving hatch. Valda had started smoking in her teens and for quite a while she used the off-licence as her own private cigarette supply. She would wait until her father was busy serving customers or down in the cellar and then slip outside where her friends would be waiting. They'd sneak into the off-licence through the door to the street and her friends would hoist her up through the serving hatch, holding onto her legs while, at full stretch, Valda pinched a packet of ten Embassy or Regal from the shelf. They'd then go off somewhere and smoke themselves dizzy.

This went on for ages and Valda, knowing nothing of stocktaking, was sure that her father would never miss the cigarettes. Eventually, though, her dad confronted her and said, 'Are you nicking cigarettes? Think very carefully before you say anything, because I might already know the answer.' Under her father's unwavering gaze, Valda stammered out a confession and waited for her punishment, but all her father said was, 'Next time, don't steal – ask – and that's a lesson for life, Valda.'

One evening, Valda was waiting on tables in the bar when she spotted a customer she hadn't seen before. He was a devastatingly handsome young man, 'the image of George Best', Valda says, and they started talking and clicked straight away. Like George Best, he was Irish, and a contract worker from Smethwick, near Birmingham. He was working in the area for just six weeks, and they saw each other every single day while he was there. When he went back to Smethwick at the end of his contract, Valda decided to follow him.

She had never left her home area before – she and her family had never even been on holiday – and even though she was only sixteen, when they saw how serious she was, her parents consented. Her mother travelled down on the train with her, made sure Valda found a decent bedsit to live in and then went back home. Valda soon found a job and spent all her time off with the Irishman, but she rapidly came to realise that the handsome, carefree man she had thought was going to be the love of her life had a much darker side. It had never come out while he was in the Northeast, but now it was all too evident.

In reality, he was a drunken, violent and abusive man, and after a few months, without a word to him, Valda simply packed her bags and went home.

Despite its unhappy end, that brief taste of life away from Blyth had been enough to ignite a desire to see more of the world, and events at home soon hardened her resolve to get away once more. All the time her parents had been running the pub, her mother had been taking in lodgers. Unfortunately, she had never declared the extra income to the Inland Revenue and Valda's parents got into serious trouble as a result. Her dad blamed her mother for that, and their relationship, already under some strain from the stresses of running a pub, never really recovered. Eventually they split up.

The Traveller's Rest did not last too much longer either. 'The pub's not there now,' Valda says. 'After we left, it was pulled down, and it made me very sad when it happened, because I loved it there.' The whole family was involved in a campaign to try to save it and give it listed status, but sadly it was in too parlous a state to repair.

During the period of turmoil surrounding their parents' split, Valda and her sister went to live with their grandmother. Valda also had to cope with the loss of her dog, Lassie, which was run over outside her grandma's house after some neighbourhood kids let it out of the garden. Valda always had work, albeit doing 'all sorts of dead-end jobs', but by 1973, when she was nineteen, she was once again bored with both her home life and factory jobs. She was desperate for a change of scene from Blyth and looking for something a bit different. That's when a friend who had worked a season at Butlin's in Skegness the year before said to her, 'If you're that bored and fed up, why don't you try Butlin's? I had great fun there.'

Soon afterwards she saw a Butlin's advertisement in the paper, with a list of available jobs. There were vacancies for redcoats, but she'd never even been to Butlin's on holiday and had no idea what a redcoat was. Among the other jobs were a few for work in the coffee bars and she thought to herself, well, I've worked in coffee bars before, so that was what she put down. Within a week she got a letter offering her a job as a coffee bar assistant at Skegness, enclosing a warrant for her train ticket there on the following Friday.

Two

Valda set off for Newcastle Central Station carrying a big suitcase in one hand and a string bag containing a flask of tea and some cheese and jam butties that her mum had made for her in the other. Her mum went with her to the station to see her off. It had been pouring with rain all morning and by the time Valda got to the station, she was already soaked to the skin. Her carefully styled hair was in rats' tails and the bell-bottom jeans she was wearing were dripping wet and splashed with mud.

By now she wasn't so much excited as terrified, because it was a real step into the unknown. Although she'd been away from home once before, she'd never gone anywhere where she didn't know a single living soul. When they got to the platform, however, another girl and her mum were waiting there. The girl was getting the same train as Valda and also had a great big case with her. So Valda said to her, 'Are we going to the same place? I'm going to Butlin's.'

The other girl smiled and said, 'So am I.' She was called Anne and came from Byker. So they travelled to Skegness together and ended up sharing a chalet as well.

The journey became increasingly uncomfortable as more and more people squashed themselves and their luggage into their compartment. The girls' wet clothes were steaming in the heat, fogging the windows, and they were both smoking, filling the compartment with a thick fug. Valda was embarrassed about having brought a packed lunch with her, but in the end she was so hungry that she got it out anyway, whereupon it turned out that Anne had brought one, too, and was equally embarrassed about hers. She had Spam sandwiches, which Valda had never tried, and cheese and jam was a new combination on Anne, too, so they ended up swapping sandwiches and eating each other's.

At each station along the way, they saw more people get on who looked as if they were also going to Butlin's. By the time they got off the train at Skegness and found their way to the Butlin's bus that was picking them up, there was a whole busful of them, as even more people had arrived on different trains from all over the country. By now the rain had long since stopped and the sun was beating down as the bus drove along the coast to the camp, which was a couple of miles out of town at a place called Ingoldmells. As it came into view, there was a collective gulp from those who hadn't seen it before, because the camp was enormous, stretching for what seemed like miles. Valda's first sight of it was, she says, 'amazing, and anyone who went to Butlin's in that era will tell you the same thing: all you could see as you approached the camp was a white picket fence and behind it this line of tall, white-painted flagpoles, with dozens of different, brightly coloured flags fluttering in the breeze. It still gives me goose-pimples to think about it now!'

Just before they reached the main gates, they passed the Ingoldmells Hotel. The bus driver, who had been keeping up a running commentary all the way, told them it was also owned by Butlin's.

They drove in through the main gates, got off the bus and then all stood there in a group looking around. In front of them was the main reception building, emblazoned with the famous Butlin's motto: 'Our true intent is all for your delight.'

'It's a quote from Shakespeare – *A Midsummer Night's Dream*,' the ever-informative bus driver told them as he unloaded their cases from the luggage compartment.

There was a gleaming outdoor swimming pool with a fountain and a cascade, a separate indoor pool, a boating lake, landscaped gardens, an amusement park, cafés, dining halls and shops, a cinema, three theatres, several bars, a gym, a riding stables, tennis courts, bowling and putting greens, football and cricket pitches, a roller-skating rink, a games room, a nursery, a playground, a hairdresser's, an ice-cream parlour, a Chinese restaurant, a bookmaker's, a bank, a tobacconist, a sweet shop and a lost-property office, and – somewhere among all this – was the coffee bar where Valda would be working. To get around the vast site there was a miniature railway, a monorail and a chairlift, and if you wanted to be more adventurous still, there was even an airfield for pleasure trips and private charters. And around all the main buildings there were endless rows of chalets that seemed to stretch away to the horizon.

'It's like a city, not a holiday camp,' Valda said, still staring around her, open-mouthed. She would probably still be standing there now, had Anne – who had worked there the year before and knew the ropes – not said, 'Come on! We need to go and get a chalet allocated to us, before the rest of them get there!'

So they left the others still in a huddle and hurried off to get their chalet keys. They then put their cases on the little Butlin's train that took them to the place where they dished out the uniforms. That felt like being in the Army. There was a long counter with a couple of grumpy people manning it, and they just threw uniforms at the new staff – which usually didn't fit. Some were so long that they were dragging on the ground; some had sleeves that were so short they finished halfway down your forearms. 'You just had to find one that was an approximate fit and do your best with it,' says Valda.

The famous red jackets and white pleated skirts were reserved for the redcoats, and the rest of the staff were given the appropriate uniform for their jobs. The ones for the coffee bar assistants were particularly hideous: a bright-orange Crimplene dress and a brown pinafore that buttoned onto it. There was also a brown-and-orange hat that was 'even more disgusting', Valda says, and looked 'like one of the old mop caps, but with a peak on it'. The men had to wear a boat-shaped paper hat, which she thought was 'slightly less repulsive', so she decided to wear that instead.

Having got their uniforms, they got back on the train, which took them up the endless chalet lines. They looked a bit like an Elizabethan's idea of beach huts, with fake half-timbering on the outside and tall, thin windows with small panes to either side of the door. They got to their chalet, unlocked the door and went inside. 'That was a real eye-opener for me,' Valda says, 'because until then I'd had no idea what to expect.' It had looked absolutely tiny to her from the outside and first impressions proved correct. When they walked in, straight ahead of them was a little metal shelf, a pair of bunk beds, one chair, a small chest of drawers, a wastepaper bin and a tiny sink with a cold tap and a mirror above it, painted with a couple of white yachts to match the ones on the curtains. That was it, nothing else.

There was no bathroom or toilet – the nearest facilities were in two concrete blocks in the next chalet line but one. One block, painted pink, was for the girls, and the other one, painted blue, was for the boys. There were toilet cubicles down one side of the room and bathrooms down the other, and the blocks were always absolutely freezing, even at the height of summer. The baths were so big that it seemed to take several hours to fill them, and if you weren't in there first thing in the morning, the hot water had usually run out.

'As anyone who went to Butlin's in that or any other era will also tell you,' Valda says, 'one of the big things was that you always had to take your own bath plug with you, because there were never any in the bathrooms. Luckily, Anne had brought one and I was able to borrow hers until I got one of my own, and usually you had to stuff tissue or paper towel around it because it was never the right size for the plughole. I don't know why there were never any plugs. I suppose either people pinched them as souvenirs or perhaps the management took them to discourage the campers from taking too many baths and using too much hot water.'

The chalets were also always freezing. There was a two-inch gap under the door through which the wind whistled, and they were such flimsy constructions that if you slammed the door, the whole chalet wobbled. There was no heating and no electric power sockets other than the one for electric razors in the light above the washbasin mirror. However, says Valda, 'It was astonishing how much electrical equipment you could run from that one tiny little socket, without setting fire to the chalet or fusing every light in the camp.' By the time she'd been at Butlin's a couple of years, Valda had perfected the art and had a record player, a hairdryer, a kettle and even a heating element all connected to the razor socket. You couldn't plug anything into it, of course, because the plugs were the wrong sort, so in a feat of improvisation that would give any modern health and safety man nightmares, the girls just poked the bare wires into the razor socket and held them in place with broken-off matchsticks.

Despite the tiny chalets, the girls still managed to make the most of what little space they had. 'We used to have some great parties in there,' Valda says. 'It was amazing how many people you could squeeze in: two- or three-dozen people squashed into a space that was only nine feet by six. You couldn't move around much, but you certainly got closely acquainted with the people standing next to you! The swimming pools were closed at night, so the reds also often used to go in there and lark around.'

The first time she had gone into their chalet, Valda had noticed that there was a round hole about the size of a ten pence piece in the bottom of the metal wastepaper bin.

She couldn't work out why it was there, since it seemed to contradict the whole object of the bin: to collect rubbish that would otherwise finish up on the floor. It took her a few days before she finally realised why it was there. If you needed the loo during the night, you had to put your shoes and coat on and blunder your way over to the toilet blocks in the dark, so most people – and Valda and Anne were no different – tended to put the washbasin in their chalets to unauthorised use. Doing so required an awkward balancing act, with one foot on the chest of drawers and the other on the pipe on the other side of the basin. You couldn't sit on the edge of the basin, because if you put too much weight on it, you would pull the basin right off the wall, as one unfortunate girl redcoat discovered. She was not only injured, but also had to bear the indignity of explaining to the security man what had happened when he appeared in response to the commotion. Using the wastepaper bin as an impromptu chamber pot would have been much easier, of course ... and it was precisely to prevent this that all the wastepaper bins had a hole drilled through the bottom!

The famous Butlin's tannoys were still hectoring and haranguing the happy campers to join in the fun in the 1970s. Originally, the loudspeakers were fitted inside the chalets, ensuring that there was no escape from the relentless jollity. There were even loud-speakers in the campers' bedrooms, which were not fitted with an on/off switch. Such regimentation soon went out of date, though, and by the dawn of the sophisticated 1960s, Butlin's was already toning it down a little. The loudspeakers were removed from the chalets and put on walls or poles outside, although this may have been more to stop irate campers from silencing them by cutting the wires than to moderate the stream of cheery announcements.

Nonetheless, the tannoys were so loud, Valda says, 'that when Radio Butlin's made announcements or played that bloody early-morning music, "Sleepy Shores" or "Cavatina", there was no way that you could avoid hearing it – it was that loud that you could have heard it in the centre of Skegness!' They stopped that practice in around 1979 and after that the redcoats manning Radio Butlin's (from a room the size of a broom cupboard) would actually play song requests from the campers.

There were two sittings for breakfast and it was 'like a cattle market'. Valda had never taken much notice of waiters and waitresses before, but the ones at Butlin's really earned their money. 'There was no self-service,' Valda says. 'All the food was delivered to the tables, and you had to carry metal stands with six full plates on each one, and you were practically running between the kitchen and the tables, because it was such a rush to get everybody fed in the available time. And if any of the waitresses dropped a plate or something, everyone in the dining hall would cheer and applaud. You were knackered by the time you'd finished breakfast, because there were two sittings, so you were on the go, flat out, for two hours. After clearing away, you'd barely got time to get back to your chalet and kick your shoes off before it was time to go back and start serving lunch, and it was the same with the evening meal as well.' She began to realise why she had hardly ever seen any of the waiters and waitresses out socialising after work – it was because they were all completely shattered!

By comparison, the coffee bar where Valda worked in Skegness proved to be fairly easy work. It was quite a big coffee bar, with a griddle for hot snacks such as burgers, poached eggs on toast and beans on toast, and also serving cakes, sandwiches, teas and coffees. When she first started, she worked as an assistant, but within a few days she'd been promoted to cashier. That meant a little more money, but even better, she got rid of the hideous orange-and-brown uniform. Her glee at that soon faded, though, when she saw the nasty blue nylon overall she had to swap it for. A week or so after that she was promoted again and made charge hand – she was a hard worker, but there was also a high turnover of staff, which meant that if you were good at your job, you could move up the ladder quickly.

Unfortunately, charge hands had an even worse uniform: 'a burgundy-coloured gabardine dress, like a sack, with a cream collar and cream cuffs'. However, within three weeks she'd been promoted again to coffee bar supervisor – mainly, she says, because, 'I've always been a pretty organised sort of person, or at least I can organise everyone except myself!' The uniform for that was much better: a pale-blue jacket with dark-blue binding and a navy-blue dress, though the dress was still Crimplene and uncomfortably hot and heavy.

Valda had about twenty staff under her and she had to do the cashing up and the running of the whole bar: stocking, ordering and so on. It was hard work and a lot of responsibility, but she absolutely loved it because of the holiday atmosphere and because there were different people coming in every day and every week. The money wasn't brilliant, but they lived on camp and got all their meals free, so their expenses weren't high.

Soon after she started work, Valda had an

encounter with Billy Butlin himself. She thinks he was officially retired by then, but he used to come round with his son Bobby on his tours of inspection. They'd been told he was going to come into the coffee bar and since he was Butlin's royalty, her boss was 'running round like a blue-arsed fly', digging out a china cup and saucer, a plate and a paper doily and a nice tray for Billy's coffee. When the man himself came in, though, he walked behind the coffee bar, ignoring the china cup and saucer, and said to her, 'How's it going–' he paused as he bent down to read her name badge '–Valda?'

'Going fine, thanks, Mr Butlin. Would you like a cup of tea or coffee?'

'I would; if the guests can drink it, so can I.' And he poured himself a coffee in one of the same plastic cups that the campers used and then sat down and started chatting to some of them.

'That really impressed me,' Valda says. 'He was so unpretentious and whoever you talked to had the same view of him; he was really well thought of by everyone. Billy Butlin, the man, was magic.'

Although many of his former redcoats, like Valda, revere Billy, those closest to him sometimes had a different view. Growing up with a distant father – both metaphorically and then later literally – may have affected Billy's relationship with his own son, Bobby,

216

who later bitterly recalled that he had been 'packed off to boarding school' at the age of five and could 'count on the fingers of one hand' the number of times his father visited him during his entire school career. He added that on 'many, many occasions when I would come home for the school holidays, my parents were away'. In the strangest irony of all, the son of the man credited with reinventing the family holiday also recalled that they 'rarely went on a family holiday'.

Three

Having not even known what a redcoat was when she first applied to Butlin's, within a few weeks of starting work there, Valda was desperate to become one herself. Her chalet mate Anne was already going out with a redcoat called Shane and Valda's first real encounter with the redcoats came when Anne took her along to meet Shane and his mates for a drink at the Ingoldmells Hotel. Valda was struck by the redcoats at once and thought they were great – full of chatter, energy, laughter and life. As she talked to them, she found herself thinking: these are my sort of people, I'm a bit like that myself. Maybe this is what I should be doing.

That was reinforced when she was working in the coffee bar one day, just going round the tables asking everyone, 'How are you doing? Everyone okay? Anybody need anything?'

A girl redcoat who was in there turned to Valda and said, 'Hey, you've got the wrong-coloured jacket on.'

'No, I haven't,' Valda said. 'We're supposed to wear these blue ones.'

'I know,' the girl said. 'I mean you should be a redcoat. You've got the patter!'

The more Valda thought about it, the more she felt that she was well qualified to do the job. She had an outgoing personality and she wasn't without talent for the entertainment side of it, because she'd been a singer all her life and loved being on the stage and taking part in amateur dramatics. She'd begun when she was at school, singing in the choir, and when she grew up, she sang regularly in the clubs and then became a vocalist with a band. She got her break when she was about seventeen, after going to see a country and western band, although she had an ulterior motive. 'I really fancied the lead guitarist,' she says, grinning. 'He was about ten years older than me, so realistically it was never going to happen, but I was too young to realise that at the time.' At the end of their set she went up to him and said, 'Your band really needs a female singer. Do you want one?'

He looked her up and down with an expression somewhere between amusement and irritation and then said, 'No.'

She wasn't giving up that easily. She said, 'Go on, can't I at least have a try?'

He still wasn't even slightly interested in hearing her sing, but the other guitarist said, 'You've got a brass neck all right, but can you really sing?'

'Of course I can,' she said. 'I wouldn't be saying so otherwise.'

'Well, go on then, let's hear you.'

Now she was thinking, God, after the build-up I've given myself, I really hope I can pull this off. They told her to turn up at the place where they rehearsed the following evening to audition for them. She was pretty nervous, but she went along and sang a couple of songs with them. She can't have done too badly, because they took her on to be their vocalist there and then. At first, she just sang a couple of numbers in their set, but she gradually sang more and more.

After she'd been doing that for a while, Valda and the lead guitarist left the group to form a duo, though she had stopped fancying him by then, so it was a strictly professional arrangement! They called themselves Lady and the Tramp and played the clubs for a while, but eventually Valda went solo. 'I came up with a pretty bizarre stage name for myself: Valli King,' she says. 'I was mad on Egyptology at the time and since Cleopatra would have been pushing it, I chose Valli King after the Valley of the Kings, where many of the ancient Egyptian royal tombs are sited.'

As well as possessing a strong voice, she was also a good disco dancer. Dressed in a black satin catsuit, she won the northeastern heat of the EMI National Disco Dance Championship at the Sands nightclub in Whitley Bay, despite a traumatic wardrobe malfunction when one of her boobs popped out of the side of her costume while she was dancing to Chic's 'Le Freak'. Without missing a beat, she popped it back in and kept on dancing. Her mum, who had gone to watch her, said, 'Well, that was a bit sly, Valda. I think you only won because you popped your boob out!' She won her quarter-final, too – with both boobs remaining firmly in place this time – but to her huge disappointment, she was knocked out in the semi-final.

So with these skills under her belt, it didn't take Valda long to realise that what she really wanted to do at Skegness was be a redcoat. From then on, she was 'never out of the face of the entertainments manager, Alan Ridgeway' she says. 'In fact, I was the original Peggy from *Hi-de-Hi!* because every time I saw him, I kept saying, "Please, Mr Ridgeway, I want to be a redcoat. I want to be a redcoat.""

If she'd gone to him in the first couple of weeks of that 1973 season, she might have been allowed to change jobs, but in those days, once the season was underway, Butlin's didn't allow you to switch jobs unless they promoted you themselves. So although she pestered the life out of him, the answer from Alan Ridgeway was always the same: 'I'm afraid not, Valda. Maybe next year.'

He'd told her to come back the next year and ask him again, so that's exactly what she did in 1974, but the answer was still the same. 'I'm afraid not, Valda. We've got all the redcoats we need for this season. Maybe next year.'

So, grumbling to herself, she did another year in the coffee bar. At the end of the season, Alan Ridgeway was still answering Valda's pleas to be a redcoat with 'Maybe next year', and at that point she thought, I'm sick of this, so she 'packed it in at Butlin's'. As soon as the season had ended, she went straight to Blackpool for a four-day holiday with her mum and her sister, and found a job on the very first day they were there. There was a flat to live in, too, so she went straight back to the bed and breakfast where they were staying, shoved her clothes into a couple of black bin bags and moved herself into the flat. She then met someone while she was working in Blackpool and soon moved in with him.

She was quite enjoying the job she was doing, so she didn't even apply to Butlin's for the next three seasons. She was singing with a band as well, but by 1978 she was getting a bit bored – with Blackpool and her boyfriend – so she applied to Butlin's again. Unfortunately, the season had already started by the time she had made the decision to apply, so she was once more out of the running for a job as a redcoat and instead had to take whatever was offered. That turned out to be work as a barmaid in the camp at Bognor Regis. 'It was very hard, relentless work there,' she says. 'You never stopped from opening time until closing time, because at a holiday camp, with thousands of people out to enjoy themselves, the bars were always very busy.'

Valda kept working in the bar right up to the end of the season. She saw some big-name acts while she was working there – The Hollies, The Four Tops, Fats Domino, Edwin Starr and Billy Ocean all appeared at Bognor over the years – and she was still in love with the whole idea of the entertainment business. She saw being a redcoat as a way of being able to work as an entertainer... Maybe she even thought it would lead to her big break into show business. So she applied to be a redcoat again the following year, 1979, and once more put Skegness down as her first choice, because she absolutely loved the place. For once, she applied in plenty of time, and now she thought: this is really it, it's now or never. If they don't make me a redcoat this year, I'm not going to go back to Butlin's again.

She sent in her application, chewed her nails for a few days and then got a reply telling her to turn up for an interview at the Highpoint Hotel in Newcastle. When her turn came, she positively bounced through the door. Determined to make a positive impression, she said a bright and breezy 'Good morning!' at the top of her voice, before the interviewer, Doug MacLeod, had even had the chance to open his mouth. He asked her a couple of questions about her previous jobs and then said, 'So, what can you do?'

'Well, I can sing and I'm a disco dancer, too.'

'Oh, right,' he said, sounding unimpressed. 'Well, go on then, can you sing me a line now?'

'Yes, if you want me to. Any requests?'

He shrugged his shoulders. 'Whatever.'

So she stood up and began to sing, but she had only sung the first line when he held up his hand and said, 'Okay, thanks, that's enough.'

Valda was thinking, blimey, I've blown it. He must really have hated my voice. In fact, as he told her afterwards, all he had really wanted to see was whether she had the nerve to get up and sing in what was quite an intimidating environment: a job interview with someone she'd never met before. If she could sing under those circumstances, he reasoned, she'd have no trouble in doing so on stage in front of a room full of campers. He must have been satisfied, because at the end of the interview he just said, 'Right, there you go,' filled in her name on one of the contracts on his desk and pushed it towards her.

When she read through it, she found that she was finally being offered a contract as a redcoat, but her joy faded a little when she saw that the job was at Ayr, not Skegness. 'Oh no,' she said, 'I want to go to Skegness.'

'Well, that was your first choice.'

'And my second choice was Bognor, and my third was Minehead. Can't I go to any of them?'

By now he was getting impatient. 'Look, do you want the job or not?' he said. 'Because if you don't, there are plenty of people waiting outside who will.'

'Yes, of course I do.'

'Well, the job's at Ayr. Take it or leave it.'

So she took the job. It was only when she got to Ayr that she discovered that although he was interviewing potential redcoats for all the camps, Doug MacLeod was actually the entertainments manager at Ayr. So he had obviously taken a shine to her and decided he was going to have her as a redcoat at his camp and not let her go anywhere else. Although she was delighted at finally being made a redcoat, she was still fuming about being made to go to Ayr, especially when she discovered that her friend who'd gone to the interviews with her had been given a contract to work at Skegness.

She was issued with her uniform, given a bit of training and introduced to the other redcoats. They were all then told whether they were to be general duties redcoats or the children's redcoats, who ran the Beaver Club for the small children and the 913 Club for the nine- to thirteen-year-olds – kids of fourteen and over joined in with the adults. There were also a few lifeguard redcoats who, as well as supervising the swimming pools during the day, did redcoat duties at night when they were needed, usually when the Redcoat Shows – the weekly cabaret nights that involved most of the redcoats – left the team short-handed for the rest of the jobs they had to do. To her relief, Valda was made a general duties redcoat, although she also had to help run the 913 Club as part of her role.

On their first day there, Doug MacLeod assembled all the redcoats, then turned to

Valda and said, 'Right then, Valda, you told me you sang with a band. Stand up, then, and let's hear you.'

So she stood up and sang a heart-rending country and western ballad about a little girl who dies, and when she finished she looked round the room and saw a couple of the other girls in floods of tears. Even Doug had a tear in the corner of his eye, but he wiped it away and said briskly, 'Absolutely lovely, Valda, but that's the last time I want to hear you singing that around here. You're supposed to be cheering up the campers and showing them a good time, not driving them to commit suicide!'

They'd all arrived on 23 April and the camp didn't actually open to the public until the end of the first week in May, so they had a fortnight to get ready, but in those two weeks there was no such thing as rehearsing a show, because they were flat out getting the camp back in shape. It had suffered a summer's worth of wear and tear the year before and had then been sitting empty all winter, so it was inevitably in need of a bit of attention. They had to spend most of the time before the formal start of the season cleaning the whole camp, repainting anything that was looking shabby, getting the dressing rooms and theatres ready and doing a million other jobs to generally spruce up the place.

The first time they actually donned their red coats was the Friday night before they opened for the season, when they were all assembled in the theatre and told to line up on the stage so that the boss, Doug Mac-Leod, could see what they looked like. So there they were: boys in red blazers, white shirts and white flannels, and girls in red jackets, white blouses and white pleated skirts, and all of them wearing white shoes. They could wear any style of shoe they liked throughout the day, as long as they were white, but the rule was that from six o'clock, when they started serving evening meals, all the girls had to wear heels and the boys had to put on bow ties. Heavy jewellery was frowned upon; you could only wear ear studs, a simple chain and a wedding or engagement ring. 'You could wear make-up as long as it wasn't too much, but believe me,' Valda says, 'getting up at seven in the morning, having only gone to bed at four o'clock, the last thing you wanted to be doing was putting on full slap.'

One of the male redcoats, Stuart, was a real ladies' man – 'at least, he thought he was', Valda says with a sardonic smile – and he didn't fancy the standard-issue, white twill trousers that the boys had to wear, so, as was the fashion then, he wore a pair of white Wrangler jeans instead, which were skin-tight down to the knee and then flared out below.

The boss marched along the line like he was a general carrying out an inspection of the troops. When he got to Stuart, he took one look at his Wrangler jeans and said, 'Get those off, now!' The sheepish Stuart had to go and retrieve his white twill trousers and put them on instead.

The only other thing the boss was worried about was whether their uniforms fitted – not from any concern for their comfort, but because of the image they would present to the campers. One of the boys, Mally Watson, was about six foot four and as thin as a pipe cleaner, and they hadn't been able to find a uniform to fit him, so he was standing on the stage with his trousers at half-mast and the sleeves of his jacket finishing just below his elbows. The boss looked him over and said, 'Is that the biggest they had?'

Mally nodded. The boss thought for a moment and then shrugged his shoulders and said, 'Well, it'll have to do for now. They'll sort you out through the week.' So Mally had to go on duty the next morning looking like an overgrown schoolboy who'd stolen someone else's uniform, though they did eventually manage to find him one that, if still not perfect, was roughly his size.

As one of the general duties redcoats, Valda was responsible for jollying the campers along, making sure that everyone – old and young, extrovert and shy – felt part of the

Butlin's experience, and keeping them entertained night and day. In the first week, about ten or twelve of the more talented redcoats put together the Redcoat Show for the season, pulling it out of thin air. If there weren't enough volunteers, the boss would conscript a few and they weren't given any time off from their other duties to do it. They could only rehearse it towards midnight, after everything else was done for the day, but that's what they did and they loved it.

To make sure there were no arguments or fall-outs, the boss, Doug MacLeod, did the whole show – 'That's the first act, that's the second act, that's the third act,' and so on. Doug put Valda together with Stuart, the 'ladies' man', who could play the guitar but couldn't sing. Doug just said, 'Right, Valda, you go with him and form a duo.' And that was it; they just had to get on and do it.

They put on the Redcoat Show every Friday night and as soon as it was over, they all went straight back to the ballroom for the Au Revoir party, because it was the last night of the week and the campers were going home the next day. There were tears every Friday night. 'They were genuine tears,' says Valda, 'because you'd made friends with these people, and a week at Butlin's was like a month in the real world.'

On a typical day, they would hear the moring reveille – 'Cavatina' – followed by the first announcement from Radio Butlin's: 'Good morning, campers. It's another lovely day. The first sitting of breakfast will be at eight o'clock.' Years later, when Butlin's finally finished playing 'Cavatina' to wake the campers in the morning, the redcoats all put their names in a hat, and the lucky winner whose name was drawn out had the honour of smashing Radio Butlin's copy of the record, because all the redcoats hated it so much. Even now, all these years later, Valda still shudders if she hears it played anywhere.

When Valda heard the hated sound in the morning, she'd fall out of bed, put on a bit of make-up and get ready to go on duty. The redcoats had to have finished their breakfast and cleared away before the campers arrived for their first sitting at 8 a.m., and then they had to do what they called 'swanning around' while the campers queued up to get in the dining room – bidding them a good morning, asking if they'd slept well and telling them what the redcoats had planned for the day, and so on.

If Valda was very lucky, she might get allocated the second breakfast duty and have a little bit longer in bed, but once the redcoats were up, they were on the go for the rest of the day, sun, rain, hail or snow – and it seemed to rain an awful lot at Ayr... Often

Valda and the other reds would be standing behind the dining-room doors giving radiant smiles and singing 'The Sun Has Got His Hat On' to the poor, bedraggled campers in their plastic rain hats and Pac-a-Macs as they stood in the pelting rain, queuing to get inside. 'It's amazing we didn't get punched,' Valda says. 'We certainly got some filthy looks and nasty remarks!'

Despite the name they gave to the pie served on Thursdays – 'Suicide Pie' – the food really wasn't that bad, all things considered. In any case, as they all used to say: 'They don't come for the food!' It was never piping hot, but then it was a long haul from where the chefs plated up to the far end of the dining room. It wasn't gourmet food, certainly, but it was substantial and the campers seemed to like it. There were three full meals a day: a full English breakfast (though the toast was like rubber, because it was made in big batches and stacked up until the waiters and waitresses got round to taking it out) and three-course meals – soup, a main and usually steamed pudding with custard – for lunch and dinner.

At mealtimes, the redcoats were allocated to a table of campers and had to socialise with them. It was one of the reasons why redcoats were sometimes disliked by the rest of the staff, because they thought they were sucking up to the campers, but it was their job to do so and they had no choice; they were not allowed to socialise with each other or other staff members when they were on duty.

The rest of the staff didn't necessarily understand this, and there was a widespread belief among the redcoats – whether it was true or not, no one could say – that if they had the chance, the kitchen staff would spit in their food. If there were no spare seats in the main dining hall, the redcoats had to go to the staff canteen for their meals, which was something they dreaded. It was often a bit of an ordeal, and for the other staff the sight of redcoats queuing up to get their food could be like a red rag to a bull. So rather than run the risk of what the kitchen staff might do to their food, the redcoats tended to starve themselves during the day and go to the chippy later on.

After breakfast, the day's events would start with a plethora of competitions. Valda's favourite one was the Knobbly Knees competition, when all the old men would get up on stage and show their knees. There was also a Lovely Legs competition, in which girls were lined up on stage and encouraged to raise the hem of their dresses so that the judges and the audience – mostly male, strangely enough – could assess the loveliness of their legs. Since the girls were understandably reluctant to raise them too far, the compère would urge them on by getting the audience to yell 'Get 'em up!'

'You didn't have to drag anybody on stage,' Valda says. 'And, as the Lovely Legs competition would suggest, it wasn't PC like it is now. We even had a competition called Miss ChiChi, and that stood for "Chubby, Cheerful and Cheeky". When my mum came for a holiday, she was little, quite chubby and very cheerful, and she was gutted she didn't win! You couldn't do it now, because you wouldn't dare call anyone chubby.'

When they weren't running events or competitions, the redcoats were just wandering around the camp, jollying everyone along and chatting to anyone who looked lonely or a bit fed up. Then in the evening they would be in the theatres, the bars or the ballrooms. The redcoats called things like the dances in the Old Tyme Ballroom and the whist and beetle drives 'punishment details', because they nearly all hated doing them. 'It was like watching paint dry,' Valda says. 'The time really used to drag. So if Doug MacLeod had caught you doing anything you shouldn't have been doing, you would be sent to the Old Tyme Ballroom or the whist drive as a punishment. The Quiet Lounge duty was even worse, because by definition that was where people had gone for a bit of quiet time to sit and think or read a book or the paper, and the last thing they wanted was a redcoat in their face going, "Everything all right? Having a good time? Do you want to join in the Knobbly Knees competition?"

'Being a redcoat looked very glamorous, and you did get to do entertainment and everything, but to be quite honest, it was damned hard work as well, particularly when you had twenty-odd kids hanging off your white pleated skirt saying, "Play with me, Valda. Play with me." You were on duty constantly, with a smile on your face, and every redcoat will tell you that it became such a habit that, when the end of the season came, for weeks afterwards we'd be walking down our own streets at home, saying, "Hello", "Good morning", "Are you all right?" to everyone we passed.'

There were pages and pages of standing orders that the redcoats had to follow as well, covering everything from their personal grooming (no facial hair of any sort for the men; no wild and wacky hairstyles for the women) to how they had to behave. Although staff were not allowed to have members of the opposite sex in their chalet, they flouted that rule two or three times a week at least. And though they were also forbidden to have any sort of relationship with a camper, that was also routinely ignored.

'You could see why the rule was there,'

Valda says, 'because if a heartless male red-coat – and most of them were! – had gone out with an impressionable young girl and broken her heart, the irate parents would soon have been banging on the boss's door. So in theory, that was grounds for instant dismissal, but of course it went on; people either went off site or were a bit more discreet about it. The management had to turn a blind eye anyway, because they could not seriously hope to control every single thing that forty-odd redcoats and up to 5,000 guests might be getting up to, especially after dark!'

Valda didn't think it was worth the risk for what could only be a very brief affair, given that the campers were usually there just for a week. The dangers were vividly demonstrated by the experience of one male redcoat. He was 'stalked' by a young girl camper, who became obsessed with him to the point where he couldn't turn around without her being there. 'She even followed him to the gents,' Valda says, 'and stood outside while he was in there; she just wouldn't leave him alone. He tried to be nice and kind to her and let her down gently, because he was afraid he would get the sack if there were complaints, but she went off sobbing to her parents. They made a fuss about it, and sure enough, the unfortunate redcoat wound up being fired.'

'If a camper complained about anything,

that was it,' says Valda. 'You were for it and there was no right of appeal. There were no unions at Butlin's in those days and there was never a problem in replacing staff; if a redcoat was sacked, there were always at least ten people queuing up to take his place.'

They worked from seven in the morning until midnight or later, six days a week, and all for terrible wages. There was also still a pay difference at Butlin's between men and women in the 1960s and early 1970s, a male-female divide, as there was in every job in those days. The pay difference was about two or three pounds a week, and though it doesn't sound like much now, it was a large amount in terms of the wages they were on at the time, as they were only paid between £9 and £12 a week then. However, a few years further down the line, and certainly by 1978 when Valda came back to Butlin's after those few years away, men and women were all on the same wages.

If you were a good, popular redcoat, you didn't really need money anyway, according to Valda. 'You never had to buy a drink, because the campers were queuing up to buy you one, and if you were friendly with somebody in the self-catering chalets, you might even get a few free meals as well!' On their days off, they had to get out of the camp altogether, because even out of uniform, the campers would recognise them as redcoats and still expect them to be chatting and entertaining them, when all they probably wanted was a bit of peace and quiet and a chance to recover. If it was a beautiful day they might head for the beach, but they usually got a bus or a taxi into Ayr and went round the pubs there, staggering back late at night.

Four

Valda did two seasons as a redcoat at Ayr in 1979 and 1980. 'I absolutely loved it,' she says. 'The redcoat job was just magical – the best job ever in the world, bar none. You can talk to anyone who was a redcoat at Butlin's in the old days, and they will tell you that it was the best job they ever did. I have so many wonderful memories of that time, but the best memory of all is of a family who came to stay at Ayr with a little boy who was only about seven or eight but had leukaemia. I made great friends with them, and the boy just loved Butlin's and loved the redcoats.' At the end of the week, his mum told Valda, 'We've got a surprise for him, because, although he doesn't know about it, when Friday comes and it's the big Au Revoir, we're going to tell him that we've

237

actually booked for another week.'

On the Friday night the little boy was 'looking absolutely broken-hearted', Valda says. 'He was saying goodbye to everybody, because he knew he was going home in the morning, and then his mum turned to him and said, "You will see them tomorrow, you know, because we're staying for another week." Even to this day, I've got goose-bumps about it, just remembering the look on that little boy's face. It was so amazing, and that's what Butlin's could do for you.'

The redcoats' job was to help everyone whatever the circumstances, but that could occasionally put them in situations where they were out of their depth. 'One Saturday, when all the new campers were piling into reception to check in and it was really, really busy,' Valda says, 'one old gentleman, who was there with his wife, had a heart attack and died instantly, right there in reception. Obviously, that was not something we had ever been trained to deal with, but trying to help, one young redcoat – I'll spare her blushes and not use her name – put her arm around the gentleman's wife and said, "Don't worry, love, try not to let it spoil your holiday." She was trying to be kind, but she just wasn't thinking!' Deaths at Butlin's camps weren't an everyday occurrence, but they weren't unknown by any means. At Minehead alone there was an average of seven deaths a year, most of them from heart attacks, but given that the larger camps were the size of small towns, it wasn't too surprising that they saw their share of births, marriages and deaths.

While Valda was at Ayr that second year, she started going out with a redcoat called Keith. 'I don't know why,' she says, smiling, 'because I had been in love with another redcoat at the time I met Keith, and he wasn't even particularly good-looking, but somehow we clicked!' They carried on a fairly discreet relationship all summer and towards the end of the season they were making plans for what they'd do together during the winter. Finding work in the off-season was always a potential problem – and the season was only five months long, so there was a lot of off-season to fill – but Valda loved being a redcoat so much that she would probably have taken her chances and kept on doing it for years, had she not been headhunted by the boss of Mecca Bingo in Scotland just before the end of that 1980 season.

He had been watching her calling the bingo and then came up to her afterwards and said, 'Do you want a proper job?'

It was coming to the end of the season and she had no work to go to in the winter, so she said, 'Maybe. Why? What are you offering me?'

'A trainee managership with Mecca Bingo.'

He told her what it would involve and how much she'd be paid and she was tempted, but she replied, 'I'll have to discuss it with my boyfriend.'

'Is he a redcoat, too? Well, if he's any good as a bingo caller, there might be a traineeship for him as well.' He watched Keith at work and then made him the same offer. Keith and Valda discussed it for a while, but it was really too good an offer to refuse, so they both said yes.

They packed their bags and had a big farewell party for all their friends and fellow redcoats, which they staged in the equipment hut on the sports field – one of the redcoats nicked the key from the offices when no one was looking. They thought that if they had the party there, well away from the chalet lines, they could make as much noise as they liked without disturbing any of the campers. Every redcoat came along, no matter what duty they were on the next day, but either someone heard them and complained to the night security man or he spotted them himself – 'He was a bit of a jobsworth,' Valda says – because he came marching across the sports field and broke up the party.

However, they weren't ready to call it a night, so after they got kicked out of there, they made a hole in the fence, crawled through it and went down to the beach. They lit a big bonfire and carried on partying until dawn. Keith and Valda were quite happy to take all the blame for the party and the damage to the fence. It didn't matter to them, because Butlin's couldn't sack them when they were leaving anyway! However, Valda didn't feel that she was cutting her ties with Butlin's completely – she was sure that she'd be back working as a redcoat again sooner or later.

Keith and Valda left Butlin's together and they both became trainee managers at Mecca Bingo, but Valda soon decided that management wasn't for her and she became a mainstage caller instead, working at the Mecca Bingo hall in Edinburgh – so she was still working in entertainment in a way – whereas Keith went away to Glasgow to train as a manager. Valda's job was well paid, and even though it wasn't as much fun as being a redcoat, it was guaranteed work for twelve months a year. Living and working in a different place from Keith wasn't ideal, though, and eventually they both resigned from Mecca.

They moved to Manchester and Valda found a job in a nightclub, while Keith went back to painting and decorating, which was the trade he'd originally trained for. Valda was still certain that she'd go back to working as a redcoat at Butlin's at some point, but then she got pregnant. She moved back to the Northeast to have their son, Daniel – and with a redcoat mum and dad, he was definitely a Butlin's baby – but with a small child to look after, she couldn't go back to being a redcoat straight away, and in the event she never went back to work at Butlin's again. 'It is the biggest regret of my life that I never did,' she says, 'because I would have just loved to have carried on.'

Keith and Valda didn't last much longer as a couple – he left in 1986, when Daniel was two and a half, and went to live in America. By then, Valda had already realised that he was not the best at committing to things for long – 'I think the responsibility of a child was the final straw for him.'

Valda had a couple of relationships after that, but then met someone she fell in love with and moved near to Manchester to be with him. He was the love of her life, she says, and they had several years together, but her dreams of spending the rest of her life with him were shattered when he abruptly left her, and within twelve months he had married someone else. 'Since then I've been on my own,' Valda says, 'which is the way I like it now, and I've no complaints at all about my life, because I've certainly had my share of good times along the way. I'm working on my autobiography at the moment, and I'm going to call it *Forty Shades of Red!*'

Still immaculately dressed, with the same slim figure she had forty years ago, Valda is a woman who knows who she is and is secure in her own judgement. She seems to know everyone at Butlin's and is one of the main driving forces behind the reunions that bring all the old friends back together in their red jackets for weekends of memories, music and laughter.

'Even when you did the whole season,' Valda says, 'you started in May and finished in September; so it was not long, but even in those few months it felt like you'd been there a lifetime, because it was very intense. There were a lot of relationships between staff at Butlin's, and there were lots of broken hearts, too, but to this day, all the redcoats from that old Butlin's era, even the men, call themselves "the Butlin's family". That connection we have remains really powerful, even with people we've never actually worked with and don't know personally. You don't need to have met someone, all you need to know is that he or she was a redcoat, or worked at Butlin's in some capacity, and that's enough – you're welcomed as part of the family.'

As an example of that, one of Valda's Butlin's friends, Liz Walsh, had a nephew with a brain tumour. The doctors couldn't do anything for him in this country, so his family were fundraising to try to get him to

America for treatment. So all of a sudden, the Butlin's reunion at Scarborough in 2012 became a fundraiser for him. They raised £3,000 just at the reunion itself, and then Rocky Mason, a great Butlin's man who worked for them for thirty years, obtained donations from the Freemasons and the Water Rats and various other organisations, and in the end they raised enough money to get the little boy to America for his treatment.

The 'old Butlin's family' is ageing now, and Valda compiles a list for the reunion every year called 'Absent Friends', commemorating all the Butlin's staff and redcoats who have died that year. 'Reading the names always brings you up short,' Valda says, 'because we knew them as such young, vibrant, dynamic personalities, and it's really hard to believe that they've grown old and died.'

There have been many changes at Butlin's over the years, but one of Billy Butlin's innovations has survived them all: the redcoats are still on duty. Roger Billington, who joined Butlin's as a redcoat in 1963 and is now the company archivist at Butlin's Bognor Regis, has an advice sheet given to men and women applying to be a redcoat in the 1960s. They were instructed: 'A redcoat is a guide, philosopher and friend to many thousands of holiday-makers. A redcoat is a good mixer, is patient and tolerant with all kinds of people. A redcoat works a hard and tiring day, [but their] ready smile is just as genuine last thing at night as it was at breakfast time.'

All that still applies today – indeed, even more so now, as redcoats have to offer a much slicker form of entertainment. Most of the redcoats at Butlin's are in their late teens (the minimum age is eighteen) or early twenties, and their energy and enthusiasm are boundless. 'I don't think I'd last five minutes today,' Roger says, 'because they run everywhere, even at midnight.'

Perhaps understandably, some of the old stagers don't share that view of their successors in the famous red jackets. As Valda says, 'It's a very different world now from when we were redcoats, so of course Butlin's has had to change, too, and the role of the redcoat is also very different. There's all sorts of legislation about hours of work, pay and conditions, so the modern redcoats don't work anywhere near the hours that we did, and there are a lot less of them, too. But again it means it's a different experience now.

'It always was a business, of course, but in my era we really did have the feeling that it wasn't just about the bottom line. It's not like the old Butlin's any more, of course, and I don't know how much of Billy Butlin's original idea still remains, but I hope it does. In any event, I'm proud to have played a small part in the Butlin's story. The man was magic and all the millions he made he deserved, because he probably brought more happiness to more British people than just about anyone else you can name.'

Sue

One

Sue Smyth's dad spent twenty-seven years in the Army, 'so I was an army brat', she says, and as a soldier's daughter from a big family, she learned early to fight her corner. Born in 1956, she had 'a very happy childhood, growing up all over the place', with her parents, her two sisters and her brother, living in the standard army married quarters on camps in Cyprus, Germany and then in Gravesend, before her dad's last posting in Shrewsbury. He came from a military family and was born in India, where his father was serving with the Royal Horse Artillery at the time. The family were originally from Ireland, but Sue's grandfather brought them to England when her dad was about four. He grew up in Leeds and joined the King's Own Yorkshire Light Infantry straight from school.

Sue's mum was a Scot and also from a military family, and like Sue's dad, she was also born in India, where her father was serving with the Seaforth Highlanders. The camps where the two families were living were only seven miles apart, but Sue's parents never met until many years later.

Britain was in the last throes of Empire when Sue was young, and there were some anxious times with revolts and rebellions against British rule. The family was given only two days to pack up everything they owned and get out of Cyprus when fighting broke out there in December 1963, and she then didn't see her dad for a year after he was posted to Aden when trouble also erupted there. 'Until then,' she says, 'wherever dad went, we always went with him, and that was the first time we'd been apart from him for a really long time, or at any rate, it seemed a very long time to a little girl.'

Her father habitually had a dour expression that gave people a misleading impression of him. 'Most people seemed to think that my dad was the most miserable bastard on the face of the planet,' Sue says, with her trademark roguish grin. 'But although he certainly didn't suffer fools gladly, he had a very, very dry sense of humour and I absolutely adored him.'

Sue was very like her mum in looks and character – her dad always said that Sue was a Macintosh, while his other children were Smyths. Her brother and sisters were all tall, blond-haired and blue-eyed, while Sue was very dark, like her mum. Sue's mum was very warm and loving. 'She had a lot to put up with. I was the naughty one out of the four children, not in a really bad way, but I always had to have the last word; I've been terrible for that all my life. If we were getting into trouble, it was usually my fault. I'd start it and then run away and leave the others to catch the flak, especially my younger sister – I could get her to do anything!' Sue was something of a handful at school as well, and her education inevitably suffered from the constant changes of school as the family moved with her father to each new posting.

When her dad came to the end of his army service, the family moved to Bristol and took over a pub, The Rose of Denmark, in the Hotwells area. They later ran The Ring of Bells in Coalpit Heath, but they then came out of the pub trade altogether, because her mum was having problems with her heart and needed an easier life.

Three of Sue's cousins joined the police force when they grew up, and given the family's military background, it's probably not surprising that once Sue had decided she didn't want to join the Army, her parents tried to persuade her to join the police as well. Had her life taken a different turn she might have done so, although it would have had to be with the mounted police, she says, since she was 'a horse-daft girl'. As it was, after she left school, she worked at a show-jumping stables in Rutland for two years, but then came back to Bristol and worked for 'an old chap in a pharmacy in Clifton', where she passed her dispensing qualifications.

However, she was always a bit rootless and restless, perhaps because of her background – they moved every two or three years when her dad was in the Army – and in 1977, she went to work as a nanny in Switzerland for two years. After she came back, she was looking around for a job and thought of her Uncle Ron, who had also chosen a career in uniform, though not necessarily one of which his father would have approved – he'd spent his entire working life at Butlin's. By 1979 he was catering manager at Butlin's in Minehead, in charge of all the food on the camp, and his wife, Sue's Aunt Kath, was in the personnel department there. 'Uncle Ron worked at Butlin's for the best part of forty years,' Sue says, 'and had also worked at the camps at Filey, Skegness and Bognor, as well as Minehead, so he and Aunt Kath were Butlin's through and through.'

Hoping the family connection would work in her favour, Sue applied for a job at Minehead. It wasn't completely a step into the unknown for her, because she had been on holiday to Butlin's in the past: once to Bognor with her parents when she was a child, and once to Minehead as a teenager. So she went along for an interview in Bristol and the interviewers told her that they had a vacancy for a nursery nurse at Minehead.

That suited her fine, but when she told her aunt what her role was going to be, Aunt Kath 'had an absolute head fit', Sue says. 'It turned out that there was a snob factor involved. The other staff jobs were thought to be inferior to being a redcoat, so Aunt Kath said, "Oh no. You're not going to be a nursery nurse; you're going to be one of the redcoats. I'll just make some phone calls." So the decision was taken out of Sue's hands, and instead of a nursery nurse's uniform, she found herself putting on one of the famous red jackets and a white pleated skirt.

Two

Sue began work at Butlin's in Minehead in March 1979. The day she arrived, she walked into the entertainments manager's office to introduce herself and discovered that her aunt had already sent him a couple of photographs of her. All the other redcoats were in there and as Sue went in she could hear the entertainments manager saying to them, 'Sue's joining us on her Aunt Kath's recommendation. Here's a picture of her in Switzerland. Oh, and it looks like she's done the London season, too!' She hadn't, of course, but the clear implication was that Sue was some posh girl being foisted on them because of her family connections.

Sue was dying inside. She felt she had to prove herself when she started, 'probably more than anybody else', she says. 'I hadn't been through the proper channels to get the job, and I definitely had to work hard to win some of the redcoats over.' However, there was one redcoat, very petite and bubbly with a shock of very tightly curled hair, who was friendly from the start. 'She told me her name was Anji,' Sue says, 'and we've been friends from that day to this.'

Before they started work as redcoats, they all had to go through an induction. 'It was a complete farce,' Sue says. 'There was a film with John Cleese playing this corny character and all these feeble scenes showing things like the right way and the wrong way to greet a customer. They were trying to be "down with the kids" I suppose, but it was just a total embarrassment,'

A force of nature, tall, beautiful and forthright, Sue called a spade a spade, irrespective of the consequences. She was always up for a prank, and delighted in bending and breaking the long list of Butlin's rules.

The redcoats weren't allowed to take their jackets off, even if it was a boiling-hot day. Sue can remember one ferociously hot August day when they were walking from the

Princess Ballroom down to the Gaiety Theatre, She said to the others, 'I don't care, I'm going to take my jacket off, I'm being boiled alive in it!'

She hadn't gone ten steps before she heard a loud banging on a window, and when she looked up, there was the entertainments manager with a face like thunder, mouthing, 'Put that bloody jacket back on!' When it rained, things weren't much better, Sue says, because they had some 'disgusting plastic Pac-a-Mac-type raincoats that we had to put on. They were white with a red collar and were absolutely vile things!'

For the first three weeks of the season, the camp wasn't open to the public, but they had what were called Kids' Weeks, when schools from all over England would come down. Their parents would pay for it, and it was a proper organised activity holiday during the school Easter break. It was all very sports-oriented, with netball and rounders, and soccer and cricket for the boys, and although it was hard work, it was also great fun. As well as the sports, there were other activities, including 'farm classes', in which the redcoats would take the kids to a local farm to learn about animals and farming.

Sue had volunteered for those, because she loved the countryside and thought she would see some horses, but she soon learned the wisdom of the old army motto, 'Never volunteer for anything', because the chief redcoat who was organising it, Keith Perron, had a particularly wicked sense of humour. He'd grown up on a farm in Devon and knew everything about animals and farming, but when he led them all into a huge barn full of Charolais bulls, he said, 'Now, Sue is going to tell you all about these animals.' He then walked out, chuckling to himself, leaving Sue facing a circle of expectant children waiting for her to enlighten them about these creatures, which she'd never seen or heard of before. 'So I started spouting the biggest load of rubbish you've ever heard in your life about these animals,' she says, 'making it all up as I went along, while the kids took it all in. I told them they came in all different colours (they don't, apparently, they're always white), that they came from Belgium (they're French), gave very good milk (they're a beef breed) and that as well as grass, they ate carrots, cabbages and sprouts, and all sorts of other nonsense. Any of them planning a career in farming or as a vet would have had some serious problems if they'd taken everything I said that day at face value! When I took them back outside, of course, there was Keith killing himself with laughter.'

One of the schools that came down for Kids' Week was Shrewsbury, which was one of Sue's many former schools. 'I was an absolute cow when I was there, because I wouldn't let anyone, including my teachers, talk down to me. I've never talked down to anyone in my life and I expected – and expect – people to treat me with the same respect I give them, but that certainly wasn't the case with a couple of the teachers at my school. So we were on a collision course and in the end I was asked to leave – expelled. The science teacher actually said to my father, "She's going to become a juvenile delinquent," so imagine my pleasure during Kids' Week at Butlin's in Minehead when I saw that one of the teachers accompanying Shrewsbury School was my old science teacher.'

On the second night they were there, after all the kids had gone to bed, the teachers were in the bar having a drink, so Sue walked over to her science teacher and said, 'Hello, remember me? Sue Smyth, juvenile delinquent in the making. Didn't quite work out like that, did it?' He laughed and offered to buy her a drink. 'So as it turned out, perhaps he wasn't all bad after all!'

When the Kids' Weeks had finished, there was then what the irreverent redcoats used to call 'Holy Joes Week', officially known as the Spring Harvest, when Christians descended on Minehead from all over the country. There were also Christian Crusade

Weeks in the autumn, when the camp was again full of the sound of hymns and prayers. 'It was all very happy-clappy, "Praise the Lord and pass the biscuits" sort of stuff,' Sue says. 'They were very different from the usual Butlin's holiday-makers.'

The normal party atmosphere at Butlin's became rather more restrained, with religious services, prayer meetings and Bible readings replacing the usual booze-ups and bingo, while the bars and dance halls were converted into temporary churches. The Princess Ballroom was even specially consecrated for the occasion. The Christian families' children had pretty much the same range of activities as on normal weeks at Butlin's, except that at regular intervals they had to stop whatever they were doing and head off to one of the temporary churches for the next religious service.

There was only supposed to be one bar open while the Christians were there, 'to avoid them falling prey to sinful temptations, I suppose,' Sue says with a smile. 'But that was a standing joke among us, because if you talked to any of the chalet-maids, they would tell you that when they were cleaning out the chalets after the "Holy Joes" had all gone home, they found many of them were full of empty bottles of liquor. So the Christians may not have been going to the bars, but they certainly weren't going short of a drink or two!'

Once the camp opened fully to the public, Sue was made one of the children's redcoats and was put in charge of the Beaver Club, which looked after the younger children, while the older children went to the 913 Club. 'They must have been innocent times back then,' she says with another grin, 'because you wouldn't get away with a name like that these days!' She was known to the kids as 'Auntie Sue'. The redcoats' duties were to organise events for the kids throughout the day, do all the competitions with them and generally keep them entertained while their parents relaxed and enjoyed themselves.

In Sue's first year, Toot and Ploot were still much in evidence – the two blue-skinned aliens with bald, rugby-ball-shaped heads and pointed ears that Butlin's advertising agency had devised as a promotional gimmick. They were even used in one of the Butlin's TV ads, with the strapline 'A holiday that's out of this world', in which they landed on Earth in their tiny flying saucer to go on holiday to Butlin's. So, to entertain the children, Sue and another unfortunate redcoat were given the task of dressing up as Toot and Ploot. 'We had to jump about wearing these big, heavy suits and heads made of latex, which were unbearably hot,' Sue says. 'We were drowning in sweat and almost suffocating inside them. I sometimes used to bribe one of the lifeguards to wear the costume instead of me because I hated it so much.'

Like all redcoats, Sue's day began bright and early, lining up to say, 'Good morning, did you sleep well? Get a big breakfast, because we've got lots of fun things planned for today,' as the campers filed into the dining hall. She was 'not the world's best at getting out of bed in the mornings' and the other reds often had to come knocking on her door to get her up in time.

Sue and the other children's redcoats were based in the children's theatre in the Beachcomber Building, and they worked pretty much non-stop from breakfast time through till midnight. They did competitions and activities with the kids all day, and put on a show for the children in the theatre every evening from six until half past eight. They then joined the other redcoats in the ballroom, theatre or bars to help keep all the adult campers happy until bedtime.

The children's shows always starred 'Uncle Maurice' and 'Uncle Ian' in the lead roles. 'Maurice was quite a character,' Sue says. 'When the TV show *Hi-de-Hi!* was on, I used to swear that they'd modelled the character of the Maplin's children's entertainer, Mr Partridge, known as "Uncle Willie", on Maurice, because they were identical. Just like his fictional counterpart, Maurice also didn't like children very much, which probably wasn't the ideal background for a children's entertainer!'

While the redcoats and nursery nurses looked after the smaller children, Butlin's was such a safe environment that the older children could take themselves off on their own; they could go on the rides or play on any equipment that took their fancy, without any adult supervision at all, either from their parents or the redcoats. That must have done wonders for their self-confidence and sense of independence. There was plenty of organised entertainment for them, too, of course, including a Junior Tarzan competition for the boys and a Little Miss Swimsuit for the girls – again, something it is hard to imagine anyone organising today.

The kids would all parade around carrying little numbers; the boys would strike 'muscle man' poses, and the girls would do 'cheesecake smiles' and then Uncle Maurice or Sue would ask them a few questions, like: 'What do you want to be when you grow up?' Then the judging panel, made up of the chief redcoat, a parent who didn't have a child in the competition and the manager of the camp, would choose the first, second and third prize-winners, and they'd get their token prizes. 'The prizes were always really naff,' Sue says, 'like really cheap toys that would break the first time they were played with.'

There was a big fancy-dress competition for everyone as well. Some of the kids – or more likely their pushy parents – would bring their costumes with them from home and take it really seriously. 'You always had the really twee costumes – little girls dressed up as Little Bo Peep, their hair in ringlets and bows, and with a fluffy lamb and a shepherd's crook over their arm, and that sort of thing – but most of the children actually made their costumes at the camp. They'd hear about the fancy-dress competition and tell their parents they wanted to enter it and some of the things they came up with, made out of nothing more than bits of Bacofoil, cardboard boxes, rubbish bags, string and Sellotape, and with plenty of their mum's make-up plastered over their faces, were really imaginative.'

There was also a junior talent show, which the redcoats used to dread, because if there was a particularly cheesy, catchy song in the charts, like 'The Birdie Song', 'Grandad' or 'Two Little Boys', almost every single one of the children would come up and sing it, one after another. Hearing the same awful song for the twentieth time, the redcoats used to exchange glances, roll their eyes and mutter the most un-Butlin's-like sentiments.

There were athletics and football competitions on the sports field, and a weekly swimming gala, and they used to play Captain Blood with the kids on Tuesdays. 'They used to absolutely love that,' Sue says. 'They all dressed up as pirates and set off in search of the infamous pirate captain who had apparently stolen all the cutlery from the dining hall – and there was me thinking it was the campers who were pinching it all! That always ended with Captain Blood being cornered by the little Beavers and carted off to be thrown in the swimming pool.'

On Fridays they had the Beaver Big Band, which was, Sue says, 'an absolutely horrendous experience, because on the Thursday night we always had the Midnight Cabaret, when we were up till the early hours and usually as drunk as skunks! So we'd stagger in on the Friday morning after a very late night, invariably nursing awful hangovers, and we then had to give all the kids wooden spoons and pans and saucepan lids, and set off all the way round the camp with them, with our heads pounding, while the kids made a terrible racket banging away on the pans and lids; it was dreadful.'

Sue also had to take part in a show for the grown-ups on a Thursday night in the theatre next to the Princess Ballroom. The head compère, Richard, played a judge, and

Sue was the court stenographer, pretending to take notes, while wearing 'glasses, a micro-miniskirt and a top that showed off my boobs'. At the end of the night Richard would say something terribly risqué and then Sue had to fall on the floor in a deep swoon. Richard then revived her by pouring a bucket of water over her so that she got soaked. 'It wasn't exactly Shakespeare, but the audience seemed to like it!'

On Saturday mornings, while their parents were packing their bags ready to go home, there was always a film on for the kids in the children's theatre. Sue saw them so many times that she claims she could recite the script of *Raggedy Ann & Andy*, *The Magic of Lassie* or *Watership Down* word for word.

During the week, the redcoats used to pick the most sensible children from the nines to thirteens and get them to help out with the little ones when they were doing the Beaver Big Band and some of the other activities. The older children enjoyed doing it just for fun, but as a reward, at about eleven o'clock every Friday morning, a couple of the redcoats – usually Sue and the camp manager – used to take them to a party, give them squash and biscuits, and present them with little certificates to take home saying, 'Thank you very much for your help.' Some of those kids loved it so much that they later became redcoats themselves.

The GD – general duties – redcoats used to say that the children's redcoats had it easy compared to them, but the children's redcoats felt that the reverse was true. The GD reds would at least have some time off during the day, whereas, Sue says, 'We were on the go with the children all day long, right from breakfast time until half past eight or nine at night. After that, as soon as the children had gone back to their chalets to get ready for bed, we had to go up to the Princess Ballroom and "swan around" with the customers, as we used to call it, until closing time.'

When they were working, they used to have their breakfast before the campers and then they were on the go with the kids all morning. They got an hour off at lunchtime, and in the afternoons it was back on competitions and activities with the children. There was a short break for their evening meal and then they were back in the theatre with the children till about nine, and then they had to go to the ballroom. 'So they were very long days,' Sue says. 'But to be honest, they never really seemed like that; we would always bitch and moan, of course, that's human nature, but it was great.'

However, Sue didn't think it was reasonable of Butlin's to expect them to work all day and all night as well, and in her second season at Minehead she 'got a bit bolshie', recruited a few of the other redcoats to back her up and then said to their boss, 'I'm not going to the Princess Ballroom in the evening, because I don't think it's fair.' The other children's redcoats all agreed with her, and although there was a huge row about it, they did get their way in the end. They still went to the ballroom on a Friday night, though, because, Sue says, 'and I'm a bit ashamed to admit it now, we used to clock the campers who loved to have a redcoat sitting at their table, and we knew that if we went and sat with them, they'd buy our drinks all night. You couldn't do it at Butlin's now, because they are not allowed to drink in red any more, but we could and did, and on Friday nights we used to come out of there absolutely out of our trees.'

There was the Midnight Cabaret on the Thursday night as well, in which every redcoat and every lifeguard had to do their bit. They would greet all the campers as they came in, check their tickets and seat them at their tables, but once they'd done that, they could then just sit there and watch the acts all night. Butlin's used to book some top professional acts, and Sue saw Bob Monkhouse, Rod Hull, Bernie Clifton, Freddie and the Dreamers, Mike Reid and quite a few others while she was there.

When the redcoats weren't on duty elsewhere, they could go to all the shows and events – everywhere except the Beachcomber Bar, which was strictly for guests. They also had their own events as well; the staff had their own version of the Holiday Princess competition, for example.

On Friday nights they did a variety show for the children at eight o'clock, then at around half past ten or eleven, all the reds would gather and do the 'Redcoat Walk' – 'our little parade around the ballroom', Sue says. 'Then we'd all get up on stage and take over from the band and do the Redcoat Show – our weekly cabaret – for the adults. It would get totally raucous, but the campers used to love it, they really did.'

Not all the redcoats were able to be in the show on a Friday night, because some had to be on other duties, but so many of them were in it that the lifeguards would have to put on red jackets as well on those evenings, to make sure all the other venues had – or at least appeared to have – redcoats in them while the show was going on in the theatre.

Saturday was changeover day, when one lot of campers went home and the new ones arrived, and it was relatively easy for the children's redcoats, because they only had to do a welcome event for the kids in the theatre. Then on the Sunday morning all the redcoats used to line up on the stage and the campers would bring their children along to have their photos taken with the camp's 'uncles' and 'aunties'.

The tannoys were still used then, particularly for the 'baby call'. Parents who'd gone out for the evening, leaving their small children asleep, would leave their top window open so that if the child woke up, their cries would be heard by the chalet patrols. The parents would then be alerted by lights flashing above the large board in the ballroom, displaying a sign such as: 'Baby Crying in Red Row, Chalet Number A10' (later replaced by an electronic display), or an announcement over the loudspeakers.

The compère would also be given a note of the chalet number and would read it out before the next song or act, just to make sure the parents had got the message. Of course, the noise of one baby crying would often set the others in the neighbouring chalets going, too, so before long the board in the ballroom would often be displaying: 'Baby Crying in Red Row, Chalets A8, 9, 11 and 12'! Risky though it might seem now, Sue says that in those days, 'It was quite routine for the parents of small children to leave them unattended in their chalets while they went out for the evening.'

The tannoys were also used for general announcements, such as mealtimes: 'But it couldn't be any other way,' Sue says, 'because it was a major logistical exercise to get thousands of people through the dining room in the space of a couple of hours. So the tannoys were still used, but not excessively, like they were a few years before, when they never stopped from first thing in the morning until the kids' bedtime.'

Some of the tannoy announcements were coded. If there was a fire, the announcement was always: 'Attention staff: X-ray. X-ray.' The redcoats didn't tell people what was going on in case they panicked, so they just got them to leave the building they were in without telling them why. One evening, there was a bad fire in the Gaiety Theatre. Fortunately, it was empty of people at the time, but there were a lot of campers in the ballroom next to it, whom the redcoats had to move fast. 'We were trying to get them out quite calmly,' Sue says, 'but as we were starting to usher them out, one of the younger redcoats got a bit overexcited and started shouting, "There's a fire! There's a fire!" which wasn't the idea at all. So then there was a huge panic and hundreds of people were stampeding out of the place. It could have been a disaster, but luckily no one was hurt.'

When the redcoats were working, they were available 24/7 for any guest on the camp, but they were never really off duty, even when it was supposed to be their day off. 'You had to go off site to relax,' Sue says, 'otherwise, whether you were in or out of uniform, the campers would still be button-holing you and expecting you to entertain them.'

The comedian Dave Allen remembered the difficulties of avoiding the campers on his day off when he was a redcoat in the early stages of his career, 'You can't get away once they know you,' he said, 'unless you lock yourself in your chalet. If you put on a moustache and dark glasses, they'd think you were doing a stunt.'

There was quite a lot of friction between the redcoats and the other staff when Sue first started working there. The two groups didn't mix with each other and that increased the tension between them. 'One of the main issues, I suppose,' Sue says, 'was that the reds could go into the Princess Ballroom on a Friday night, sit with the campers and have our drinks bought for us by them, but the other staff weren't allowed to do that. They were only allowed in the staff bar, so that was bound to lead to resentment, and if the reds went into the staff bar – and I very rarely did, in the early part of the season – we were made to feel very, very uncomfortable.'

That soon began to change, however, partly because of a stunt Sue pulled at the Pontin's camp at Brean Sands. It was not far away from Butlin's and there was always a bit of rivalry between the two camps – 'nothing that serious', Sue says. 'But we definitely saw them as the opposition and they probably felt the same way about us.' One day, Sue and a couple of the other redcoats had gone to the Wookey Hole caves on their day off. On the way back, just around sunset, they were passing by Brean Sands and Sue said to the lads, 'Why don't we see if we can get in there?'

They weren't wearing their Butlin's uniforms, just normal clothes, but all the camps had fairly tight security to stop people using the facilities for nothing, so the others said to her, 'Don't be daft, we'll never get in there.'

She just grinned back at them. 'Well, let's try and see what happens. We'll just tell them that we're day visitors and we've lost our passes.'

In the event, it was easy to bluff their way past the security man on the gate, so they wandered around the camp for a bit and then went to the ballroom.

The Pontin's bluecoats were running a competition when they got inside and the boys kept saying to her, 'You've got to enter the competition.' Sue kept saying no, but in the end they wore her down and persuaded her to try.

Sue volunteered and went up on stage. The compère asked her name and then got one of the Pontin's bluecoats to take her into a back room so that she couldn't hear what the compère was saying to the audience. What he actually said to them was, 'The secret question that Sue is going to have to guess the answer to when she comes back on stage is: what would you say to your husband on your honeymoon night?'

When one of the bluecoats brought her back on stage, the compère shoved the microphone right into her mouth, banging it against her teeth, so, a bit irritated, the first thing Sue said was, 'Get that thing out of my mouth,' and of course the whole audience collapsed in hysterics. So they gave her the first prize in the competition: a voucher to spend in the gift shop. Unfortunately, the gift shop was closed when they left the ballroom and Sue thought she might be pushing her luck to come back the next day, but before they left, they peered through the windows of the shop and saw that the prizes were 'a whole lot better than the ones they handed out at Butlin's. There were really good-quality toiletry sets and soaps and perfumes,' Sue says. 'Things that actually looked nice instead of what we had, which looked like a job lot of cheap, fairground tat that someone had bought at knockdown prices.'

They strolled nonchalantly out of Brean Sands past the same security man on the front gates and went back to their own camp. The next morning it was all round the camp that Sue had entered the Pontin's competition at Brean Sands and actually won it.

When he heard the rumours, the manager called Sue in and said, 'I could sack you for this. This is like espionage between camps and we just don't do that.' That wasn't strictly true, since according to long-standing redcoat and entertainments manager Rocky Mason, Billy Butlin always made a point of sending some of his employees out at the start of the season to check what the competition – not just holiday camps, but hotels and other tourist venues – were charging, since he always liked to try and undercut them.

'It was only a bit of fun,' Sue said.

The manager thought for a moment and then gave her a shifty smile. 'So ... what were their prizes like, then?'

'They were better than ours, a lot better.'

A couple of days later, one of the other redcoats took a photo of Sue in her Butlin's red jacket and posted it to the chief bluecoat at Pontin's. The bluecoats were furious that they'd been conned, and from then on they were always trying to sneak onto the Butlin's camp and put one over on the redcoats in revenge, but they never succeeded.

Sue thinks that her prank really helped to break the ice between the redcoats and the other staff. 'It brought us all together,' she says. 'Butlin's had put one over on Pontin's and we could all enjoy that!'

The redcoats also started going into the

staff bar regularly and socialising with the others. It didn't get rid of the jealousy or resentment altogether, but the atmosphere was certainly a lot friendlier from then on. 'I also think the people who were becoming redcoats weren't quite so "up themselves" as some perhaps had been in the past,' she says. 'I don't think most of us saw it as a possible career – though some certainly did. For most of us, during the months the season lasted, we were just there to have a laugh and a good time. We were all in the same boat together and so the barriers started to erode.'

The redcoats tended to be friendly with the lifeguards in any case, because they all dressed up in reds and whites on Friday nights to help with the Redcoat Show, and in turn, the lifeguards were friends with the people who worked in the fast-food outlets, because they used to hang around them all day. So through the lifeguards, they'd get to be friends with the redcoats, too, and gradually it all became more integrated and less hostile.

There was never any crime on camp that Sue can remember and she never saw policemen there either. Butlin's own security men handled any trouble there might be, though it was rarely more serious than a couple having a domestic argument or someone who'd had too much to drink. 'Perhaps people were generally more honest then,' Sue says, 'but there also weren't the drug problems that there are today. As soon as the drugs began to appear, the crime rate started to climb as well.'

The head of security, a man called Phil, looked like an ex-military man; he was always well groomed, suited and booted. He seemed very old to the redcoats at the time, though given their relative youth, he might only have been in his late thirties or early forties. A strict disciplinarian, he used to absolutely hate Sue, she says, 'because I was always winding him up to fever pitch'.

The redcoats weren't supposed to have friends in their chalets, let alone parties, but there was always something going on in Sue's chalet, and Phil would invariably appear, call her outside and say, 'Miss!'

'My name is Sue,' she'd say, helpfully.

'Miss! If this happens again, I'll be reporting you to the manager.'

And Sue would say, 'Terribly sorry, I'll make sure it doesn't happen again.' Of course, by the next night they would all be back in there, chatting and laughing and drinking again. However, although they weren't scared of Phil, they knew they couldn't push him too far, and Sue says she wouldn't have had his job for anything, because it could get 'very raucous on the lines'.

If the redcoats' feelings about Phil were a mixture of resentment and respect, there was no such equivocation about the matron at the camp, who, according to Sue, was 'a hideous creature... Her whole purpose in life seemed to be to refuse to sign anybody off work, calling them "malingerers", no matter how sick they might be.'

Sue had an accident in her first couple of weeks at the camp. Her Aunt Kath was having a party and Sue went along with her friend Kim. They had a couple of glasses of Cinzano, no more than that, so they certainly weren't drunk, Sue says, but on the way back to their chalet, Kim tripped and stumbled. Sue tried to catch her but only succeeded in falling over herself. She didn't have time to put her hands out to break her fall and hit the ground face first. She knocked out her front teeth and bust her nose and had cuts and bruises all over her face. When she realised what had happened, she was scrabbling about on the ground, with blood pouring from her mouth and down her face, trying to find the teeth she'd lost.

Kim took her to the first-aid centre where the duty nurse stitched up the cuts on her face. She then told her to report back there in the morning to have her wounds looked at again. When Sue did so, the matron was on duty. Straight away, before Sue had a chance to even open her mouth, the matron started saying, 'You were drunk last night. That's why you fell over.'

When Sue denied being drunk, the matron called her a liar. 'She made no effort to examine me or treat me,' Sue says. 'She just kept on being vile to me and in the end I left the first-aid centre in tears.'

On her way back to her chalet, she met the camp manager and her Aunt Kath coming in the opposite direction. They asked her what was the matter and when Sue told them, the manager went to the first-aid centre and sacked the matron on the spot. Sue felt bad for her in one way – she'd lost her job – but, she says, 'She was as foul to the people who came to her for treatment as her successor in the job was lovely to them... And, of course, after that happened, all the other staff absolutely loved me!'

Sue wasn't allowed to wear her reds for a couple of weeks after that, because her face was so cut and bruised. 'I looked like Frankenstein's monster, and they were afraid I'd scare the customers and terrify the children!' The camp photographers were monsters in a different way; they kept following her around, trying to get photos of her hideously swollen face!

There was a monorail and a chairlift at the Minehead camp, both of which were very popular with the holidaymakers. Sue hated the chairlift because she was terrified of heights, but one day, after her face had healed enough for her to return to normal duties, she had to get to the other end of the camp in a bit of a hurry, so she swallowed her fear and got on the chairlift. Unfortunately, some of the other redcoats decided it would be funny to keep her up there for as long as possible, so when she had almost reached the other end, where there was a little 'shed on stilts' where you could get on and off, they threw the lever to stop the chairlift and then sent it back in the opposite direction. The same thing happened when she got to the other end. As she looked down, white with fear, all she could see was Keith Perron and some of the other redcoats, laughing like drains as they sent her back the way she'd come.

She was stuck on the chairlift for what seemed like about an hour and a half, while they kept shuttling her backwards and forwards but always stopping short of the point where she could get off. By now Sue was 'shaking with fright, absolutely hysterical, screaming and begging them to let me get off, and in the end they did, though probably more because they got bored with their game than from any sympathy for me. Or perhaps they thought I was ready to jump off it if they didn't let me down! Once I finally got on solid ground, I went absolutely potty about it and never went near the chairlift again, though in retrospect it did seem to help cure me a bit of my fear of heights, so perhaps it wasn't all bad after all.'

Three

Like every redcoat, Sue knew that relationships with the campers were outlawed, because it could lead to all sorts of jealousies and frictions – and complaints from parents – but that didn't stop them from happening. 'The redcoat lads had strings of conquests among the female campers. Some of the lads were terrible; they even carved notches in a post in the gents for every conquest they made, and on a Friday they used to award the "Ropey Trophy" to the redcoat who had got off with the worst-looking girl that week.'

Every Saturday morning girls from the Yorkshire wool mills, the Lancashire cotton mills, the West Midlands car factories, the London dockyards, or whichever industrial region was just finishing its annual holiday, would set off for home. The callous redcoats all lined up, waving and crying crocodile tears for the benefit of their departing girl-friends, and trying – though usually failing –

to look suitably broken-hearted. A couple of hours later they'd be back in place to assess the new arrivals – fresh meat – as they began checking in. By the following day, or even the same night, new affairs would have begun.

'The girl redcoats weren't really like that at all,' according to Sue. 'We tended to form a relationship with one person and stick to them for the season.' In her first year at Butlin's, 1979, she started going out with Paul Derrick, a lifeguard at the camp. He had a friend called Ian whom he'd been at university with and who was now working in IT. He came down to stay for a weekend in 1980 and got along so well with Sue that she was soon having a change of heart. 'Before you knew it, I'd stopped going out with Paul and started going out with Ian instead!' Despite that, Sue remained close friends with Paul – who later became a teacher – for many years.

She was fully intending to go back to Butlin's for the following season – she'd already signed her contract – but Ian had started working in a good IT job in London, and it was a choice between staying with him or going back to Butlin's. What made her decision a little easier was that many of the people Sue was really close to, like her best friend Tracy, weren't going back either, so in the end she stayed with Ian in London and never returned to work at Butlin's.

Her friend Tracy was, Sue says, 'the most wonderful person. She was one of the youngest redcoats ever, absolutely scatter-brained and a proper dippy blonde! She was a trained dancer – a wonderful dancer – who appeared in the Redcoat Shows and also did a couple of solo skits. She was the most beautiful person, too, inside and out.' Sue managed to badger her into entering the Miss Butlin's competition, even though Tracy kept saying, 'I'm not doing it, I'm not doing it.' Sue kept on begging her to do it and in the end Tracy gave in – she came second in the grand final of the whole competition.

Tracy had been going out with a redcoat called Gordon, but when she left Minehead at the end of the 1980 season she was offered a job as a dancer in Argentina and broke up with him. 'I think he really loved her,' Sue says, 'but Tracy wasn't ready to settle down then. She wanted to do different things and see more of the world, so off she went. She hadn't been in South America long when the Falklands War broke out – she always seemed to be in the wrong place at the wrong time!'

Sue had only known Tracy for those two years at Minehead, in 1979 and 1980, but in that time they became the closest of friends and remained that way for the rest of Tracy's life. Ian and Sue stayed together and moved around a lot. It was just like it had been when Sue was growing up and they were constantly moving whenever her father was given a new posting; the whole family seems to have inherited itchy feet as a result. Sue's brother emigrated to Australia in 1981 and is now living in Japan as the CEO of an oil company. Her sister Jane married an Australian and lived there for twelve years before coming home a few years ago, and Sue has had her share of overseas living as well. She and Ian lived in London together for two years, then moved to Sweden for another two years before returning to England. They got married in 1983 and bought a house in Harlow, where their son was born, but in 1988 Ian's job took them to Oklahoma, where their second child was born, and they stayed there until 1995.

Sue had never missed England while she was away, but when her dad became very ill, she began to feel extremely homesick. They promptly came back home to Bristol so that she could be nearer to him. She'd lost her mum back in 1986, but her dad lived for almost twenty years after that, dying in 2004, although he was in poor health for the last few years of his life.

Wherever Sue went in the world, she always tried to keep in touch with the people she met at Butlin's, because, she says, 'I made the best friends of my life when I was working there.' After leaving Butlin's, she lost touch with Anji for a little while before meeting her again at the wake for a Butlin's friend of theirs, Keith Perron, who died tragically young. 'Anji and I are very close friends again now,' she says. When Sue got to the wake, she found all sorts of other people there that she hadn't seen in years, and yet it felt like she'd only said goodbye to them the day before; they all hit it off again, right from the first moment.

However, the one friend she 'never, ever lost touch with', Sue says, was Tracy. 'When I got married in 1983, Tracy was my bridesmaid, and she was godmother to my children.' Tracy had gone through some changes along the way. She started off as Tracy Gosling, then changed her stage name to Tracy Lee, then changed it again to Tracy Carrington and finally got married and became Tracy Spencer. She phoned Sue up one day, breathless with excitement, 'I've met someone,' she said, as soon as Sue answered the phone. 'He's called Frank Spencer.'

Sue burst out laughing. 'Frank Spencer? You're having a laugh, aren't you? Does he say "Ooh, Betty" and wear a little black beret?'

'I'm not having a laugh,' Tracy said. 'I'm deadly serious.' And by the next time Sue saw her, she'd married him. Although they were comfortably off, Tracy was always trying new things and coming up with ideas for new businesses, but 'she didn't have the best business brain in the world, and was often too eager to get things started without thinking them through first', says Sue.

She phoned Sue once and said, 'I've had a great idea for a business making pickles. I've spent the last few days making them and putting them in jars.'

'Erm, you did sterilise the jars first, didn't you?'

'Oh no, but I've had lovely labels made.'

'Tracy,' Sue said, 'you can't sell them.'

'Of course I can. In fact, I already have. I took some to the market and sold them.'

'Well, you'd better go and get them back, because you might kill someone!'

Her next idea was making cushions, which wasn't any more successful. 'Although she bought reams of beautiful material, the cushions were dreadful, because she couldn't use a sewing machine to save her life!'

Tracy had only just turned forty when she became seriously ill. She had never smoked or drank alcohol, and she was a very fit, healthy, active person, and yet she was struck by cancer. It started off as just a cough, but it got steadily worse and Sue said to her on the phone quite a few times, 'Tracy, you've got to go and see the doctor about that cough.'

Tracy would always just say, 'Oh, it's nothing. Stop making a fuss.'

Eventually, though, Tracy said to Sue, 'I've been to the doctor and had some X-rays. There's nothing wrong with me.' But her cough kept getting worse, and when she went back to the doctor she was eventually diagnosed with cancer. It was a really rare form of the disease, which was probably why it took such a long time to diagnose – her specialists said they had only ever seen three other people with that form of cancer, though Sue did wonder whether, if she'd been diagnosed earlier, they might have been able to save her. A surgeon came over from the States especially to examine her and operate on her, but he couldn't save her either. He said that every case of the disease he had seen was linked in some way to the appendix, and while she'd been on holiday in Ireland with her mother a couple of years earlier, Tracy had got appendicitis and had her appendix out, so that may have been the trigger. Whatever the cause, it spread fast and proved incurable.

Sue was with her the day she died, on 16 August 2005. Tracy was in hospital in Basingstoke, very ill, and her husband, Frank, called Sue at home in Bristol that morning to say that there was nothing more that the doctors could do. They had stopped her medication and they were going to switch off the life-support machines later that day. Sue's husband was about to drive to London, but Sue said, 'You can forget that, I have to get to Basingstoke straight away,' and so she set off to say goodbye to her friend. She got there within about an hour and twenty minutes, at around half past eleven, and ran to the intensive-care unit where Tracy was being treated.

It was even more heartbreaking for Sue when she saw Tracy, because Frank hadn't told her how much she'd deteriorated. It was a real shock, she says. 'Tracy no longer even looked like herself any more; she was so swollen with the disease that she was almost unrecognisable. I was so upset at the sight of her that I had to leave the room for a little while until I could get myself under control, but I was there in the room with her, alongside Frank and her mum, Ros, when Tracy passed away at about ten past three that afternoon.

'I was in a terrible state afterwards. I'd only buried my father in March of that year and now I was losing my best friend, too. I knew I was going to lose it and I didn't want to make things worse for Frank and Ros, whose grief was already so intense, so in the end I had to say to them, "I have to go now," and then I just fell apart when I got outside.'

Sue says she didn't cope with the funeral very well either. Tracy's favourite colour was purple, so the coffin was draped with purple fabric and there were purple flowers everywhere. 'I absolutely lost the plot at the funeral. I was just sobbing and sobbing and sobbing, and I've never been like that in my life. Anji was there and was trying to console me, but in the end I just had to go out of the church, because I felt I was distracting people from what it was supposed to be about.'

She'd pulled herself back together a little by the time the service was over, and she went on to the wake that was being held for Tracy in a local pub. Despite the grief they all felt, there was a lot of music and laughter as they tried to celebrate her life. Friends of Tracy's had come from all over Britain and beyond – someone had flown in from America for the funeral – and from every stage of her life. A gospel choir and an Irish band both played, and Sue got up and sang one of Tracy's favourite songs with the band.

When it was all over and almost everyone else had gone home, Frank and Sue just sat together with a glass of wine, talking about Tracy. Frank wanted to give her Tracy's wedding ring as a memento of her, because they'd had no children and there were no daughters to pass it on to. 'I was very touched by that,' Sue says, 'and if I'd taken it, I would have worn it for the rest of my life, but I still said no, because I just had this feeling about it. "You must keep it, Frank," I said, "because you never know what may happen in the future, and it's funny how things can work out."

'Tracy never wanted children,' Sue says. 'She'd had a very bad time with her father as a child. He was in and out of her life and it was her mother who brought Tracy up, and I think she'd decided that she didn't want to run the risk of inflicting that kind of childhood on anybody else. So she and Frank never had children, but when Frank remarried, his second wife, Polly, gave birth to two lovely daughters, and one of them will have that wedding ring of Tracy's one day, on her own wedding day. Tracy's mum was over the moon about it and is very involved with them. It's given her a new focus in her life.'

It took Sue a very long time to get over Tracy's death. She still telephones Tracy's mum every year on the anniversary, and also keeps in regular touch with Frank. 'It was such a tragic waste of a life,' she says, 'when she was so young, and she was one of the most lovely people, in every way, that I've ever met. We were best friends from 1979 until she died in 2004, and we never had an argument or a cross word in all that time. She was the only person in my life who genuinely never had a harsh word to say about anyone – I never heard her say anything bad about anyone or anything. All the redcoats' funerals are sad, because we remember them when they were so vibrant and so young, but none of the people we've lost has been more tragic than the loss of Tracy. She was the baby of the group and it just didn't seem right that she should be one of the first to go.'

Sue is now the landlady of a pub in Whitchurch, near Bristol, so she's still entertaining the public, just as she did as a redcoat over thirty years ago. Like many of her peers, she thinks that Butlin's is not the same now – not necessarily better or worse, just different from how it was in her era. She thinks that she caught 'the last wave of the old Butlin's before it all started to change. Obviously, the layout of the camps has changed a lot and the customers have changed, too, so it's a very different atmosphere from when we were there, but the times are very different, too. There was an innocence about that era and a feeling of all being in it together, and though in material terms we're much better off today, I think we've lost a lot of that spirit along the way.'

The tragically early deaths of Keith Perron and Tracy had brought the redcoats of Sue's era back together for the funerals, and, shocked at how many years had passed almost unnoticed, they resolved to keep up their friendships in the future, so Sue's still very close to her Butlin's 'family'. 'I've been back to Minehead a few times for reunions,' she says. 'I made many great friends there, and though the years have gone by and they've all grown older, they haven't changed inside – none of them – and when we get together, we're straight back into redcoat mode.

'There will be a pause during the weekend when we'll drink a toast to absent friends. Another of the Butlin's girls, Valda, keeps a roll of honour of redcoats that goes right back to the earliest Butlin's eras, and each of us will name someone we worked with who is no longer with us and is much missed, and, of course, I always say Tracy's name then. However, that's the one sombre moment in the weekend, and the rest of the time we just laugh and reminisce together, and we even put on a Redcoat Show, just like we used to all those years ago. Laughter gets you through it, and we were all of a very similar ilk. We were all very extrovert and used to have so much fun, and the friendships we formed have really stood the test of time.

'It's very special, because we're like a family. We didn't all grow up together, and I'm not saying we all got on like a house on fire, because we didn't – there were frictions sometimes, just like there are in any family.

But we all came together at a certain time, in a certain place, and the ones who we became close to, and who became important in our lives, formed a bond with us that is so strong I don't think it'll ever be broken.'

Terri

One

Terri Tasker first went to Butlin's on holiday in the very early 1960s and started working as a redcoat in 1963. An only child, she was born in 1945 and grew up in Northampton. Her dad was a banker, a six-foot-two, ramrod-straight former guardsman, which made him and Terri's mum look like a bit of an odd couple, because she was, says Terri, 'about four foot nothing, but if they looked mismatched that was far from the case; they were a really happy, loving couple'.

Terri admits that she wasn't the keenest of students and left school at fifteen with absolutely no qualifications at all. She landed her first job, working in a local estate agent, by sheer fluke.

She had been a really keen swimmer ever since she was a kid, and can still remember the day she learned to swim. There were two instructors at her school, one very short and fat, and the other very tall and thin – they looked like Laurel and Hardy – and on the basis of no real evidence other than their imaginations, the kids had all decided that the short and fat one was as jolly as he looked, while the thin one was nasty and horrible. So when they were on their way to the pool, they'd be peering through the windows, saying, 'Is it the fat one or the thin one!' It turned out to be the thin one who taught Terri to swim.

In those days, when you were learning to swim, they had a sort of canvas belt with a rope attached to it that they put around your middle, so they could haul you out of the water if you got into difficulty. The day she learned to swim she was about ten or eleven years old and she remembers thinking to herself, I'll either sink or swim, and if I sink he'll pull me out. So she jumped in. She didn't sink; she splashed her way across the pool and, hey presto, she could swim!

The thin man, who was called Jim Hardwick, had seen something in her that he could develop and he went to see her parents and offered to coach her in swimming. She did think at the time, oh no, not him, I don't want to work with him, but actually, she says, he was 'lovely, an absolute darling, and he coached me right up to county level. I never got beyond that level, but I've loved swimming all my life and funnily enough, in later years, I even became a swimming teacher myself.'

She kept up her swimming all the way through school and was always at the local pool at lunchtimes and in the evenings. There was, she says 'a lovely old chap called

Mr Ashby, a very small man who used to swim there as well for fitness'.

One day she got talking to him and told him that she was just about to leave school. 'I don't think I had much clue about what I was going to do,' Terri says, 'apart from wanting to be an air hostess – the sort of airy-fairy thing that one wanted to do in those days!' She certainly had the looks – she had grown into a poised, cool, classic beauty who turned heads wherever she went – but back then you couldn't become an air hostess until you were twenty-one years old. 'Well,' Mr Ashby said, 'I'm looking for a junior in my estate agency, if that might interest you.' So she went home that night and said to her parents, 'Guess what – I've got a job!'

Terri knew lots of people who'd been to Butlin's, but her parents would never take her there. By the time she was seventeen, in 1962, she was absolutely desperate to go because all her friends were going on their own that year, but even though she had left school and begun full-time work, her dad, who was 'more than a bit strict', wouldn't let her go. She was devastated, but she kept pestering her parents and in the end her mum said, 'Oh, all right, you can go to Butlin's, because I'll take you there.'

'My dad didn't want to come with us,' Terri says, 'probably because he thought

Butlin's was a bit beneath a banker's dignity. There was certainly a bit of snobbery about it in those days – "nice girls" didn't go to Butlin's.'

So she went on holiday with her mother, and although it wasn't quite the same experience it would have been with her friends, they both had a wonderful time. She was still a competitive swimmer back then, so she entered all the swimming competitions at the camp and won them all. She won second and third prize in the Miss *She* and Holiday Princess competitions as well – the other parents and their kids must have been sick of the sight of her getting all the trophies!

The redcoats must have been just as fed up with her. 'When I became a redcoat myself,' Terri laughs, 'I came to appreciate how irritating it was when one kid was monopolising the prizes.'

Her mum was a very friendly, outgoing type who would strike up a conversation with anyone, so in the evenings Terri often left her chatting to people she'd met and went to dance in the Rock 'n' Roll Ballroom. A group called Rory Storm and the Hurricanes were the resident band. The drummer had a teddy-boy quiff, a prominent nose and a beard, and Terri barely gave him a second glance. Had she known what was going to happen, she would probably have paid rather more attention to him, because round about the time that Terri and her mum were going home at the end of their holiday, Rory Storm's drummer, Richard Starkey, who had just changed his name to the rather more rock 'n' roll-sounding Ringo Starr, was also saying goodbye to Butlin's.

That August, two other leather-jacketed Liverpudlian lads, John Lennon and Paul McCartney, bought day passes to the Skegness camp and met Ringo. Butlin's had proved to be a happy hunting ground for Paul in the past, because he'd made his stage debut singing 'Long Tall Sally' in a squeaky treble voice at a Butlin's Junior Star Trail talent contest.

A couple of days after they'd met Ringo, John phoned him at the camp and invited him to join their band. When he came off the phone, Ringo said he'd been told that his facial hair didn't suit the Beatles' image and he'd have to get rid of it. He went straight to his chalet and shaved it off, and his next stop was the hairdresser's at the camp, where he had his quiff restyled into a Beatles moptop. Four days later, on 18 August 1962, he sat down behind a Beatles drum kit for the first time, and their first Top Twenty hit record, 'Love Me Do', was released on 5 October. Strangely enough, Ringo never played drums at Butlin's again.

Oblivious to all this, Terri and her mum carried on with their holiday. They'd had such a good time that when they went home, Terri's mum set to work on her dad and persuaded him that Butlin's wasn't beneath his dignity after all. The three of them then went back to Skegness for another week's holiday at the end of August, when Terri added a few more prizes to her haul and irritated the redcoats still more!

Terri had got to know some of the redcoats in her first week at the camp. She met up with them again when she went back and when she told them she'd decided that she wanted to be a redcoat herself, they set up an interview with Frank Mansell, the entertainments manager.

Terri had a bit of a chat with him and two of her redcoat friends helped her to fill in an application form. She couldn't really sing, but could just about carry a tune, and she could do a bit of ballet and tap dancing, but she didn't really have any other talents apart from swimming. Nonetheless, her friends were busily ticking every box, saying, 'Yes, you can do that, and you can do that,' until they'd said that she could do absolutely everything.

Frank Mansell then offered her a job as a redcoat, to start the following season, after her eighteenth birthday – Butlin's didn't employ anyone under that age. However, the form listing her multitude of alleged talents, came back to haunt her when she was working there, because Frank had a standard saying whenever a redcoat tried to get out of doing something: 'You said you could do it when you wrote your application form. Now get on with it!'

Two

As soon as Terri turned eighteen the following year, 1963, she handed in her notice to Mr Ashby. 'Lovely though he was,' she says, 'I couldn't see myself working in an estate agent's for the rest of my life; showing potential house buyers the particulars of a semi-detached house in Northampton didn't have quite the same glamour for me as posing in a redcoat's uniform at a seaside holiday camp!'

She worked out her notice and then started work as a general duties redcoat at Butlin's in Filey, on the windswept Yorkshire coast. She was really excited and even her dad did his best to look pleased on her behalf, but he wasn't the only person in Northampton to have traces of snobbery about Butlin's. Some of the comments Terri heard were really cruel and hurtful – none more so than the barbed remarks from one of her mother's supposed friends. According to her, 'Only slappers went to Butlin's,' and Terri was 'bound to come back pregnant'. She was quite right about the second of those, although her timing was a little off. Terri started at Butlin's in 1963 and she did get pregnant, though not until 1971, by which time she'd already been married for five years!

Terri's mum and dad drove her up to Filey and she was given a chalet sharing with another girl. 'The chalets were awful,' Terri says. 'They were bearable if you were only there for a week on holiday, but living there for months on end was an ordeal. They were so tiny that you couldn't even swing a cat in them, really primitively furnished with iron bunk beds, flimsy furniture and a wardrobe that was just a tiny curtained alcove in which two people were supposed to be able to store enough clothes to last the entire season.'

Like the other Butlin's camps at the time, there were no facilities in the Filey chalets other than a washbasin. If the weather was cold and wet – and on that exposed North Sea coast it wasn't exactly unknown – the chalet was absolutely freezing.

The toilet and bathroom blocks were even less welcoming than the chalets. There were no bathrooms as such; they were just partitioned off from the main room. They were cold, draughty and crawling with spiders, and you always had to clean the bath before you got into it. Shivering in their chalet, while the east wind whistled through the chinks in the flimsy walls and the rain rattled against the window panes, their only consolation was that, except on their day off, they worked such long hours that they only went back to the chalet to sleep. 'We worked really hard in those days,' Terri says, 'and just about all the hours there were. There were no union rules at all, we just did what we had to do.'

Billy Butlin made regular tours of inspection of his camps, and whenever he arrived at Filey, Terri and the other redcoats would try to keep well out of the way as he strode around the camp trailing a retinue of anxious managers behind him. 'He was certainly feared,' Terri says. 'Whether it was true or an urban myth that had grown over time, we'd all been told – and we certainly believed – that in the old days he would sack people on the spot if they weren't carrying out their work the way he expected. And people were still sacked like that even when I was there. It could never happen now, of course – there would have to be verbal and written warnings and all sorts of procedures – but back then it would simply be "You're fired", and the person would be escorted to their chalet to pick up their possessions and then marched straight off the camp, whatever time of day or night it might be.'

The girl redcoats tended to modify their uniforms to look as fashionable as they could within the constraints of a pleated white skirt and a red jacket, and they would often roll up the waistband of their skirts to raise the hems a little nearer to the fashionable 1960s length, but they had to be especially careful when Billy was around, because he was really hot on enforcing the strict rules about uniforms.

The girls were allowed to wear white shorts instead of pleated skirts when they were doing sports and other events during the day, though after six o'clock in the evening they had to be 'properly dressed' in their skirts. The only drawback with the shorts was that their red jackets were very long, so if they wore cropped shorts with them, it looked as if they were wearing nothing but the jackets. So the Butlin's rule was that the girls' shorts had to be long enough to show three inches below the jacket. However, the girls thought these looked terrible, so they kept on wearing their short shorts, and whenever Billy or one of the managers from head office was around, Terri says, the girls had to keep wandering around adjusting their hair, keeping their arms raised so the jackets rode up and you could see the regulation three inches of shorts.

Terri fell foul of another of the Butlin's

rules during her first season. She had 'a bit of a thing' about the lead singer with the band in the Rock 'n' Roll Ballroom and thought, it's midnight, what the hell, I'm going to sit down and chat to them. The next minute, Frank Mansell walked in, looked at her and said, 'I'll see you in my office in the morning, Terri,' and then walked out again.

She didn't sleep a wink that night, convinced that she'd be sacked and marched out of the gates in the morning. When she got to his office, he said, 'Come in and sit down. Now, you know what you did wrong, don't you?'

Terri nodded, choking back the tears. 'I'm so sorry, I'll never do it again.'

'Right,' he said. 'I think you've been punished enough. Off you go.' And to her great surprise and relief, that was the end of it.

Terri had begun working at Butlin's just as the 'Hi-de-hi' era lampooned in the TV show was waning. 'There were still traces of it there,' she says. 'They still did keep-fit classes on the playing fields with rows of campers in their vests and skirts or trousers – not many of them had shorts back then – and they still divided the campers into different "houses" to compete in the team competitions.

'It wouldn't work now, I'm sure,' Terri says, 'but back then people really bought into it and got behind it. However, it was pretty regimented and people were beginning to get to the point where they didn't want to do that sort of thing on holiday any more.'

When the BBC started screening *Hi-de-Hi!* in 1980 (the writers, Jimmy Perry and David Croft, had both been Butlin's red-coats themselves in the past), the Butlin's camps had already changed a lot and much of the old regimentation had gone. Still, when Terri sat down to watch it, she kept seeing little things and incidents and thinking, God, that used to happen to us!

In one episode, a senior hostess came down to visit Ruth Madoc's character, Gladys Pugh, and caused chaos at 'Maplin's', and exactly the same thing happened in Terri's time at Filey when their senior hostess paid them a visit. 'The couple who did the ball-room dancing in *Hi-de-Hi!* were also classic, absolutely typical; every Butlin's camp I went to, the ballroom dancing instructors were exactly like that! I wouldn't have been surprised if the ones I met in my first year at Butlin's hadn't had wallpaper on their chalet walls, too!'

Terri says she always identified with Gladys Pugh, because she was like her for a while, too, if only in being attracted to her boss! The company always found their permanent staff winter work, whereas only a few of the red-coats were kept on out of season, so at the end of her first year at Butlin's, Terri went back to Northampton and took a job working for Avon cosmetics to see her through the winter. She spent the next two seasons at Filey, where she became assistant hostess, and in 1965 she was promoted again and went to the Butlin's hotel in Margate as chief hostess.

The following season, she was sent to Skegness as chief hostess. The first person she met there was the assistant entertainments manager, Dave, who was to be her new boss. He was working at Minehead the previous Christmas and Terri was supposed to be going there as well, but in the end, she says, 'I chickened out and decided I didn't want to go, and had Christmas at home with my parents instead. So I didn't meet Dave until I got to Skegness at the start of May. He had joined Butlin's at the same time as me, but he was at Pwllheli when I was at Filey.'

Terri went into his office to report to him. She introduced herself and asked what chalet she was in. Dave immediately took her suitcase and carried it down to the chalet for her, which she thought was 'a bit strange, because usually the entertainments managers just said something like, "Your chalet's number Y47, down there on the right," and left you to carry your own bags.' They were chatting away as they walked down there. Dave came from Dublin and 'was very slim, dark and handsome', she says, 'with a very gentle, soft Irish voice. We just looked at each other and clicked, and we started going out together in true *Hi-de-Hi!* style!'

They had to be a little discreet about their relationship, not because they needed to keep it hidden from the other employees, but because of the Butlin's rules about staff not spending time together when on duty. 'We were supposed to be there for the campers, not each other,' Terri says. 'Butlin's didn't even want you sitting together, let alone being all over each other, but when you were off duty it was another matter. Butlin's really didn't mind staff forming relationships, and in fact most of the managers, not just in entertainment but in all areas of the company, were married to former or current Butlin's staff.'

Even though they worked such long hours, the redcoats and the other entertainments staff would often be still buzzing long after the campers had gone back to their chalets for the night. So there was quite a lively after-hours social life, usually involving a party in one of their chalets, with as many people as they could squeeze in. A bunch of them were having a few drinks in Terri's chalet one night when there was a pounding on the door. When she opened it, the night security man gave her a real rollicking for disturbing the campers and said, 'I'm reporting you to the general manager in the morning.' Terri had a struggle to keep a straight face, because all the time the security man was lecturing her, the general manager was sitting behind the door with a drink in his hand!

Midway through the season, Terri was sent up to the Butlin's hotel in Blackpool after someone on the entertainments staff there made a serious mess of the book-keeping. Knowing that Terri had book-keeping skills from her time at the estate agency, Butlin's sent her to sort out the mess.

'I wasn't too thrilled about that,' Terri says, 'because I'd only just met Dave and was madly in love and now I was being shipped off to Blackpool. The entertainments manager there was a singer called Russ Hamilton, who'd had a hit with "We Will Make Love" back in 1957 – and didn't he love reminding everyone of that! He'd worked at Butlin's before his big break and came back to work there when his career fizzled out, but he absolutely lived on his former glories and he really did fancy himself something terrible!'

So Terri hated being there, but although it was quite a long job, it proved fairly straightforward, and she and Dave were then reunited. In case Butlin's wanted to ship her off again to Blackpool or somewhere else, they got engaged soon afterwards, with Dave proposing while they were lying in bed on their day off. They didn't have a lot of money – the ring only cost £20 – but they didn't care. When they told Dave's boss the news, he just said, 'It'll never last.' He could not have been more wrong; Terri and Dave had over thirty happy years together.

Three

When the 1966 season ended, Dave was sent to work at the Butlin's hotel near Brighton – the Ocean Hotel at Saltdean – for the winter, and Terri did freelance sales promotion work with several companies, including John Player & Sons, Polaroid and Danish Bacon.

They got married on 11 March 1967, at St Giles Church in Northampton. Like a lot of couples then, they chose a March wedding because they got a full tax rebate if they married just before the end of the financial year. Some of their Butlin's friends came, though it was difficult to get everybody there because as usual, as soon as the previous season had ended, everyone had scattered to the four winds for the winter and wouldn't normally reappear until the next season began in May.

Dave and Terri worked together at Clacton for the next couple of years, where Dave was entertainments manager. The comedian Jimmy Cricket, or Jimmy Mulgrew as he was then, was a redcoat there at the time. He was 'a little Irish lad', Terri says, 'and it was the first year he'd ever spent away from home. He used to send all his wages home to his "Mammy" in Ireland every week, so he never had any money at all. He had his redcoat uniform given to him, so he was all right for that, but redcoats had to provide their own socks and shoes and he didn't have any white socks. Dave was passing him one day and he suddenly did a double take and walked back to him. "Jimmy," he said, "what on earth have you been doing to your feet?" It turned out that Jimmy had tried to solve the sock problem by using some white emulsion paint from the maintenance department to paint his feet and ankles white! So they bought him some socks and the white emulsion went back to the maintenance department.'

Among Terri's duties as chief hostess was a rather strange task: handing out budgerigars as prizes to campers' children. Billy Butlin was a keen budgerigar fancier and at one time there was an aviary in the reception of every Butlin's camp. In the mid 1960s, he came up with the bright idea of giving budgerigars away as prizes. So one of Terri's jobs was to catch one of the budgerigars, put it in a metal cage and present it at the prize-giving at the end of the week.

'Billy Butlin was a great man,' Terri says, 'but that wasn't one of his better ideas. A lot of campers came on the train and probably had more than enough to carry already with their luggage, holiday paraphernalia and souvenirs, without a budgie in a big metal cage as well. If they'd come by car, then the cage had to be squeezed into that, so most people would probably have preferred something smaller, or cold, hard cash instead. There were also regular escapes by the budgies – I lost a few myself while I was struggling to catch them. There are probably whole colonies of them living around the sites of Butlin's camps to this day!'

One of the perks – or, very occasionally, the drawbacks – of Dave's job as entertainments manager and Terri's work as chief hostess was that they often had to hold open house at their home for some of the cabaret acts and stars who came to perform at the camp. Bob Monkhouse appeared at Butlin's a lot, and in common with several of the other Butlin's girls, Terri thought of him as 'a good friend and a lovely man. Jon Pertwee – Doctor Who at the time – and his little boy also came for lunch one day when we were in Clacton, causing wild excitement in the street. They stayed in Clacton overnight and I remember the little boy asking for "strangled egg" for his breakfast!' Dave also brought the guitarist Bert Weedon and his wife home for lunch with him one day. The fact that it was Christmas Day did not get in the way of his duty to keep 'the talent' happy, even though it meant sharing their turkey and Christmas pudding.

Even the stars sometimes found themselves performing other duties aside from their acts. Years later, Matt Goss of Bros fame was appearing at Butlin's Minehead when one of the redcoats, Paul, asked him if he'd propose to Paul's redcoat girlfriend, Ami, for him. She was a huge Bros fan, a 'Brosette' in fact, and was very excited about seeing her hero. Matt was happy to do it, so Paul let Ami's boss in on the secret and he told her to look after the press to keep her busy until the crucial moment. Matt was in the Green Room, signing some T-shirts and CDs for giveaways, while Ami was on the other side of the room, but every time she looked up, Matt Goss was looking at her. Finally, he picked up one of the T-shirts, walked over to Ami, looked deep into her eyes and said, 'Can I sign this one to you?'

Convinced that she'd 'pulled' Matt Goss, Ami managed to stammer out a yes and he then wrote on it: 'To Ami, Will you marry

Paul? Love Matt Goss.' Paul, who had been hiding in a rather unromantic location – the gents toilet – then emerged with a bunch of flowers and a ring, and Ami, masking any disappointment she might have felt that it wasn't Matt Goss who wanted to marry her, immediately said yes. Just to round off the day, when he was performing that evening, Matt Goss called Ami up on stage and sang to her on bended knee. She and Paul are now happily married and have two small children.

Terri became pregnant while she and Dave were living in Clacton. They moved on to Minehead soon after that, and as Terri was still pregnant, she began working as a wardrobe mistress with the revue company there – her bump was too big for her to fit into her chief hostess's uniform by then. The company was run by Chesney Allen, of the old Flanagan and Allen music-hall act, and Terri's weekly cheque was signed by him. 'I always wanted to keep one of the cheques and frame it,' she says, 'because it had his signature on it and I thought that was quite wonderful, but I could never afford to, because we were just too broke!'

At the end of the season, Dave stayed on in Minehead, while Terri went to stay with her parents in Northampton for the last few weeks of her pregnancy. She was due to give birth on New Year's Eve, but in the event, perhaps wanting to see his first Christmas, their son Roger was born early, on the afternoon of Christmas Day, 1970. Like his mother, he's an only child.

Employees didn't get the compassionate leave then that is routine today, and in any case, Dave had to work on Christmas Day; as entertainments manager, he couldn't take time off for the birth at Christmas, when the camp reopened for the holiday and was always packed, so he didn't get to see his son until Boxing Day. He celebrated the birth on Christmas night, then got up early and, nursing a hangover, drove all the way to Northampton to meet his son for the first time.

With their new baby, Dave and Terri moved to Filey for the next few seasons. Terri didn't work at all in the first year, but by the second, even though Roger was still only tiny, she began teaching swimming for a couple of hours in the evening while a neighbour looked after the baby. No money ever changed hands; the neighbour looked after Roger in the evening and in return Terri looked after the other woman's child during the day.

Dave was a full-time Butlin's employee and so always had winter work, and after they were married, Terri often found winter employment somewhere within the Butlin's organisation. She had spells at almost all of the camps over the years; Barry Island and Ayr were the only ones where she didn't work at one time or another. She also worked in virtually every department. She had a spell in bookings at Skegness, worked in the accommodation department at Pwllheli and also taught swimming there.

She worked as Dave's secretary one year, using her background in office work from the estate agency days, and she went back to Blackpool one winter as well, to work at the annual Dancing Festival, the grand final of the dancing competitions held at all the camps. Butlin's sponsored the final and before the dance-offs began, Terri and another Butlin's girl, Mavis, were given the plum job of leading all the dancers – formed into two columns – around the Tower Ballroom. It was a very glitzy occasion, with all the men and women immaculately groomed and dressed, and Frank and Peggy Spencer's famous formation dancing team all lined up in matching outfits. Mavis and Terri had to dress in 'red jackets, tiny satin hot pants and shiny white boots – very 1960s! – and parade around at the head of the column of dancers. I'm pretty sure I wouldn't get away with wearing that outfit now,' she says, 'but I think we managed to carry it off at the time!'

While Billy Butlin's son Bobby presented

the prizes at the end of the competition, Terri and Mavis had to stand around looking suitably decorative. 'We didn't have to do anything else,' Terri says, 'so I suppose we were just there as a bit of eye candy! I never worked with Mavis other than on that occasion, but I thought she was a lovely, gentle lady, and of course I'm back in touch with her now through the Butlin's websites and the reunions.'

While she was working at the Butlin's hotel in Margate, they put on the Miss *She* fashion competition. If they didn't have enough judges, they would just grab people out of the audience who had no friends or family members in the competition. Terri saw a smart-looking lady sitting in the audience with her friend and said to her, 'Would you like to be a judge?'

'Yes, I'd like that very much,' she said. 'As a matter of fact, I run a fashion house myself.'

Terri used to 'dink about' on the catwalk herself, just to show the competitors what to do, so she 'walked down the catwalk, did a turn this way and that, dinked back, struck a pose and that was it'. When the judging was finished, the woman said to her, 'Have you ever done any modelling?'

'No, never.'

'Well, would you like to?'

It turned out that she ran a fashion house,

Horrockses, just off Regent Street in London. They were a bit of an old-fashioned house, but they had a high-end clientele and a royal warrant; if the Queen and Princess Margaret wanted off-the-peg sundresses – and they often did, particularly when making royal tours to sunnier climes – Horrockses was what they bought.

So Terri and another redcoat, Judy, packed their bags and went off to London together. Judy had a different job, but as Terri was to model for Horrockses, her employer let both girls live in a flat that was part of her own house. They didn't stay there very long, however, because her husband was 'a bit batty!' according to Terri. 'So we moved out and found ourselves a grotty little bedsit in Earls Court.'

Terri's job was mainly just to sit in the showroom waiting for customers to arrive and then put on the dresses they chose and 'glide around the showroom' so the customer could see what they looked like. She worked at Horrockses for most of the winter, but didn't enjoy modelling the clothes that much, mainly because they were so old-fashioned; Horrockses was becoming so out of touch with modern tastes and trends that the company eventually closed down altogether.

The real highlight for Terri came when her employer lent her to Mary Quant, who needed an extra model for a day's work. Instead of being paid in money, Terri was given one of Quant's little 'Dolly Rocker' dresses. She was so proud of it that she wore it for years. Going back to Horrockses after that only made their clothes seem even more old-fashioned, and in the end Terri left. She could have timed her departure better, though, because as she was leaving, her employer let drop that she was getting the collection ready to take to St James's Palace to show to Princess Margaret!

When Dave was moved from Filey to the Butlin's camp at Pwllheli, Terri worked for the winter in the accommodation department. Her dad had retired early from the bank because of ill health – he had angina – so her mum and dad came and lived with them in Pwllheli for the 1974 season. Dave and Terri had a really nice, big bungalow there, with plenty of room for them all. It was right on the camp, which Terri was quite pleased about, because at that time a Welsh nationalist group calling themselves *Meibion Glyndwr* (Sons of Glyndwr) were burning down a lot of English-owned or occupied houses in rural parts of Wales. British Coal were running an ad – 'Come home to a real fire' – at the time, and Terri can remember it being spoofed on *Not the Nine O'Clock News* with an ad saying,

'Come home to a real fire – buy a cottage in Wales' ... which was very funny, if you didn't happen to be living in Wales at the time.

Her dad's heart was, Terri says, 'like a ticking time bomb' that he – and they – knew would claim him one day. However, he didn't want to just sit around waiting passively for the end, so Dave found him a gentle part-time job, working in Sports Issue. There were a couple of wooden huts inside the sports hall where the campers would go to get their games equipment: golf putters, tennis rackets, bowls, table-tennis bats and snooker cues. Terri's dad did the rotas for the other people working there and took his turn at issuing the equipment as well. 'He had always been very good with his hands,' Terri says. 'He could make absolutely anything, so he also took charge of repairing the damaged and broken things, and there were a lot of those, because they took a real hammering. So Dad would mend the broken table-tennis bats and snooker cues, and so on, and it was a nice gentle little job for him.'

One day he came back to the bungalow for his lunch, as usual. Dave was at work, but Terri, her mum and Roger were all there. 'Dad sat down on the sofa,' Terri says, 'complaining about a bit of a pain in his chest, and the next moment he had a massive heart attack. He didn't cry out or show any signs of pain at all. It was as if someone had just thrown a switch and he stopped breathing and toppled over.'

Terri had had to learn first aid to work as a swimming teacher, so while her frantic mum rang the nurse at the camp and dialled 999, Terri began mouth-to-mouth resuscitation, but she could not revive her dad and he had passed away before the medics arrived. All their Butlin's workmates and friends held a collection to buy flowers for the funeral. Her dad was cremated in Bangor, but he'd said that when he died, he wanted his ashes to be in Northampton where he'd grown up and lived almost all of his life. So after the cremation, her dad's brother and sister drove back to Northampton with the urn holding his ashes and honoured his last wish.

Her mum was 'a very strong lady', Terri says, and after her father's death she carried on working for the general manager at the Pwllheli camp, dealing with complaints. 'When anyone came in jumping up and down and demanding to see the manager, she was very good at fending them off. I suppose she was such a tiny little lady that it made everyone calm down a bit when they saw her, whereas if it had been some big bloke, fights might have broken out sometimes.'

Her mum also helped her look after Roger when he was little. As he grew up, he didn't take much looking after any more, and would disappear onto the camp for the day and Terri would not even know where he was! She never worried about him, because all the staff knew him and Butlin's was such a safe environment for children. There can't have been too many better places to grow up from a child's point of view: a giant playground with almost every facility you could ever imagine within easy reach.

While they were in Pwllheli in 1976, R Company of the Royal Marines, came to the camp to do promotional displays. 'It was a great jolly for them, and they were like a breath of fresh air for us as well,' Terri says. 'There was an air of excitement all round. They were all young and fit, and most of them were handsome lads as well, so all the girl redcoats suddenly started taking extra care with their hair and make-up!'

The Marines set themselves up on the camp and flew their regimental colours from a pole fixed to the top of the kids' climbing wall. 'Of course, the colours are sacrosanct for any regiment,' Terri says, 'and were guarded night and day by a couple of Marines, but we had a big Kiwi lifeguard called Kevin working there that year, and for no apparent reason, he and a few of the other boys decided it would be a good idea to pinch the colours.' Dave and some of the other male redcoats had formed what they, in those unreconstructed sexist days, called 'The Willett Watchers Club'- Willetts being code for boobs. When they were wandering round the camp and saw a scantily clad young woman approaching, one of them could say, 'Willetts at nine o'clock,' without (if they were lucky) offending anyone. 'Heaven knows why, but I'd made them a shocking-pink silk flag with "Willett Watchers Club" on it,' Terri says, 'and they all decided it would be great fun to replace the Marines' colours with it.'

The plan they formed was that on the night of the Midnight Cabaret, Terri would keep the Marines' lieutenant entertained, while Kevin the lifeguard sabotaged the two men guarding the colours by plying them with drink. Obviously, they weren't supposed to drink while on guard duty, but Kevin was very persuasive and they drank so much that they eventually fell asleep. Kevin and a few others then scaled the climbing wall, pinched the colours and flew the Willett Watchers flag in its place. 'The next morning all hell broke loose,' Terri says. 'The Marines didn't see the funny side of it at all – understandably, because it wouldn't have looked too good if their senior officers were to discover that the Marines' finest fighting men had been outwitted by a bunch of Butlin's redcoats. So they were stomping around the camp threatening all sorts of dire reprisals if the colours were not restored to them pretty damn quick, and eventually the boys gave them back ... though not before posing with them on the seasonal group photograph! The atmosphere was a bit strained for a while, but then there were rueful smiles and then belly laughs and everyone was the best of friends again.'

Four

Dave ended his Butlin's career in the head office at Bognor, and Terri ended her own long career by working in administration there as well. Her mum moved there with them. She lived for many years after Terri's dad had gone, and any fine day in summer would find her pottering about on the Esplanade or the gardens on the Steyne, or sitting in the sunshine chatting to people strolling by. She eventually died peacefully in Bognor.

When Roger was old enough, he kept up the family tradition by working for Butlin's himself, doing a few odd jobs at the Bognor camp. First, he worked as a barrow boy on Saturdays, moving the departing campers' luggage in the mornings and the new arrivals' cases in the afternoons. Later, he worked in the fairground and in the camp's catering department for a while. However, he'd probably seen quite enough of Butlin's while he was growing up, so instead of becoming a redcoat, he eventually opted for a different kind of uniform and joined the Royal Navy.

Terri worked for Butlin's for twenty years, but in the mid 1980s she had a complete change of pace and went to work as PA to the director of the Onyx motor racing team in Formula 3000. 'We were the Red Bull of that era,' she says, smiling. 'Absolutely unbeatable!'

By then Butlin's had fallen out of fashion. The camps were losing money and were closing one by one, and staff were being laid off left, right and centre. Eventually, in one of the management's frequent cost-cutting purges, Dave was made redundant. 'It was very upsetting, almost like a death in the family,' Terri says, 'because Butlin's had been his life for so long. However, he got a job as a brewery rep in the Southwest and really enjoyed that. So we moved down to Exmouth, where I've lived ever since.'

Terri gave up her motor-racing job when they moved to Devon, and set up a swimming school, teaching kids and training those who wanted to become competitive swimmers. The school was soon doing very well and was over-subscribed, so when Dave was made redundant for the second time, he trained as an assistant teacher and came to work with Terri. 'He absolutely loved teaching the kids,' Terri says. 'He said it was the best job he'd ever had in his life!'

Sadly, though, Dave then developed prostate cancer. Terri didn't spot the symptoms herself and Dave didn't tell her about them until it was too late. 'Prostate cancer is so curable,' she says, her frustration and anguish still strong today. 'But by the time he said anything, it was already too late. He died fifteen years ago. Many of our old Butlin's friends were at the funeral, and though Bob Monkhouse wasn't able to come, he sent a lovely wreath. A few years later he died of prostate cancer himself.'

Terri was on her own for a few years, but then she met Mike, the assistant manager at a hotel where she was teaching Aquacise classes. 'We got talking and he seemed really nice,' Terri says. 'Since Valentine's Day was coming up, I sent him a card. I didn't know whether he was married, or anything about him at all, and I couldn't really ask anyone, because hotels are such hotbeds of gossip that word would have been all around the building before I'd finished asking the question. So I just wrote a little note on the card saying, "You seem a bit lonely and if you'd like some company, give me a call." I didn't sign it, so how I expected him to work out it had come from me I don't know, but somehow he did and he rang me. He had been married but was now divorced, so that was it, off we went, and we've been together ever since.'

They got married seven years ago. They were on a Grand Prix holiday to Australia and Malaysia, and were having dinner on their last night in Sydney in the revolving restaurant looking out over the city skyline, when Mike proposed. On the flight to Penang the next day, they were talking about how they would organise the wedding and about all the people they'd need to invite, and Mike said, 'It's a shame we can't just run away and get married without all that fuss.'

It was dark when they arrived in Penang, so they couldn't see much when they got to their hotel, but when they opened the curtains the next morning, they found they were looking out across a pristine white sand beach to the beautiful turquoise waters of the Indian Ocean. Half an hour later, they were having breakfast on the terrace, drinking in that fabulous view, when Terri suddenly said, 'I bet people pay a fortune to come out here and get married.'

'Well,' Mike said, 'we're already here. So let's do it!'

They told their tour guide, and he went off and fixed things with the hotel coordinator.

Five days later they were married, just off the beach in Penang. They had sent emails to their families and closest friends, saying, 'We're going to get married in five days' time and if you can get here, please come!' They didn't really expect that anybody would be able to, though.

Terri sent a message to Roger, of course, but he'd changed his email address without telling her, so he never received it. She was trying to get hold of him as they also needed faxed copies of documents like Dave's death certificate and Mike's divorce papers. She tried ringing him, but Roger was now working as a fire fighter and doing unusual shifts, so that plus the time difference between England and Malaysia made it impossible for her to speak to him. In the end, Terri had to ask her neighbour, who had a set of keys to her house, to go over and find the documents for her. When the neighbour saw Roger, she said, 'Isn't it wonderful news about your mum?' It was the first he'd heard about it, so understandably he was 'more than a little miffed at the time', but once Terri had explained the email mix-up, he was fine.

Mike and Terri have had some very happy years together, but sadly Mike is now suffering from a degenerative condition. Initially, the doctors thought he had carpal tunnel syndrome, because he was losing the use of his fingers. 'They were months trying to sort that out,' Terri says, 'before they realised that it wasn't and eventually found the right diagnosis.' Mike is suffering from corticobasal degeneration, a very rare condition in which the brain cells become damaged over a period of time and sections of the brain start to die. 'It's like dementia, Alzheimer's and Parkinson's all rolled into one,' she says, 'and it's incurable. The doctors say that it takes about eight years to run its course, but they can't pinpoint when it started, so we have no idea how far along that track we are.

'He's already lost the use of one arm and the other one is going, and his memory's gone to pot as well. He's on morphine for the pain and understandably gets very depressed. It's a horrible, horrible disease. Obviously, he couldn't carry on with his job as assistant manager at the hotel, but they have been really good to him and he has a little job, for four hours, four days a week, which is really good for him, but obviously the longer-term prospects are bleak.'

Her son and her friends are a great support to Terri and though her life is tinged with sadness at Mike's inevitable fate, she retains a positive outlook. She speaks to her best friend from Butlin's on the phone every Sunday, just as they've done for the last thirty-three years, and she looks back at her time at Butlin's with nothing but affection and gratitude.

'I left school at fifteen with nothing,' she says. 'I had no qualifications at all and I could do nothing beyond a bit of secretarial work, but I went to Butlin's and I've never been out of work since. I learned a lot there, too – talk about the university of life! I've never regretted it for an instant, because it was a wonderful time in my life. There was a real bond between all of us who worked there and a real family feeling. We felt we were all in it together, a bit like in wartime, I suppose, and you just don't get that any more. It took over my life, really, from being an eighteen-year-old camper to being a middle-aged lady, and I loved it!'

Anji

One

Petite, with a mass of hair that seems almost as big as she is, Anji Hartnell is an irrepressible and effervescent bundle of energy with a mischievous sense of fun. She was born in 1954 and grew up with her parents and her older brother, Geoffrey, in a large Victorian terraced house on Monk's Road in Exeter. There was an old-fashioned kitchen, a scullery and an outside loo in the yard, though there was also a bathroom upstairs with a big iron bathtub. There were fireplaces in all the rooms, which was wonderful, Anji says, 'because on cold winter weekends when my father was home, he lit the fires all over the house, and my friends were always coming round to play because their houses were not as warm as ours'. There was a half-size snooker table in the front room, and Anji and her brother had a playroom at the back of the house. Beyond it, through the French doors, there was a conservatory where her father's upright piano had been banished because her mother wouldn't allow it in the main house.

By day, Anji's father was a traffic manager for a coach company, Greenslades Tours, but he had a second job as a professional musician: as a drummer and the leader of his own dance band. He also played the piano 'absolutely brilliantly', Anji says. His name was Rick and he had all the band-stands draped with ornate maroon covers with his initials 'R.H.' picked out in gold lettering. The band played regularly at the Rougemont Hotel and Anji's dad used to joke that the only reason they'd taken the band on was because he had the same initials as the hotel, so it looked as though they were the house band.

'My dad was lovely,' Anji says. 'He was round and jolly and red-faced, just like a big Santa! In fact, we used to do Santa and his helper together at Christmastime, with me dressed as an elf. And if anyone should have gone on the stage, it was my father; he was an absolute natural and he was a real character, too.'

When Anji was young, the house always seemed to be full of music and laughter. Her parents loved to have their family and friends around them and every family gathering would inevitably end with an impromptu singsong around the piano.

Monk's Road was very long and Anji recalls it being 'like a little community on its own'. When she was young, it seemed to her as if the road went on for ever; she lived at Number 61 and her friend lived at Number 251, and the journey between the houses was a marathon for Anji's little legs. There was an equally long, wide lane that ran along the back of the houses; the coalman, the vegetable man and the fish man all drove their carts and lorries through there, but the children played there, too. 'We used to build all sorts of things, like rafts, out in the lane,' Anji says, 'tying together bits of scrap wood and old tins and anything else we could find. We were always going to go to America and Australia on this raft, even though there was no water within a mile of us.'

In summer, their mothers would take their chairs out to the back and peel their potatoes or cut up their veg or do some other chore while sitting in the lane, chatting to their friends, but also keeping an eye on the kids. Mrs Hendy, who lived at the top of the lane and had lots of boys, might come out for a while and she'd wave to Anji's mum, and when Mrs Hendy went in Mrs Potter might come out and Anji's mother might go in. There was never a rota or anything as organised as that, but there was always somebody there keeping an eye out for all the kids.

Anji's grandfather on her father's side had died when he was only forty-two and her grandmother was left with eight children to bring up – 'plus any waifs and strays that she'd taken in,' Anji says, 'and there were always a few of those'. Her grandmother had to fight very hard to keep the family together and from the moment her husband died, every inch of her garden was turned over to growing vegetables. She had fruit trees, currant bushes and rows and rows of potatoes, carrots, cabbages, onions, beans and peas, and that was how she fed her family.

'She was a survivor all right, and that survival instinct is a Hartnell family trait,' Anji says. 'It's one that my dad and I both shared. She instilled in us all a willingness to bend; you don't have to be rigid all the time – better to bend than to break. She had a dining table and chairs that used to be hocked every year. They were always brought back for Christmas and New Year, but as soon as the holidays were over, they would be hocked again. The rest of the time she would sit her children all the way up the stairs when it was mealtime and they'd eat their dinner sitting on the steps, because then they had a natural lap to put their plates on!'

Many years later, when Anji's grandmother died, her obituary was headed 'Mother of thirty-three', because as well as her own children, she took in all sorts of others who needed a home. 'So there was always someone else who needed feeding at my grandma's house,' Anji says. 'And it didn't stop with children, because she used to take in all sorts of animals as well – a stream of dogs with one leg or cats with one eye, that sort of thing. That's something I've inherited from her!'

Her grandmother was living in Somerset when Anji's dad was young, but after the war, with her large brood of children to provide for, she moved to Exeter and bought a fish-and-chip shop in Alphington Road, 'My grandma used to make the most fantastic food out of the bits of fish and trimmings that she couldn't sell in the shop,' Anji says. 'She fed the family on them. She'd make fish patties with the leftover chips, and the fish pie she made was absolutely to die for.' The family lived above the shop for a while and then moved to a council house on a huge estate in the St Thomas's district of Exeter. The pub on the estate was called The Green Gables and was run by Frank and Kate Vale, whose daughter, Lil, became a lifelong best friend to Anji's dad.

Even though there was never much money, Anji's dad had grown up in a really good family environment, and he was very family oriented himself, though he had a very flexible definition of 'family' that embraced friends and neighbours – including 'Auntie Lil', as she was known by the kids. She lived in a large house on the bottom corner of Monk's Road, with her husband, 'Uncle George'.

Uncle George and Auntie Lil played a big part in their lives. Anji's dad and Lil were such close friends that when he met Anji's mother, he even took Lil with him on their second date, so Lil could run the rule over her! Although they were not 'proper family', they were the closest family they had. 'I think sometimes that the family you choose for yourselves are often the ones that you're closest to,' says Anji.

Her dad had met her mum when he was playing at a gig in Tiverton. He was going in through the doorway carrying his bass drum just as she was coming out. She was struggling to get past him, but wanting a closer look at her because he obviously liked what he saw, her dad used the drum to block the doorway and started chatting to her. They started going out and eventually got married. After Anji was born, the bass drum case also sometimes doubled as an impromptu cot for her. If her dad was playing at a gig and her mum wanted to go along, she could tuck up Anji in a blanket inside the case and let her sleep while she enjoyed the music or had a quick dance.

Anji's friends became part of the extended family, too. It was not unusual for them to come over to the house unannounced, and even if Anji wasn't there, they'd be made to feel welcome.

They were one of the first families in the area to get a television and on Saturday nights it would be like a cinema in their living room, packed with people. If he wasn't playing with the band, Anji's dad would be playing snooker in the front room with the lads, but the rest of them would be sitting around watching television. So there was always a real family atmosphere in the house and always lots of people there. 'If I've taken nothing else from my dad, I've had that example from him, and my grandma before him,' Anji says.

Christmases always involved a huge get-together in somebody's house, with Christmas Day at one house, Christmas Night at another and Boxing Day at another, and Anji feels 'very, very lucky to have grown up in that environment', she says. 'It's stood the test of time, too; all the cousins, whether they are real cousins or just the children of family friends, have all stayed in touch; we're godparents to each other's children, and so on.'

When Anji was a teenager, they moved out of the city to a tiny little Devon village called Thorverton, and both there and when they lived in Exeter, as far back as she can remember, her family always went on holiday to Butlin's. Those holidays were really important to all of them; they talked about nothing else for weeks before they set off and for weeks after they came home. Before their departure, everyone's best clothes would be looked out, washed and ironed, and then put away, with no one allowed to wear anything they were taking with them until the holiday actually began.

They didn't just go to the nearest one, Minehead; they went to all the camps at one time or another. At first they just went for a week every year, but then they began taking two separate weeks in different camps, or sometimes a whole fortnight in one place. It was expensive during 'the factory closes', as they used to call them, when the northern mills and factories closed for the annual clean-up and overhaul during the last week in July and the first week in August, and avalanches of mill and factory workers descended on every Butlin's camp. So they'd often try to avoid those times, though it depended on her dad's work commitments. Through her father's day job they used to get coach holidays as well, but she says they never quite seemed to match up to their holidays at Butlin's.

Anji can still vividly remember her first ever sight of Butlin's. The first camp they went to was Pwllheli. They got there quite late, after dark, and all she can remember seeing is miles of what they called 'fairy lights' – coloured light bulbs – everywhere. 'I just couldn't believe it,' she says. 'I had never seen anything as colourful and wonderful in my entire life.' They didn't even stop to unpack;

they just set off to explore this magical kingdom.

When they went on holiday, every member of their extended family came, too – 'I don't think my parents would have dared to book a holiday for just the four of us without involving the rest of the family,' Anji says. As well as her mum and dad, and Anji and Geoffrey, there were their grandparents, Auntie Lil and Uncle George, and their daughter Margaret with up to five of her friends. Various other friends of her parents came, too. There could be up to twenty of them altogether, all the way from babies right up to grandparents.

'In those days, the families all stayed together and played together, and our holidays were always the whole lot of us,' Anji says, 'like a home from home. Our chalets were all in a great long line, with Nan and Granddad at one end, my mum and dad and me and Geoffrey at the other end, with Auntie Lil and Uncle George next door, and our other close friends in between. My cousin Margaret even brought her boyfriend Brian with her sometimes, which was almost unheard of, though they had to sleep in separate chalets, of course.'

Her mum didn't learn to drive until Anji was six, and her dad never drove at all, so Auntie Lil and Uncle George used to take them all on holiday. George drove a bright-yellow van, like a Transit, for his work and he was allowed to bring it home at weekends, so they'd all set off in that. George and Lil would put a single mattress and the settee from their front room in the back of the van and then they'd all pile in. 'There was always at least a dozen of us packed in,' Anji says, 'and not a seatbelt in sight!'

Anji grew up being sardined with other children, because they'd often go to the beach or the moors like that as well. 'We'd always take a picnic,' she says, 'and for some reason Auntie Lil always insisted on taking a jelly, though with the heat and the vibration, it had always turned back to liquid by the time we got there and we'd be wearing it instead of eating it! All the kids got covered with it, so we'd all be sticky before we'd even started.'

When they got to Butlin's, the whole family were always up for every scrap of entertainment laid on for them. Anji's nan was always the first up on stage for the Glamorous Granny competition, though she never won it, and her granddad's knobbly knees were just as regularly on display! They were a very sociable, outgoing family and Anji thinks that later stood her in good stead for socialising with the campers at Butlin's.

When Anji was a bit older she was often recruited to be a team leader at Butlin's and help the redcoats with some of the smaller children. 'Of course, I used to love that,' she says. 'They had little button badges and a Dymo machine that would click your name out on a strip of plastic. So they'd do one of those for me, and I thought I was "it" with one of those on, but I could never have dreamed that I might one day become a fully-fledged redcoat myself!'

There were tip-up cinema seats around the edge of the ballroom and some more comfortable seats at the back, but Anji and the other children used to sit on the edge of the dance floor in the evenings, watching her mum dance with their friend Ronnie, who was her dance partner and 'a wonderful dancer', says Anji. 'My mum was a ballroom dancer and absolutely loved dancing, but Dad was nearly always playing with the band on evenings and weekends and so couldn't dance with her. Anyway, he had two left feet and it would have been easier to get a camel to dance than my dad!' Because he was working all the time, her mum either had to sit on her own or get herself a dance partner, so Ronnie would often take them all out at the weekend and dance with Anji's mum, while her dad's band provided the music.

Since Anji had been to the Ida Tremain School of Dancing and learned to do ballroom and Latin American dancing, she and Ronnie would also often glide around the ballroom at Butlin's together, though it was a bit of a struggle for Ronnie, as he was about a foot taller than Anji at the time. The dancing helped later on when Anji went to work as a redcoat, because many of the older campers used to love to ballroom dance and not many of the other redcoats could do it.

Anji's mum was a dressmaker and she would make wonderful outfits for herself and matching ones for Anji, particularly while she did competitive ballroom dancing. 'You had to have a certain type of dress,' says Anji, 'with layers of petticoats, and they had to be above the knee so that the judges could see your feet and leg movements.'

Going home from Butlin's was always very painful. The children would stay up late on their last night, the Friday, as a treat, to enjoy the big farewell party for the campers. 'The Au Revoir was wonderful,' she says. 'We'd see all the redcoats together, and of course you always had your own particular favourite. The redcoats were such stars to me that I really wouldn't have been surprised to see them on TV back at home! It always broke my heart when we left, and you could see that some of the redcoats who'd looked after us were genuinely upset, too, because we'd get really close to them in the course of the week. Years later, when I was a redcoat myself, I always said to myself, "I'm not going to get so attached to children that I end up crying when they go home," but it was a total waste of time, because I was in floods every week!'

Anji's dad had two great regrets in his life: he'd never fought in the war and he'd never become a Butlin's redcoat. He missed out on active service during the Second World War because of ill health. When war broke out, he and his brothers (there were five of them altogether) tried to enlist together, but Anji's dad failed the medical, first for the RAF, then the Navy and finally the Army, when he was also arrested by the military police, because they'd been alerted by the RAF and Navy recruiting offices that he was a medical risk and was refusing to go to hospital.

He was suspected of suffering from TB, which was a notifiable disease and still a considerable threat to public health in those days – the first really effective antibiotic was not introduced until after the war, in 1946. So the military police made sure he went to Southernhay Hospital, and the doctors there confirmed the diagnosis of TB. Instead of joining the Army, he was forced to go to an isolation hospital at Wickden. To alleviate his boredom while he was there he started his own entertainments committee, putting on shows and performing songs and sketches to keep the other patients and the staff amused.

Anji's dad was lucky to survive – many people still died of TB in that era – but when he came out of hospital, he was still not fit enough to enlist in the forces, so he joined the Home Guard instead, training in a Nissen hut at Exwick.

He also put on a lot of entertainment during the war, doing gang shows for the troops. He used to tell Anji that it was vital that things like the shows had gone on, not only to boost the morale of the fighting troops, but also that of the men, like himself, who for various reasons weren't able to go to war with their friends and brothers, and felt their lack of active involvement acutely.

So Anji's dad could sing, play music and tell a joke, and he absolutely loved entertaining people. He used to say to Anji, 'Before I met your mother, I wanted to run off and join the circus ... and after I met your mother, I definitely wanted to run off and join the circus!' He had also always wanted to be a Butlin's redcoat, but earning a living and feeding his family had to take priority, because Anji's brother Geoffrey was born when her mum was only twenty-one and her father wasn't much older. So he bought a house, and, faced with the responsibility of paying the mortgage and feeding his family, he had to put his redcoat dreams on hold.

They were never to be fulfilled.

However, having not been able to do it himself, he was determined that Anji would become a redcoat, so as soon as she was old enough, he was continually badgering her, saying, 'You would make a good redcoat. You would make a really good redcoat.'

In June 1975, when she was twenty years old, Anji saw an advert recruiting for redcoats. She showed it to her dad, who, as usual, pestered her to go for it. 'I'll ring up if you want,' she said, 'but I really don't think they'll want me.'

To Anji's surprise, after chatting to her on the phone for a few minutes, they asked her to go along to an interview at Minehead the following Saturday morning. A friend of Anji's borrowed her parents' car and drove her up there from Exeter. She was interviewed by a man called Brett Creswell, and after talking to her for five minutes and asking her to stand up and sing something in front of him, he said, 'Right, you're now a redcoat. Go and get fitted out with a uniform and get a chalet allocated, and be quick about it, because you're on duty in the ballroom tonight.'

There was always a 'natural spillage', as her boss used to call it, because the redcoats started the season in spring and by June some of them would inevitably be beginning to fall by the wayside for one reason or another. So a couple of the Minehead red-coats must have quit or even been sacked, and Anji filled one of the vacancies and embarked on her redcoat career.

Within an hour of getting there, Anji's friend had set off back to Exeter on her own, carrying a note from Anji to her parents, asking them to pack all her things and send them back to Minehead. Her long-suffering friend then had to make a second 100-mile round trip to deliver it. So Anji had her job interview on the Saturday morning and by the Saturday night she was working as a redcoat. One of the reasons she found it so easy to go there when she was offered the job was because her holidays at Butlin's had been so magical when she was young.

Two

The other redcoats at Minehead had all been there since the start of the season at the end of April, and the training had already been done, so they were very pol-ished and professional. Anji, on the other hand, must have looked like a rabbit in the headlights to start with, because she didn't have a clue what she was supposed to be doing, but the other redcoats looked after her. A lot of the reds had already worked a couple of seasons together when Anji started, so they knew that it was in their interests to look after any new recruits and ensure that they stayed around, because that made everyone's life easier. If they left, then the remaining reds were short-handed and everyone had to work harder, so they went out of their way to help the newcomers learn the ropes.

That camaraderie and friendliness really did make Butlin's feel like a family to Anji, and it was a feeling she never lost in all the years she worked for them. 'It was', she says, 'as if I had all these extra brothers and sisters – that's really what it felt like to me from the very beginning, and that was really important to me, because wherever I'm working, I always want to create a family atmosphere around it. My grandma used to say, "Wherever you are, it's really important that anybody in your company feels comfortable," and I used to think about that when I was starting as a redcoat.'

Despite this, Anji can remember ringing her dad on her very first night at Butlin's and saying, 'I don't know what I'm doing. I can't do this. I can't speak to strangers.'

Her dad just said, 'You always speak to strangers. You talk to anybody. Why is it so different now that you've put a red jacket on?'

'But who should I be?'

'Just be you.'

There were other times when she rang her dad just for some reassurance, and it could have been at one or two in the morning, but he was never angry, she says, even if she'd woken him up. 'He'd just say, "Hello, darling, what's the matter, what's up?" And I'd talk it out with him and feel so much better afterwards.' To offer further support, the first year that Anji was a redcoat the whole extended family also came on holiday to Minehead, just like they had when she was small, though it was the first time they'd done so for years.

When Anji started, the redcoats' hours were very long and their pay was 'absolutely ridiculous, but we weren't in it for the money', Anji says. 'We did it because we loved it, and I've got friends – redcoats and campers – who I was friends with then that I'm still friends with today.'

Each work group within the camps formed a close bond and they often had quite different dreams and aspirations from the other groups. Waitresses often tended to live on their tips and save their wages, using work at the camps as a means of putting together a nest egg for a deposit on a house or car, or sometimes to pay off a debt.

Among the other employees, a surprising number of kitchen porters seemed to be on the run from missed alimony payments or troubled pasts. One former Minehead camp manager, Bryan, used to tell staff who looked like they'd come to Butlin's to run away from their problems: 'If you've got a problem, bad luck, it's in your suitcase, so you've brought it with you.' As if in confirmation of that, the arrival of a police car through the front gates at some camps would sometimes signal an exodus of kitchen porters out of the back gate or over the fence!

The cleaners and chalet-maids were usually local women, living off site, but the redcoats and other staff might come from anywhere, and the high turnover meant that there were nearly always jobs to be had at the camps, even for applicants turning up unannounced. Even those locals who had no connections with the camps would sometimes make use of the facilities, with or without the blessing of the staff. Undeterred by the fences surrounding them or the patrolling security men, locals would sometimes still manage to sneak into the Saturday-night dances.

Although the different work groups tended to stick together, the one thing the other staff usually had in common was their resentment of the redcoats. During the first two seasons that Anji worked there, two people had to share each chalet– 'They were called chalets,' she says, 'but they were really just little boxes, tiny huts, like garden sheds.' In her third year, however, the redcoats were given the luxury of a chalet each, which didn't go down at all well with the rest of the staff, who all still had to share theirs.

That certainly deepened the hostility towards the redcoats that already existed. At Minehead, though, Anji inadvertently helped to bridge that divide. 'A lot of the other staff at Butlin's used to think that redcoats had a charmed life,' she says, 'perhaps forgetting that we were working seventeen or eighteen hours a day and were constantly on show, whereas most of them worked shorter hours. There was certainly hostility between the staff and the redcoats, but my passion is that people shouldn't be judged until you actually know them, and I was – and still am – totally opposed to people working together and having an "us and them" situation.'

Anji tried to avoid any bad feeling with the other staff by defusing some of the most fractious situations. The redcoats had chalet-maids to clean their chalets for them. It was one of the perks of their job, but it certainly didn't help relations with the other staff, who had to clean their own chalets. So Anji told her chalet-maid, 'Listen, you can tell your boss that you're doing my chalet if you want to, but it really isn't your respon-sibility; I've got to tidy up after myself. You take your time, go and sit on my bed if you like and have a few minutes off, but don't clean the chalet. From now on, I'll be doing that.'

The staff bar, where all the non-redcoat staff used to go after work or on their nights off, was effectively off limits to redcoats at the time, which only fuelled the hostility between them and the other staff further, so Anji set out to do something about that as well. 'It was pretty much taboo for a redcoat to go in there,' she says, 'unless you were a twenty-two-stone lifeguard and could hold your own in a punch-up – and I was one of the smallest redcoats of all – but one night I asked the boss if I could go to the staff bar. Although he thought I was asking for trouble, in the end he reluctantly gave his permission.'

As Anji walked into the staff bar, there was a sullen silence at first, just like in the old Hollywood Westerns when the bad guy walks into the saloon, the pianist stops playing and everyone swivels round to fix the intruder with hostile stares, but she soon managed to break the ice. 'It may have helped that I was a woman and too small for anyone to pick a fight with, but I was soon accepted and, in fact, I met some really nice friends there who I've kept in contact with ever since.' After that, redcoats were actually encouraged to go up to the staff bar. They had broken down the division between 'them' and 'us', and from then on, Anji says, they all saw themselves as being part of the same family.

All the redcoats had to be up for breakfast duty, but Anji soon got put on Radio Butlin's duty, so she couldn't go down to the canteen; she was in the tiny studio doing the famous tannoy announcements. She was supposed to wake the campers up gently with the regular piece of music, the soothing 'Cavatina', but, she says, 'being very rebellious by nature – I always have been – I decided to wake them all up one morning with the *1812 Overture* instead – the full version, complete with cannon fire!'

Her boss gave her a ticking-off about it, but he was laughing as he was doing it and trying and failing to look stern. 'You know I have to tell you off,' he said, 'and I have to tell the camp manager that I've chastised you. You won't do it again, will you?'

She promised she wouldn't, but it wasn't very long before she was 'up to her old tricks' again and putting on the *Pink Panther* theme and various other unauthorised songs. However, she wasn't the only one sabotaging the morning reveille music. To save time in the mornings, she often set everything up the night before, putting the record on the turntable and even putting the needle on it, so she just had to switch it on when she first went in, but she had to make very sure that she always locked up the Radio Butlin's office before she went to bed, because more often than not someone would get in and tamper with the LP. If she didn't notice in time, she'd find Elvis's 'All Shook Up', or 'The Laughing Policeman', or something equally inappropriate, blasting out of the speakers instead of the gentle strains of 'Cavatina'.

When Anji started work, she says, 'They really used to shuffle the campers around then. It was as if they had to know what they were supposed to be doing at every minute of the day.' So as well as waking them up and getting them into meals at the right time for their sitting, Radio Butlin's would also be broadcasting announcements like, 'Well, campers, we are all going to get together now in the Princess Ballroom, because we're having "Meet the Redcoats".' Some people really liked to be organised like that and Anji remembers it well from when she was a child on her own holidays there; they were always getting moved around.

'Meet the Redcoats' was always on the Sunday morning, just after the campers had all arrived, and the regular redcoats would all be out in force, backed up by the life-guards, musicians and dancers, also dressed in red jackets and doing the general duties they had to do to qualify for a free chalet on site.

Every camper they could find would be cajoled, encouraged or dragooned into the ballroom until as many as 1,000 people were packed in there. The compère would then invite thirty-two couples to come onto the dance floor to take part in the fun and games. If there weren't enough volunteers – and there never were – the redcoats would coax couples onto the dance floor until there were enough. There was then an hour of non-stop games.

The redcoats would line up the campers into teams and they'd have to pass a football over their heads to the next person behind them as fast as they could, and then do the same, passing it between their legs. They also had them in piggyback races and in relay races where they'd spin them round to make them dizzy so they couldn't run in a straight line as they tried to get back to their team-mates.

They'd then put the individual couples on the spot and ask them embarrassing personal questions about themselves and their partners. If they didn't answer or gave a different answer from the one their partner had given, they were eliminated until eventually they were left with just four couples. In turn, the four men then had to sit their partner on their knees and serenade them with 'If You Were the Only Girl in the World', and the winner would be chosen by the volume of applause from the audience. After all that, their prize usually turned out to be nothing more than another round of applause.

As the grand finale, the redcoats would get all the contestants back onto the dance floor and tell them they all had to kneel down and rest their heads on their hands, close their eyes and pray for good weather during their week's holiday. Some of the redcoats walked around making sure that the campers weren't peeking, while the others put all the microphones and equipment away. They'd then make 'Sssshhh!' gestures to the rest of the audience and all sneak off, leaving the contestants still 'at their prayers', heads down and eyes closed. Eventually the contestants would open their eyes and lift their heads to find out what was going on, only to be greeted by roars of laughter from the remaining audience.

After a pause for Sunday lunch, the campers would be rounded up again for one of the biggest competitions of the week – The Holiday Princess. The girls were always encouraged to wear bathing costumes for it, ensuring that the male campers all turned up to watch, but even girls in their normal clothes who had only come as spectators would often find themselves gently persuaded to take part. A lot of the girls needed no encouragement, however, since they knew that there was a prize of a free week's holiday for the winner, plus the chance of a really big prize for the 'all camps winner' after the grand final at the end of the season.

Following the crowning of that week's Holiday Princess, the men would undergo their own ritual humiliation in the Knobbly Knees contest. They not only had to parade around with their trousers rolled up to expose their knees, but also might find themselves dressed in tutus or mimicking Tarzan and his chimpanzee. The competition was always judged by the girls who came first, second and third in the Holiday Princess competition, and the winner would get a kiss from the winning girl as well as his prize, or sometimes as his only prize.

Every so often the redcoats would also have to do a promotion on behalf of one of Butlin's corporate sponsors. There was a regular one for the *Daily Express* when Anji started, where she found herself having to dress up as Rupert Bear first thing in the morning. The *Express* paid the redcoats an extra £5 a week for dressing up, and that was 'an absolute fortune' at the time, so Anji was very happy to do it, even though it was 'really hot and sweaty' when wearing the full costume: a bear's head, which was really itchy on the inside and so hot that she could hardly breathe, and Rupert's traditional costume of a scarf, a jacket and a pair of checked trousers. One of the other redcoats made those for her just by drawing black checks on a pair of waterproof yellow trousers with a magic marker pen. It looked fine, but when Anji took them off, the checks had transferred to her legs and they wouldn't wash off!

Dressed as Rupert Bear, she would go into the dining room at mealtimes, and any children who brought her the little crusader logo torn from the top of the *Daily Express*'s front page were given a draw ticket in return. On the Friday night at the end of the week they held a big prize draw, with fantastic prizes – £25 in cash for the holders of the lucky numbers, which was almost a month's wage for a redcoat. They had blocks of tickets to give out and every block they gave away yielded another £25 prize, so they were often giving away four or five prizes on a Friday night.

Anji was also involved in all the competitions, though the Knobbly Knees competition was 'my forte', she says. 'Probably because I was a woman, I found it easier than the male redcoats did to persuade the male campers to put on tutus, fairy wings and leotards and things. Mind you, some of them didn't need persuading at all, they were right into it from the start!' She would get them all dressed up and then have them re-enact *The*

Dying Swan. So the chosen swan would 'die' and then the others had to pick him up and carry him off the stage. 'We would invariably choose the heaviest man to be the swan,' says Anji, 'so there'd be grunting and groaning as they tried to pick him up and more often than not they would drop the poor chap, which was great entertainment for the audience, but often left the swan and his attendants with a few scrapes, bumps and bruises.'

The redcoats were always playing tricks and pranks on each other as well; it was great fun and good for staff morale, though sometimes, Anji says, 'the tricks did go a bit wrong. There used to be a donkey derby on the Gaiety Green and one time we borrowed a baby donkey from the man who looked after them and brought it all the way up through the theatre while everyone was watching a film. Nobody even batted an eye – it must have been a very good film.'

They put the donkey in the manager's office while he was out for lunch and tiptoed away, giggling to each other. Unfortunately, he was delayed on his way back from lunch, and then things got progressively worse. 'The donkey either missed its mum or had eaten something that didn't agree with it, because it got upset and its stomach got upset, too. By the time the boss came back, his office was half-full of donkey poo. It had seemed very funny when we'd thought of doing it, but the boss didn't think the joke was quite so funny, and nor did I, when I and several of the other redcoats had to spend most of the rest of the day cleaning up his office again.'

Anji says that her boss at Minehead, Brett Creswell, was 'probably the third most important male influence in my life'. The first was her father and the second was a maths teacher at her school, Paddy English, who, when her parents split up for a brief while and she 'went completely off the rails', got her back on track again. And so the third was Brett Creswell. 'He was a big, big influence on me. When you're young and impressionable, which I was when I went to Butlin's, I thought I was invincible, and he taught me that you are not going to win every argument, and while you can't always like the people that you work with, you have to remain professional and you have to find common ground with them.

'When you have a lot of extroverts together, you often find a clash of personalities, and it would have been quite easy to fall out with a lot of people. However, doing that could send a damaging ripple through the whole department, so the redcoats were made very aware of the need to avoid that. It was a family atmosphere among us,' Anji says, 'but just

361

like your real family, there were members that you'd avoid. Ninety per cent of the people you meet do come in and out of your life, and you like them well enough, but it's the other ten per cent that you take into your heart and become a big part of your life.'

They all had flare-ups from time to time, of course, but in nearly every case they would be all over and forgotten in seconds. If there was a more lasting grudge, Anji says, the great thing about Brett 'was that if you went to him and said, "I have this clash of personalities with someone," he would make sure that you weren't put on duties together, and it gave the other person as much space as it gave you, so it was a two-way street.'

Brett Creswell always made it clear to the redcoats that they were the people in the front line, the ones that the customers saw first and most often, so it was very important that any relationships they got themselves into were 'in good taste'. Anji actually 'fell madly in love' with a staff member during one season, but they had to keep it 'terribly quiet'. He was a dish washer in the kitchens, but eventually he went off with one of the singers in the band, leaving Anji to nurse a broken heart.

There were relationships between the staff and the campers, but that was mainly with the male redcoats. From 1979 onwards, Anji had a boyfriend at home, anyway – she met her future husband, Rick, at a party while she was at home in the autumn of that year. His birthday was 4 October, the same day as Anji's, and he was going to the party of another friend who also had the same birthday. The friend said to Anji, 'It's your birthday, too; why don't you come to the party as well?' So there were three of them, all with the same birthday. Anji actually went to the party with a boyfriend, a male model turned redcoat from Birmingham. Anji had persuaded him to become a redcoat, but 'he turned out to be a complete ladies' man', she says. 'He got carried away and the call of all those pretty faces got to him!' So Anji ended up dumping her boyfriend – though they are still very good friends – and started going out with Rick instead.

Even before that happened, Anji would never risk going out with one of the campers. In any case, she says, 'I was lucky enough to be wrapped up in my work; I loved my job, absolutely loved it. It was my own personal choice, but however much I might have fancied somebody, I knew that they would only be there for a week, and you can't really build a relationship in that time.'

The Butlin's security men kept a close eye on the redcoats, but that was as much for their protection as anything else. 'The biggest problem for us was the married campers,' Anji says. 'If I had a penny for every one who told me that his wife didn't understand him, I could have bought Butlin's myself! So you had to be able to cope with that. You had to stay very public and be very professional. They'd say, "Can I buy you a drink?" and I'd say, "Well, actually, I'm not drinking at the moment." If they were very persistent and insisted on buying her an alcoholic drink, Anji would say, 'All right, I'll come up to the bar with you.' She had an arrangement with one of the barmen, so she'd wait until that particular barman was free to serve her and then she'd ask him for a vodka and lemonade, and he knew to pretend to give her a vodka but actually just give her a glass of lemonade. He'd still charge the camper the price for a vodka and put the money in his tips jar.

The girls would often pretend to have a relationship with one of the other redcoats, just to put off the more tenacious male campers. On Friday nights, after the Au Revoir, Brett Creswell would pair them all off, lining up male redcoats with female ones, pretty much at random, just because they were safer that way and he'd say, 'I want you out of the ballroom, back to the chalet line and changed out of your reds. After that you can go back to the ballroom if you want, or up to the staff bar, but I don't want any lone redcoats left around the place.' He was afraid that some of the male campers who'd had too much to drink and were heading home the following day might get too amorous or out of control.

Anji used to pair up with a guy who was gay, and if she was in a tricky situation in the ballroom with some male camper pestering her, she'd just say, 'Hang on, I've just got to give a message to my boyfriend,' or, 'Can I introduce you to my boyfriend?' and that would solve the problem. It was always worse towards the end of the week, as a lot of the men would go carefully with their money early in the week, but later they'd be thinking, I've got all this money left for the last couple of days, and they'd start drinking much more on the Thursday and Friday night.

Despite the precautions they took, Anji did know some redcoat girls who got themselves into very sticky situations. One or two of those who really enjoyed a drink found it became their downfall, as they were sacked either for being drunk on duty or for being caught in a compromising position with a male camper.

Although it was seasonal work, Anji had done well enough in her first season to be offered winter work within the Butlin's organisation. 'If there were any jobs to be had and you were good at your job, they would try to keep you on and give you work in the hotels or somewhere,' she says. So at the end of the season, and over the next few years as well, she would do the Horse of the Year Show at the Empire Pool at Wembley (now the Wembley Arena), because Butlin's always sponsored a trophy in the show. Redcoats came from each of the camps as part of the Horse of the Year Show, and even though it was staged at Wembley, when Anji was doing it they would all stay in the Butlin's hotel at Saltdean near Brighton and travel up to London when they were needed. So in the evenings 'the hotel would just become Butlin's again', she says, 'Complete with a nightly Redcoat Show.'

During the rest of the off-seasons, Anji worked in one or other of the Butlin's hotels, and she and her redcoat friends from Minehead would sometimes all go off and work in the same place together. She worked in the Saltdean hotel during one off-season and did two winters at Scarborough, at the Butlin's hotel there. 'There's a famous banister at the hotel,' she says, 'and you really haven't lived until you've slid down that banister!'

Anji's next season at Minehead was a really hot summer – 1976, the year of a long drought. The heat wave made life very difficult for the redcoats, who were expected to wear the full uniform no matter how hot it was. 'Redcoats were fainting left, right and centre,' says Anji. There was also a severe water shortage, with hosepipe bans and standpipes erected in the streets of some towns and villages.

One afternoon, as Anji was walking back to her chalet, one of the other redcoats lobbed a cup of cold water at her. This simple act set off a chain of retaliation and before long all the redcoats, lifeguards and entertainments staff were engaged in a full-blown water fight. Anything that could hold water – from buckets and pint pots to plastic top hats, caps and bags – was filled and then thrown all over the place. 'The guys were taking no prisoners,' Anji says. 'All our screams and pleas for mercy were ignored. I have never laughed so much in all my life!'

Breathless both with laughter and from trying to outrun someone with a masterblaster water pistol, Anji ran straight into the path of Brett Creswell, the entertainments manager. 'I can't begin to tell you how angry he was,' she says. 'There was a water drought and we were having a water fight! My career as a redcoat flashed before my eyes. Was I sacked? No, but only because there were just two members of staff missing from the water fight. One was in Radio Butlin's, and the other was in the sickbay having a boil on his arse lanced. However, we were all given written warnings and lost a whole day's pay. Were we remorseful? Were we hell! That water fight was one of the funniest days of my life!'

Three

Anji's last year at Butlin's was 1982. By then, she and Rick felt that they wanted to start a family, so she decided it was time for her to leave. She said to herself, 'Right, I'll go home, and all that energy I put into being a redcoat, I'm going to put into raising a family instead.' When she left, she hoped she would be able to have her family and then go back to work at Butlin's in a different capacity. She would have had no hesitation in moving her family to Minehead, even though it might have led to a few arguments, because Rick didn't share her love for Butlin's, but in any case it was not to be.

It was a very, very emotional finish to her Butlin's career. The season ended on the Saturday, and on the Sunday they folded up, cleared their belongings out of their chalets and everybody started to leave – and Butlin's had been such a big part of her life that it was a huge wrench for Anji to leave. She finished at Butlin's that day, 3 October

1982, and she and Rick got married the following day – 4 October – their joint birthday, so neither of them would ever have an excuse for forgetting their anniversary!

It was a relatively quiet wedding, because some of their Butlin's friends had already scattered to start their winter jobs, but quite a few of them came along. Anji was on the way to the church in the car with her dad when she suddenly shouted, 'Stop the car!'

Her dad panicked and said, 'What's up? Don't you want to marry him?'

She said, 'Yes, I do, it's not that. I've just noticed that you've got Sandtex in your hair!'

He had been decorating that morning before getting ready for the church and his head must have brushed against the ceiling, because he did indeed have white Sandtex stuck in his hair. So Anji had to pick it all out before they drove on to the church, where he walked down the aisle with her and gave her away.

Although she'd officially finished as a redcoat at Butlin's, Anji was still on the roster for Christmas, but seven weeks after the wedding, on the day before Christmas Eve, when she should have been on her way to Minehead, she suffered a miscarriage. She was only seven weeks gone and hadn't even known she was pregnant. Her friends at the camp were ringing to find out what had happened to her, but they couldn't get through because she was still in hospital.

The doctor who treated her advised her not to go to Minehead, so she stayed at home that Christmas. 'I really felt like I should have been back at Minehead working with them again,' she says, 'because Christmas at Butlin's was always a magical time, but I wasn't able to. In fact, I don't think Christmas has ever been quite the same for me since I left Butlin's. It's still difficult, even now, when it comes round to the season and Christmas, when I know they are going to be gearing up and getting ready. I don't think I've ever stopped being a redcoat; I just changed the colour of my jacket, that's all.'

The following year, Anji went back to Minehead for a week at the start of the season to help them prepare and rehearse the Redcoat Show, but it felt very strange to be leaving the camp again a few days later without taking part. It was to be the last time that she went there to work, because, in the end, the plan to return there after having her family just didn't work out.

Having lost that first baby to a miscarriage in December, Anji got pregnant again quite quickly, but in May she was told that it was an ectopic pregnancy and the surgeon would have to remove one of her fallopian tubes. Already facing the heartbreak of a second lost baby, she was also told that the removal of one of her fallopian tubes would make it very difficult for her to conceive naturally in the future.

She was still determined to try for a baby but knew nothing about infertility treatments at that stage. It was a steep learning curve for her and she found it very difficult psychologically, because while she was battling to try and have a child, she says, 'my friends and my sister-in-law were having babies like shelling peas'. However, Anji began a regime of fertility treatments. They were very painful and she had to go to hospital for the injections and the scans to see if she had ovulated, but she was still assuming that she and Rick would have a baby eventually. She duly became pregnant again with triplets, but lost all of them quite quickly, and then underwent another long period of fertility treatment in vain.

Going through all this trauma led Anji to two bouts of anorexia, which only made things worse. She had been told that she was slightly overweight – she'd been slim to start with, but as is often the case, the fertility treatment caused her to put on weight. She tried to counteract this by going on diets, but they didn't work, as she was still having the treatment, so she then began almost starving herself. 'I think it was mainly the result of low self-esteem,' she says. 'Every woman is put on this earth to have children and if you think that is not going to happen, it can make you do extreme things to yourself.'

She gained some perspective on her own problems by going to work at a centre for 'down and outs'. She told herself, 'As bad as times are for me, there are other people who are a lot worse off.' She also knew that there were other women at the infertility treatment centre who had been told that they would never have children, and one of them – a woman she'd got to know well through having treatment at the same time – had been forced to have a hysterectomy.

After an interval of several years since her last pregnancy, Anji was going through another bout of anorexia and had almost given up hope of ever having a child when she discovered that she was pregnant once more, this time with twins. Strangely enough, she'd stopped the fertility treatment shortly beforehand – her doctors had told her to have a little break from it – but she'd got pregnant anyway.

Yet again, further weakened by the anorexia, she lost one of her twins when she was about eleven weeks pregnant, and she was told that she would almost certainly lose the other one as well. She had bouts of depression as a result and her health was very poor. She also had to deal with the nagging fear that every new day would be the day she lost her other baby. She had pretty much resigned herself to the thought that if she lost this baby as well, she would just give up and wouldn't even try to have a child any more, but still, in desperation, she went to see a fortune teller. 'I suppose I was clutching at any straw by then,' she says. The fortune teller looked at her and said, 'This child wants to be born. He is going to be born.' And illogical though it was, Anji took strength from that – as she says, 'You have to take comfort where you find it.'

The baby was due around Christmas and on 4 December 1989, Anji decided to go into Exeter to do all her Christmas shopping. She planned to bring it all home, wrap it up and get it out of the way ready for when the baby arrived. The final thing she had to get was a book for her father, so she went to pick it up while Rick went back to the car with their other parcels.

When she came out of the bookshop, she got a little disoriented and went the wrong way, ending up on the wrong side of the multi-storey car park from the pedestrian entrance. Preoccupied, she was about to step off the pavement and cross the road without looking when she felt a hand on her shoulder, pulling her back just as a lorry rumbled past within inches of her. 'It would certainly have hit me,' she says, 'because I felt the draught as it passed, and I and my son would both have been killed. I looked round, stammering out my thanks, but this old man in a long black coat who was standing behind me just said, "Have you got the right time?"'

Anji glanced at her watch and said, 'Yes, it's 4.10.'

He said to her, '1954.'

She thought that was a bit odd, because it was nowhere near five to eight, but as she turned away, she thought about it again: 4 – 10 – 1954: her birth date. She whipped around again but he was nowhere to be seen and the whole street was empty of people. 'I hurried up the only stairs nearby, but there was no sign of him there either,' she says. 'I'm shaking now, just thinking about it.' She offers no explanation for it, leaving the possible reasons hanging in the air, but it's clear she believes that something extraordinary happened that cold, bleak December day.

She didn't tell Rick straight away, because they were wet and cold and it seemed too strange a topic to broach in a casual conversation on the way home. When they got back, she went to bed with what seemed to be a cold, but was admitted to hospital a couple of days later with a chest infection that turned into pleurisy and then pneumonia. Had she lost the baby as a result, it would probably have been the end of the line for her. There were no other easy options, because adoption was a lot harder to arrange twenty years ago than it is now, 'What would have happened had I lost my other baby, I'm not sure,' she says, 'but the fortune teller was right and my beautiful son was finally born, almost a month late, on 23 January 1990.'

She had the reward of a healthy little boy, but she had endured a very long, painful time while trying for a family; it took nine years out of her life altogether. For all those years, her career was on hold, because she never knew when she was going to be called into the hospital for treatment. By the time her son was finally born, it was too late for her to go back to work at Butlin's, but in most cases, her friendships from that era had continued, and her trials and tribulations had helped her realise who her true friends were. 'I've been through a few crises in my life,' Anji says, 'and it's not always the people you expect to step up to the plate who do so. Sometimes people who you never thought were really close friends will really be there for you, while others are nowhere to be seen.'

Her son is now grown up, and Anji has often said to him, 'You should be a redcoat. You would make such a good redcoat,' just like her father always used to say to her. 'He really would,' Anji adds, 'but his career's gone in a different direction. He did a degree in film and television and works in the industry now, but although he's very good behind the camera, I like him the other side of it even more, because I think he's a very good actor. He would be fantastic in a situation comedy, if only because, in addition to his acting talent, just like his grandfather, he can also pull some very strange faces!'

Although she was never able to go back to work there, Anji says, 'Butlin's has definitely played a major part in my life, not just while I was working there, but ever since. It made me more extrovert, though that wasn't always an advantage. I discovered that once you've been given the freedom to be an extrovert, it's a very hard habit to break!'

In common with many other ex-redcoats, for weeks and months after each season had ended, and even when her career at Butlin's was over and she was back at home, Anji would still be walking along the street with her friends, saying, 'Good morning. How are you?' to absolutely everyone she passed.

Her friends used to say to her, 'Will you stop it? You're not at Butlin's now!'

'You also find out who your friends are when you've taken on a job like being a redcoat,' Anji says. 'When I went back to my home village, I was given a very hard time by some people who felt I'd got above myself, even though I was still just the same person

I'd always been. I'd been fortunate enough to follow my dream, but I'd been brave enough to follow it, too, and when I look at some of the people in the village who I've known since childhood and who haven't done that – some of them have never left the village at all – they're probably my biggest critics, but with me, what you see is what you get. If you ask me a question, you are going to get an answer and it may not always please you.'

When Anji was growing up, her life was very family-oriented, and because of that, all through her life, even today, she still wants that family atmosphere around her, and that was certainly the case during her time at Butlin's. 'It wasn't all touchy-feely there, of course,' she says. 'There were people who didn't get on with other redcoats, and there were clashes of personality and things like that, but as the boss used to say to us: "If you want to be professional, this is where you learn."' It could be a hard lesson sometimes, but it was a great training ground. Butlin's was also a perfect stepping stone for Anji and many others, a halfway house between the cosy security of family life and the big, wide and often cold world outside.

Anji met another Butlin's girl, Sue, when they were redcoats at Minehead together and they've stayed friends ever since. She also met her very best friend, Lynn Manton, at Butlin's. Lynn used to come on holiday to Minehead with her family every year when she was young, and they were all very keen on entertainment – her sister Heidi took over from Cheryl Baker in Bucks Fizz. Anji got to know Heidi because she used to perform with her brother Jamie in the Butlin's Junior Star Trail competition, and when she was older she entered the adult Star Trail a couple of times, too. Jamie and Heidi got to the final of the Junior Star Trail in 1979, but in the end they were beaten by a ten-year-old girl who had also won the grand final of the Beaver Showtime Talent Contest at the tender age of eight. Her name was Catherine Zeta Jones, and she went on to become very famous indeed.

One year, Anji got chatting to Heidi's sister, Lynn, at the side of the stage and didn't think any more of it at the time, but it was the start of a lifelong friendship. Lynn also had a beautiful singing voice – 'though I'm not sure she'd be able to say the same about me with a straight face', Anji says with a rueful smile – and they sang together in the Redcoat Show. Lynn did two seasons at Minehead, but then started a relationship that was the cause of a bust-up between Lynn and Anji that lasted for years, although they are once again inseparable now.

They were both appearing in a huge production at the time, a pantomime brought to Butlin's from the West End, along with several of its stars. Lynn and Anji auditioned for the rather less grand roles of Munchkins and were chosen to be Munchkin One and Two. Their characters were very tactile – 'a bit like the Teletubbies, really', Anji says. 'When we came on stage we had our arms around each other and were all cuddly and affectionate.'

However, Lynn had started going out with a male redcoat whom Anji didn't feel was right for her at all. She thought he was with Lynn not because he loved her, but because she was very popular, with a beautiful singing voice, and it was a bit of a feather in his cap to be Lynn Manton's boyfriend. 'In fact, he always used to introduce himself that way; he didn't mention his name, he'd just say, "I'm Lynn Manton's boyfriend,"' Anji says, 'and that rang alarm bells with me.'

Towards the end of the season, Lynn was on stage when her boyfriend walked on from the wings, stopped the show and proposed to her. She said yes, and the audience went absolutely mad, but there was still something about him that Anji just didn't like, so she tried to talk Lynn out of it. They had a big row about it, and so there they were, not speaking to each other, but still having to go on stage every night as the cuddly, super-affectionate Munchkins. They managed to smile, laugh and do the Munchkin act so well that the stage manager even said, 'I'm so glad that you two have made up again,' but as soon as they came off stage they went back to not speaking to each other.

Lynn was going to be Anji's bridesmaid, but that fell through because of the row, and in the event, she didn't come to the wedding at all.

Lynn went ahead and married her boyfriend, but, as Anji had predicted, they were not right for each other and eventually split up. Anji knew that Lynn was married and living in Bath, but still she didn't speak to her for several years. 'It broke my heart,' Anji says, 'but I never let go of the thought that Lynn was my friend and we'd make up some day.'

The key to their reconciliation was provided by the untimely death of one of their redcoat friends, Keith Perron, in 1998. Always a larger-than-life character, he sadly died much too young, after suffering fatal head injuries in a fall. Almost all of his old friends got together for his funeral. All the redcoats from the camp carried his coffin, Anji's friend Sue read the eulogy and the organist played Rod Stewart's 'Maggie May' on the church organ in tribute to Keith, who had always said that he loved only three things in his life: his mum, cricket and Rod Stewart.

After the service was over, the redcoats were all saying the same thing to each other: 'How come all these years have gone by without us meeting up?' So they arranged a reunion at Minehead as a wake for Keith. Almost all the redcoats that Anji knew had been at the funeral, but there was no sign of Lynn. Anji went up to Minehead early to help prepare for the reunion, and a former redcoat and lifeguard, Mickey, who knew both Anji and Lynn, was also there. He took her to one side and said, 'I've got something for you. I've got Lynn's phone number and address, and I want you to ring her.'

'No, I can't, not while she's still with that guy,' said Anji.

'But she's not with him any more,' he said. 'She hasn't been with him for years.'

So Anji rang Lynn. 'It was just like nothing had happened and we'd spoken the day before,' Anji says. 'From that moment on we were fast friends again. She's remarried now to a man called Pete, who I do like, and who is really good for her.'

Having re-established contact, they agreed to go to the Minehead reunion together. Lynn arranged to pick up Anji from Taunton station. 'What will you be wearing?' she asked her.

'A Teletubby outfit and some *Batman* slippers,' Anji replied.

And when Anji got off the train, that's

exactly what she was wearing. Lynn took one look at her and burst out laughing, saying, 'I knew it! Pete was saying to me, "Don't be daft, she won't be wearing that," and I said, "Oh yes, she will!"'

'We have been the best of friends again ever since then,' Anji says, 'and I absolutely adore her. Some people even say that we've got our own language, as we spend so much time together and we're such good friends.'

The bond Anji feels with people who worked at Butlin's also extends to people whom she never even met when she was working there. 'A lot of redcoats met up again through Facebook, which has made it so much easier to find people you've lost touch with, but I've met other redcoats who I never worked with,' Anji says, 'and we have become really close friends simply because of that Butlin's bond we share.' One such person is fellow Butlin's girl, Valda. 'I've still never actually met Valda face to face, but we text each other and Facebook each other all the time, and I value her as one of my closest and most trusted friends. I've told her things about me that I perhaps wouldn't tell anybody else in the world apart from Lynn – and I tell her everything! That shows the bond that many of the redcoat girls were able to achieve.'

Valda introduced Anji to the Butlin's re-unions, which are open to anyone who worked at Butlin's in any capacity and in any era, but the Minehead redcoats have had their own reunions as well, their first one being in 1998 because of the sudden death of Keith Perron.

Anji lost her father, too, a while ago. He had at least fulfilled some of his frustrated ambitions to be a redcoat by getting heavily involved in amateur dramatics. He was a popular performer. One of his signature turns was sitting in a rowing boat on stage doing a piece called 'Three Little Fishes'.

After he died, Anji wrote a revue in tribute to him, staged at the Thorverton Memorial Hall. The cover illustration just showed the empty boat – 'Everyone got the allusion straight away,' she says. The show was called *Summer Holiday* and was based on a Butlin's holiday camp, with half the audience in 'Red Camp' and half in 'Blue Camp'. Lynn came down from the Devon town where she lives to appear in the show, and they revived a lot of the old Butlin's sketches, and things like the Knobbly Knees contest, which was Anji's forte when she was a redcoat.

Anji's time at Butlin's seems so long ago now, and yet it's stayed with her and still inspires her. Last year she put a picture on Facebook on the anniversary of Billy Butlin's birthday, with a caption that read: 'Happy Birthday, boss! Thank you for letting me share your dream.' She did so because, she says, 'Billy Butlin wanted to give people who didn't have much in life the chance to forget all their worries and woes for a few days and just enjoy themselves; that was his dream, and it was one that I feel privileged to have been allowed to share. Mind you, I met some very affluent people at Butlin's as well, but they also went there to experience that bond, that friendship, that sense of family.'

The friendships that Anji has formed with the other redcoat girls 'are not just because we once worked together,' she says, 'but because we all shared that dream. We might have worked in different places and at different times, but we have an empathy and a bond that draws us together, makes us friends and almost makes us family.'

According to Anji, and many other former redcoats, 'Butlin's is now a far cry from what it was when I was working there. That doesn't necessarily mean it's worse, of course, but it is a different world. The people who go on holiday there are also very different from the ones we used to entertain; they go for different reasons now and expect different things from it. But in my era there was something about Butlin's and the feeling you got when you put on that red coat that got under your skin.'

She still has pictures of Billy Butlin on her phone even now, and she remains very close to her friends from the Butlin's days. Those friendships have survived everything they've experienced; they've lasted through thick and thin. 'So for me,' Anji says, 'Billy Butlin is right up there. Yes, Butlin's became commercial, yes, Butlin's has changed, but I firmly believe that though the times may have changed, the friendships and bonds that were formed between the redcoats, and those who worked at Butlin's in other capacities, will stay and endure for ever.'

Epilogue

At the height of Billy Butlin's fortunes there were ten Butlin's holiday camps: Skegness, Clacton, Filey, Bognor Regis, Minehead, Barry Island, Pwllheli, Ayr and Mosney on the Irish coast, and there was even, briefly, a Butlin's in the Bahamas. The company also owned amusement parks, several hotels and even the revolving restaurant at the top of the Post Office Tower in London. However, despite Billy's showman's flair, since the dawn of the Swinging Sixties, his camps were living on borrowed time and by the late 1970s the writing was already on the wall for Butlin's as a whole.

Butlin's potential customers were not only

developing more sophisticated tastes, but package holidays were making the beaches of Spain and elsewhere in Europe cheap, available and very desirable to those seeking guaranteed sunshine for their annual holiday – the one thing that even Billy Butlin could not provide. As Rocky Mason says, 'The packages were half the price of Butlin's holidays, the drinks when they got there were half the price as well, people had sunshine every day and were seeing palm trees and flying on aeroplanes for the first time in their lives – well, we just couldn't compete with that.'

Most British families now owned a television set, and compared to the star names and high production values of television entertainment shows, Butlin's often more homespun brand of entertainment inevitably suffered in comparison. By the late 1960s, Butlin's was losing its audience.

'When we used to do the Au Revoir on Friday night,' one former redcoat recalled, misty-eyed, 'people were on the last night of their holiday and I'd often see tears in their eyes because they knew they were going home the next day. All the redcoats would march in together and we'd link arms in front of the campers and do a slow kicking dance, singing the old Butlin's song "Goodnight Campers" to the tune of "Goodnight Sweetheart".'

Goodnight Campers, I can see you yawning,
Goodnight Campers, see you in the morning,
You must cheer up, or you'll soon be dead,
For I've heard it said, that folks die in bed!

So I'll say, Goodnight Campers, don't sleep in
* your braces,*
Goodnight Campers, soak your teeth in Jeyeses,
Drown your sorrows,
Bring the bottles back tomorrow,
Goodnight Campers, Goodnight.

'They had to stop doing that routine, because you just couldn't get away with singing things like that to an audience any more – they were as likely to cringe as laugh or sing along with us. At one time many of them would be in tears, shaking your hand and swearing that they'd be back to see you again next year ... but by the mid to late 1960s, it had all begun to seem very old-fashioned.'

Bobby Butlin succeeded his father in 1968, after Billy made an abrupt exit to Jersey for tax reasons. Bobby made efforts to adapt the Butlin's brand to the modern era, including the introduction of self-catering accommodation. 'He was a nice bloke,' says Butlin's girl Valda, 'but we could see the way it was going when he took over and it wasn't up-hill.' Bobby's attempts to promote a more upmarket image for the camps met with only limited success. Although he stayed on as chairman for a few more years, Butlin's ceased to be a family business in 1972, when the company was taken over by the Rank Organisation, but the camps continued to struggle and then began closing. Clacton and Filey both shut in 1983, and most of the others soon followed. As one former redcoat said: 'The most dreadful thing was losing all your friends. I mean, we didn't know Filey was closing. We closed at the end of the season, all of us thinking we were going to go back the following season, and then suddenly we were all informed: "That's it, Filey has closed and you are redundant. End of story." It was dreadfully, dreadfully sad.'

Many of the hotels and ancillary businesses were also sold off, and so unfashionable had Butlin's become that even the name was dropped for a while – the camps were given different, faintly ludicrous names, with Skegness becoming Funcoast World and Minehead Somerwest World. One 1980s television advertisement even showed one of the old camps being blown up, but this attempt to show that Butlin's was changing fast was probably too radical and led to more complaints from existing Butlin's holiday-makers than bookings from potential new ones.

Skegness was revamped in 1987, and again in 1998, including the first of the Skyline

Pavilions, bringing all the entertainment venues, restaurants, bars and shops together under a weatherproof white canopy. The Butlin's branding was also reintroduced, and over 1,000 brand-new apartments were also built at Skegness, sweeping away almost the last of the old-style chalets. Never comfortable or luxurious, they had now become hopelessly outdated. However, one of the original 1936 chalets has been lovingly preserved and is now a Grade II listed building – presumably for its historical importance, rather than its architectural merit!

In 2000 Butlin's changed hands again. The new owners, Bourne Leisure, have invested heavily in further updating and upgrading the facilities, and building new hotels at the three resorts still operating under the Butlin's name: Skegness, Minehead and Bognor Regis. Bourne Leisure has retained brands like Costa Coffee and Burger King, familiar to Butlin's holiday-makers, but they have also introduced fine-dining restaurants to appeal to more upmarket customers.

The days when Butlin's dominated the British holiday scene are certainly long over and will never return. Yet the modern Butlin's resorts are thriving in a very different environment, simply by doing what Butlin's has always done, ever since Billy Butlin opened his first camp in that turnip field outside Skegness almost eighty years ago:

adapting to changing times, and giving the public what they want. Their 'true intent' is still 'all for your delight'.

BUTLIN'S RULES

<u>To be observed by Members of the Entertainments Staff</u>:

<u>GENERAL DUTIES</u>:
As a redcoat, you are a host or hostess and as such should behave exactly as if you were host at your own home to any guests who may be there. This consists of being good-mannered, knowing where everything is, to direct those who do not know, <u>mixing with as many guests as possible and not remaining with any one person or persons for too long</u>.

1) Always make a note of your daily detail. To 'not know' is not an excuse.
2) Use your own common sense about smoking. The general rule, however, is <u>NO SMOKING ON DUTY</u>.
3) Do not linger in the bars too long. Ten to fifteen minutes is the maximum and mix around. Always sit with guests when in uniform. <u>WE DO NOT WANT BAR FLIES</u>.
4) Do not 'switch duties' without permission from the Entertainments Manager or

his Deputy.

5) Spend your day off in a relaxing way and don't hang around the Centre. You deserve a change and if you have been doing your job properly you will feel like one.

ABOVE ALL – BE ON TIME – REMEMBER IF YOU ARE LATE YOU ARE KEEPING THE GUESTS WAITING – 'WOULD YOU LIKE IT'.

POINTS TO WATCH ON SPECIAL DUTIES:
BALLROOM:
a) Mix with as many guests as possible. Do not single out the young and attractive partners all the time – think of the lonely guests – especially the elderly ones.

b) Do not congregate in groups of redcoats.

c) Never dance with staff and always prevent men from dancing together.

DINING HALL:
a) Be at the Dining Hall five minutes before the start of the meal. MEALTIMES ARE DUTIES.

b) Do not impede waitresses who are working hard at their job.

c) Make a point of talking to the guests waiting to enter the Dining Hall.

Try to take an interest in, and enjoy,

whatever you are doing. This will make the job easier and more satisfying. Being a redcoat really boils down to having good manners and using them with your own common sense.

Acknowledgements

Thanks are due above all to our cast of 'Butlin's girls': Hilary, Mavis, Valerie, Valda, Terri, Sue and Anji. Our thanks, too, to James Silverstone of Bourne Leisure; Roger Billington and Judith Rodway, keepers of the Butlin's Archive at Bognor Regis; Gail Everett, Kyran Jesson, Rocky Mason, Bryan Leaker, Lorna Tiffany, and many other former Butlin's holiday-makers and staff who shared their recollections with us. Thanks also to Rebecca Bailey, a former student at York St John University, who recorded the first interview with Valda on our behalf.

Our grateful thanks also to Mark Lucas, Julian Alexander and Alice Saunders at Lucas Alexander Whitley, to Anna Valentine, and to Natalie Jerome, Laura Lees, Julie MacBrayne, Holly Kyte, Virginia Woolstencroft and the entire team at HarperCollins.

The publishers hope that this book has given you enjoyable reading. Large Print Books are especially designed to be as easy to see and hold as possible. If you wish a complete list of our books please ask at your local library or write directly to:

Magna Large Print Books
Magna House, Long Preston,
Skipton, North Yorkshire.
BD23 4ND

This Large Print Book, for people
who cannot read normal print,
is published under the auspices of

THE ULVERSCROFT FOUNDATION